ONE NATION
UNDER THERAPY

ONE NATION UNDER THERAPY

HOW THE HELPING CULTURE
IS ERODING SELF-RELIANCE

CHRISTINA HOFF SOMMERS
AND SALLY SATEL, M.D.

ST. MARTIN'S PRESS ✺ NEW YORK

www.stmartins.com

Library of Congress Cataloging-in-Publication Data

Sommers, Christina Hoff.
    One nation under therapy : how the helping culture is eroding self-reliance /
Christina Hoff Sommers & Sally Satel.—1st U.S. ed.
        p.   cm.
    ISBN 0-312-30443-9
    EAN 978-0312-30443-0
    1. Mental health—United States. 2. Psychotherapy—United States. 3. Self-
reliance. I. Satel, Sally L. II. Title.

RA790.6.S66 2005
155.8'973—dc22

                                                                    2004051305

10   9   8   7   6   5   4   3

To Christopher DeMuth

Contents

One Nation Under Therapy

In 2000, five Canadian psychologists published a satirical article about Winnie the Pooh entitled "Pathology in the Hundred Acre Wood."[1] At first glance, say the authors, the hero of A. A. Milne's 1926 children's classic appears to be a healthy, well-adjusted bear; but on closer and more expert examination, Pooh turns out to suffer from attention deficit/hyperactivity disorder, binge eating, and borderline cognitive functioning ("a bear of very little brain") to name just a few of his infirmities. Pooh's friends are similarly afflicted: Rabbit fits the profile of narcissistic personality syndrome; Owl is emotionally disturbed, which renders him dyslexic; and Piglet displays classic symptoms of generalized anxiety (a diagnosis that is admittedly difficult to dispute). Eeyore the donkey has low self-esteem and an inability to enjoy himself, a condition known as anhedonia—which the authors refer to as anhe(haw)donia.

The Canadian spoof makes a serious point: the propensity of experts to pathologize and medicalize healthy children en masse has gotten way out of hand. The past decade has seen a cascade of books and articles promoting the idea that seemingly content and well-adjusted Americans—adults as well as children—are emotionally damaged.

Mary Pipher, the best known of the child-crisis writers, describes American society as a "girl-poisoning" culture.[2] Her book *Reviving Ophelia: Saving the Selves of Adolescent Girls* (1994) was on the *New York Times* best-seller list for three years, selling more than 1.5 million copies. According to Pipher, "Just as planes and ships disappear mysteriously into the Bermuda Triangle, so do the selves of girls go down in droves. They crash and burn."[3]

Not to be outdone, Harvard psychologist William Pollack soon followed with *Real Boys: Rescuing Our Sons from the Myths of Boyhood* (1998). Pollack's book claims to show that adolescent boys who appear to be healthy and happy, are really emotionally deprived and quietly in despair.[4] Looking at young American males, Pollack sees "Hamlets [who] succumb to an inner 'state of Denmark.'"[5] The boys who shot their classmates at Columbine High, according to Pollack, are "the tip of the iceberg, and the iceberg is all boys."[6]

For more than three decades, various experts and popular writers have been telling us that adults are miserable too. For example, in 1993 the prestigious Commonwealth Fund, a New York philanthropy concerned with public health, released the results of a poll on women's health.[7] This "important" study, as then secretary of health and human services Donna Shalala called it, reported that in any given week, 40 percent of American women are "severely depressed."[8]

But then, in 1999, feminist author Susan Faludi, a veteran of the best-seller lists, called attention to the devastating emotional problems of yet another group of fragile Americans: adult males. In *Stiffed: The Betrayal of the American Male*, Faludi contended that American men cannot live up to the conventional stoic ideal of manliness and so, en masse, they lose their sense of self. "No wonder men are in such agony," she says.[9]

And no one has been more successful in making a career out of an alleged national anguish than Daniel Goleman, a former *New York Times* science writer. His best-selling 1995 book *Emo-*

ONE NATION
UNDER THERAPY

tional Intelligence described a nation suffering from profound "emotional malaise" and in the grip of "surging rage and despair."[10]

In an article in the *Wall Street Journal*, *New York Observer* editor Jim Windolf tallied the number of Americans allegedly suffering from some kind of emotional disorder. He sent away for the literature of dozens of advocacy agencies and mental health organizations. Then he did the math. Windolf reported, "If you believe the statistics, 77 percent of America's adult population is a mess. . . . And we haven't even thrown in alien abductees, road-ragers, and Internet addicts."[11] If we factor in the drowning girls, diminished boys, despondent women, agonized men, and the all-around emotionally challenged, the country is, in Windolf's words, "officially nuts."

One Nation Under Therapy offers a more sanguine view of American society. It points out that there is no evidence that large segments of the population are in psychological free fall. On the contrary, researchers who follow the protocols of genuine social science find most Americans—young and old—faring quite well.[12] If they are crashing, burning, in agony, or trapped in medieval Denmark, they do not seem to know it.

Of course, we are not suggesting that everyone is perennially happy or possessed of an abiding sense of well-being. Many, if not most, human beings are mildly neurotic, at times self-defeating, anxious, or sad. These traits or behaviors are characteristic of the human condition, often emerging in different life circumstances—they are not pathological. And they are certainly not new. What we oppose is the view that Americans today are emotionally underdeveloped, psychically frail, and that they require the ministrations of mental health professionals to cope with life's vicissitudes. The crisis authors offer only anecdotes, misleading statistics, and dubious studies for their alarming findings. Yet they are taken very seriously.

Goleman, for example, has become a secular apostle of the

credo that continuous monitoring of one's feelings is healthful and liberating. He is founder and cochair of the Consortium for Research on Emotional Intelligence in Organizations, which promotes and evaluates self-awareness workshops for managers in companies such as American Express and Johnson & Johnson.[13] One "model" program uses a variety of "teaching modalities" to help managers learn how to identify and "reframe" their own "inner dialogue."[14] Modalities include drawing pictures, role-playing, and visualization. Emotional Intelligence training has been hugely popular. Its value for adults is questionable at best; its effect on children may be quite harmful.[15]

Goleman endorses many standard, commonsensical, and uncontroversial child-rearing practices that go back at least to Aristotle—e.g., teaching a child to control impulses and to temper anger; but his distinctive and original contributions concern not just emotional regulation but emotional self-expression and focused emotional awareness. For example, he champions classroom exercises that encourage children to talk at length about their feelings. He praises a school program called "Self Science," which he calls a "model for the teaching of emotional intelligence."[16] Its purpose is to get teachers and students to focus on "the emotional fabric of a child's life."[17] In a typical self-science exercise, when the teacher calls the roll, the students do not say "here," but take the opportunity to identify their feelings at that moment.

Here is Goleman's description of a roll call in one Northern California classroom:

TEACHER: Jessica.
JESSICA: I'm jazzed, it's Friday.
TEACHER: Patrick.
PATRICK: Excited, a little nervous.
TEACHER: Nicole.
NICOLE: Peaceful, happy.[18]

Goleman appears not to recognize the intrusive nature of such seemingly innocent programs. Nor does he seem to consider the possibility that what healthy children need most is guidance on how to be civil and ethical—not how to be self-obsessed (something many children have no problem learning on their own).

These would-be healers of our purported woes dogmatically believe and promote the doctrine we call "therapism."[19] Therapism valorizes openness, emotional self-absorption and the sharing of feelings. It encompasses several additional assumptions: that vulnerability, rather than strength, characterizes the American psyche; and that a diffident, anguished, and emotionally apprehensive public requires a vast array of therapists, self-esteem educators, grief counselors, workshoppers, healers, and traumatologists to lead it through the trials of everyday life. Children, more than any group, are targeted for therapeutic improvement. We roundly reject these assumptions.

Because they tend to regard normal children as psychologically at risk, many educators are taking extreme and unprecedented measures to protect them from stress. Schoolyard games that encourage competition are under assault. In some districts, dodgeball has been placed in a "Hall of Shame" because, as one leading educator says, "It's like *Lord of the Flies*, with adults encouraging it."[20] Tag is also under a cloud. The National Education Association distributes a teacher's guide that suggests an anxiety-reducing version of tag, "where nobody is ever 'out.'"[21]

It is now the practice for "sensitivity and bias committees" inside publishing houses to expunge from standardized tests all mention of potentially distressing topics. Two major companies specifically interdict references to rats, mice, roaches, snakes, lice, typhoons, blizzards, and birthday parties.[22] (The latter could create bad feelings in children whose families don't celebrate them.) The committees, says Diane Ravitch in her book *The Language Police*, believe such references could "be so upsetting to some children that they will not be able to do their best on a test."[23]

We suggest that young people are not helped by being wrapped in cotton wool and deprived of the vigorous pastimes and intellectual challenges they need for healthy development. Nor are they improved by educators, obsessed with the mission of boosting children's self-esteem, telling them how "wonderful" they are. A growing body of research suggests there is, in fact, no connection between high self-esteem and achievement, kindness, or good personal relationships. On the other hand, unmerited self-esteem is known to be associated with antisocial behavior—even criminality.[24]

Therapism tends to regard people as essentially weak, dependent, and never altogether responsible for what they do. Alan Wolfe, a Boston College sociologist and expert on national mores and attitudes, reports that for many Americans nonjudgmentalism has become a cardinal virtue.[25] Concepts of right and wrong, good and evil, are often regarded as anachronistic and intolerant. "Thou shalt be nice" is the new categorical imperative.

Summarizing his findings, Wolfe says:

What the Victorians considered self-destructive behavior requiring punishment we consider self-destructive behavior requiring treatment. . . . America has most definitely entered a new era in which virtue and vice are redefined in term of public health and addiction.[26]

One Nation Under Therapy does not advocate a return to a harsh judgmentalism. Wolfe may have a point when he says that an emphasis on tolerance has made Americans "nicer." We shall note, however, that this emphasis also induces a moral inertia that can be the opposite of nice. Consider, for example, the supposedly enlightened, compassionate view that drug and alcohol addiction are "brain diseases." We challenge the brain disease model on the grounds that treating addicts as morally responsible, self-determining human beings free to change their behavior is, in the end, more effective, more respectful, and more compassionate.

We also reject therapism's central doctrine that uninhibited emotional openness is essential to mental health. On the contrary, recent findings suggest that reticence and suppression of feelings, far from compromising one's psychological well-being, can be healthy and adaptive. For many temperaments, an excessive focus on introspection and self-disclosure is depressing. Victims of loss and tragedy differ widely in their reactions: some benefit from therapeutic intervention; most do not and should not be coerced by mental health professionals into emotionally correct responses. Trauma and grief counselors have erred massively in this direction.

In the wake of mass tragedy, therapism's "grief brigades," as *Time* magazine calls them, swoop down on victims.[27] Helping professionals—many with questionable credentials—have become fixtures at scenes of disaster. The trauma industry operates on the assumption that the principal lesson to be learned from suffering is that one must exorcise it. But suffering is sometimes edifying. In his profound and moving book, *Man's Search for Meaning*, psychiatrist Viktor Frankl, himself a survivor of the Nazi death camps, wrote that, "Suffering is not always a pathological phenomenon . . . suffering may well be a human achievement, especially if it grows out of existential frustration."[28]

It was in the same spirit that *Time* writer Lance Morrow wrote in the wake of 9/11, "For once, let's have no 'grief counselors' standing by with banal consolations, as if the purpose, in the midst of all this, were merely to make everyone feel better as quickly as possible. We shouldn't feel better."[29] Finding solace and strength after grief without professional help has become an anachronism—like setting one's own broken bone.

The trauma industry routinely flouts Morrow's wise injunction, and applies with abandon the diagnosis of "post-traumatic stress disorder." PTSD is a legitimate clinical condition marked by intense reexperiencing of a horrific, often life-threatening event in the form of relentless nightmares or unbidden waking images. PTSD is not to be applied to people who are acutely distraught—a perfectly normal reaction—after a terrifying ordeal, but to the minority who go on to develop disabling, pathological anxiety because of it. Worse, clinicians often diagnose PTSD in individuals who haven't even been exposed to horrific events but are simply upset by troubling incidents. For example, professional journals are rife with examples of "PTSD" patients who have been sexually harassed on the job, moviegoers upset by seeing *The Exorcist*, and motorists involved in minor accidents—treated as if they were survivors of the Bataan Death March.[30]

Where did it come from, this current preoccupation with feelings? It has many roots. One is the eighteenth-century Romantic philosophy of Jean-Jacques Rousseau. For Rousseau, the expression of emotion is crucial to any moral and spiritual development. It can also be traced to nineteenth-century evangelical movements that offered nostrums for liberating their followers from negative emotions.[31] However, a detailed account of the remote origins of therapism is beyond the scope of this book. What we will examine are its more immediate and familiar progenitors. In particular, we shall discuss the new psychologies that flourished and were popularized in the United States after the Second World War—notably, Freudian psychoanalysis and a successor that came to be known as the "human potential movement."

Colorful academic psychologists like Abraham Maslow and Carl Rogers introduced into American life their ideal of "self-actualization." Their work and that of colleagues seems at first optimistic, positive, and suitable to a dynamic and energetic society like postwar America. But a closer look shows that both these thinkers were precursors to today's crisis writers. They were of the opinion that the vast majority of Americans led "unactualized" lives in spiritual wastelands from which they needed to be rescued. Said Maslow, "I sometimes think that the world will either be saved by psychologists—in the very broadest sense—or it will not be saved at all."[32]

We reject the idea that psychology, however humanistic and liberationist, can be a general provider of salvation. This is not to say that psychology has not made impressive progress. We understand very well that the same half century that incubated an unwholesome therapism also saw remarkable developments in the knowledge of the brain and in new medications for severe mental illnesses such as schizophrenia. And we appreciate that the various talk therapies have real value for many patients. But this approach can be, and has been, taken too far. The popular assumption that emotional disclosure is always valuable, and that without professional help, most people are incapable of dealing with adversity, has slipped its clinical moorings and drifted into all corners of American life.

We are not the first to notice these encroachments. Social critics such as Philip Rieff, Christopher Lasch, Allan Bloom, and, more recently, Charles Sykes and Wendy Kaminer, have chronicled many aspects of what Rieff called the "triumph of the therapeutic."[33] Our book builds on their insights and shows how the growth of therapism continues apace, affecting contemporary culture in ways that might surprise even these observers.

One Nation Under Therapy describes the incursion of therapism and the growing role of helping professionals in our daily lives. It rejects the presumption of fragility and challenges the dogma of self-revelation; it exposes the folly of replacing ethical judgment with psychological and medical diagnosis, save for instances where individuals are truly mentally ill. The book contends, in other words, that human beings, including children, are best regarded as self-reliant, resilient, psychically sound moral agents responsible for their behavior. For, with few exceptions, that is what we are.

1

The Myth of the Fragile Child

In 2001, the Girl Scouts of America introduced a "Stress Less Badge" for girls aged eight to eleven. It featured an embroidered hammock suspended from two green trees. According to the *Junior Girl Scout Badge Book*, girls earn the award by practicing "focused breathing," creating a personal "stress less kit," or keeping a "feelings diary." Burning ocean-scented candles, listening to "Sounds of the Rain Forest," even exchanging foot massages are also ways to garner points.[1]

Explaining the need for the Stress Less Badge to the *New York Times*, a psychologist from the Girl Scout Research Institute said that studies show "how stressed girls are today."[2] Earning an antistress badge, however, can itself be stressful. The *Times* reported that tension increased in Brownie Troop 459 in Sunnyvale, California, when the girls attempted to make "antianxiety squeeze balls out of balloons and Play-Doh." According to Lindsay, one of the Brownies, "The Play-Doh was too oily and disintegrated the balloon. It was very stressful."[3]

The psychologist who worried about Lindsay and her fellow Girls Scouts is not alone. Anxiety over the mental equanimity of American children is at an all-time high. In May of 2002, the principal of Franklin Elementary School in Santa Monica, California, sent a newsletter to parents informing them that children could no longer play tag during the lunch recess. As she explained, "The running part of this activity is healthy and encouraged; however, in this game, there is a 'victim' or 'It,' which creates a self-esteem issue."[4]

School districts in Texas, Maryland, New York, and Virginia "have banned, limited, or discouraged" dodgeball.[5] "Anytime you throw an object at somebody," said an elementary school coach in Cambridge, Massachusetts, "it creates an environment of retaliation and resentment."[6] Coaches who permit children to play dodgeball "should be fired immediately," according to the physical education chairman at Central High School in Naperville, Illinois.[7]

In response to this attack on dodgeball, Rick Reilly, the *Sports Illustrated* columnist, chided parents who want "their Ambers and their Alexanders to grow up in a cozy womb of noncompetition."[8] Reilly responds to educators like the Naperville chairman of physical education by saying, "You mean there's weak in the world? There's strong? Of course there is, and dodgeball is one of the first opportunities in life to figure out which one you are and how you're going to deal with it."

Reilly's words may resonate comfortably with many of his readers, and with most children as well; but progressive educators tend to dismiss his reaction as just another expression of a benighted opposition to the changes needed if education is to become truly caring and sensitive. This movement against stressful games gained momentum after the publication of an article by Neil Williams, professor of physical education at Eastern Connecticut State College, in a journal sponsored by the National Association for Sports and Physical Education, which represents nearly eighteen thousand gym teachers and physical education professors. In the article, Williams consigned games such as Red Rover, relay races, and musical chairs to "the Hall of Shame."[9] Why? Because the games are based on removing the weakest links. Presumably, this undercuts children's emotional development and erodes their self-esteem.

In a follow-up article, Williams also pointed to a sinister aspect of Simon Says. "The major problem," he wrote, "is that the teacher is doing his or her best to deceive and entrap students."[10] He added that psychologically this game is the equivalent of teachers demonstrating the perils of electricity to students "by jolting them with an electric current if they touch the wrong button." The new therapeutic sensibility rejects almost all forms of competition in favor of a gentle and nurturing climate of cooperation.

Which games, then, are safe and affirming? Some professionals in physical education advocate activities in which children compete only with themselves such as juggling, unicycling, pogo sticking, and even "learning to . . . manipulate wheelchairs with ease."[11] In a game like juggling there is no threat of elimination. But experts warn teachers to be judicious in their choice of juggling objects. A former member of The President's Council on Youth Fitness and Sports suggests using silken scarves rather than, say, uncooperative tennis balls that lead to frustration and anxiety. "Scarves," he told the *Los Angeles Times*, "are soft, nonthreatening, and float down slowly."[12] As the head of a middle school physical education program in Van Nuys, California, points out, juggling scarves "lessens performance anxiety and boosts self-esteem."[13]

Writer John Leo, like Reilly, satirized the gentle-juggling culture by proposing a stress-free version of musical chairs:

> Why not make sure each child has a guaranteed seat for musical chairs? With proper seating, the source of tension is removed. Children can just relax, enjoy the music and talk about the positive feelings that come from being included.[14]

Leo was kidding. But the authors of a popular 1998 government-financed antibullying curriculum guide called *Quit*

It! were not.[15] One exercise intended for kindergarten through third grade instructs teachers on how to introduce children to a new way to play tag:

> Before going outside to play, talk about how students feel when playing a game of tag. Do they like to be chased? Do they like to do the chasing? How does it feel to be tagged out? Get their ideas about other ways the game might be played.[16]

After students share their fears and apprehensions about tag, teachers may introduce them to a nonthreatening alternative called "Circle of Friends" where "nobody is ever 'out.'" If students become overexcited or angry while playing Circle of Friends, the guide recommends using stress-reducing exercises to "help the transition from active play to focused work."[17] Reading through *Quit It!*, you have to remind yourself that it is not satire, nor is it intended for emotionally disturbed children. It is intended for normal five- to seven-year-olds in our nation's schools.

Our Sensitive and Vulnerable Youth

But is overprotectiveness really such a bad thing? Sooner or later children will face stressful situations, disappointments, and threats to their self-esteem. Why not shield them from the inevitable as long as possible? The answer is that overprotected kids do not flourish. To treat them as combustible bundles of frayed nerves does them no favors. Instead it deprives them of what they need.

Children must have independent, competitive rough-and-tumble play. Not only do they enjoy it, it is part of their normal development. Anthony Pellegrini, a professor of early childhood education at the University of Minnesota, defines rough-and-tumble play as behavior that includes "laughing, running, smiling, jumping . . . wrestling, play fighting, chasing, and fleeing."[18] Such play, he says, brings children together, it makes them happy and it promotes healthy socialization. Children who are adept at rough play also "tend to be liked and to be good social problem solvers."[19] Commenting on the recent moves to ban competitive zero-sum playground games like tag, Pelligrini told us, "It is ridiculous . . . even squirrels play chase."

The zealous protectiveness is not confined to the playground. In her eye-opening book *The Language Police*, Diane Ravitch shows how a once-commendable program aimed at making classroom materials less sexist and racist has morphed into a powerful censorship regime.[20] "Sensitivity and bias" committees, residing in publishing houses, state governments, test-writing companies, and in groups like the American Psychological Association, now police textbooks and other classroom materials, scouring them for any reference or assertion that could possibly make some young reader feel upset, insecure, or shortchanged in life.

In 1997, President Bill Clinton appointed Ravitch to an honorary education committee charged with developing national achievement tests. The Department of Education had awarded a multimillion-dollar contract to Riverside Publishing, a major testing company and a subsidiary of Houghton Mifflin, to compose the exam. Ravitch and her committee were there to provide oversight.

As part of the process, the Riverside test developers sent Ravitch and her fellow committee members, mostly veteran teachers, several sample reading selections. The committee reviewed them carefully and selected the ones they considered the most lucid, engaging, and appropriate for fourth-grade test takers.

Congress eventually abandoned the idea of national tests. However, Ravitch learned that several of the passages she and her colleagues had selected had not survived the scrutiny of the Riverside censors.

For example, two of the selections that got high marks from Ravitch and her colleagues were about peanuts. Readers learned that they were a healthy snack and had first been cultivated by South American Indians and then, after the Spanish conquest, were imported into Europe. The passage explained how peanuts became important in the United States, where they were planted and cultivated by African slaves. It told of George Washington Carver, the black inventor and scientist, who found many new uses for peanuts.

The Riverside sensitivity monitors had a field day. First of all, they said, peanuts are not a healthy snack for all children. Some are allergic. According to Ravitch, "The reviewers apparently assumed that a fourth-grade student who was allergic to peanuts might get distracted if he or she encountered a test question that did not acknowledge the dangers of peanuts."[21]

The panel was also unhappy that the reading spoke of the Spaniards having "defeated" the South American tribes. Its members did not question the accuracy of the claim, but Ravitch surmises, "They must have concluded that these facts would hurt someone's feelings."[22] Perhaps they thought that some child of South American Indian descent who came upon this information would feel slighted, and so suffer a disadvantage in taking the test.

Ravitch's group had especially liked a story about a decaying tree stump on the forest floor and how it becomes home to an immense variety of plants, insects, birds, and animals. The passage compared the stump to a bustling apartment complex. Ravitch and the other committee members enjoyed its charm and verve. It also taught children about a fascinating ecology. But the twenty sensitivity panelists at Riverside voted unanimously against it: "Youngsters who have grown up in a housing project may be distracted by similarities to their own living conditions. An emotional response may be triggered."[23]

Ravitch presents clear evidence that our schools are in the grip of powerful sensitivity censors who appear to be completely lacking in good judgment and are accountable to no one but themselves. She could find no evidence that sensitivity censorship of school materials helps children. On the contrary, the abridged texts are enervating. "How boring," she says, "for students to be restricted only to stories that flatter their self-esteem or that purge complexity and unpleasant reality from history and current events."[24]

The idea that kids can cope with only the blandest of stories is preposterous. Staples like "Little Red Riding Hood," "Jack and the Beanstalk," and "Hansel and Gretel" delight children despite (or because of) their ghoulish aspects. Kids love to hear ghost stories on Halloween and to ride roller coasters, screaming as they hurtle down the inclines. Therapeutic protectiveness is like putting blinders on children before taking them for a walk through a vibrant countryside.

Excessive concern over imagined harms can hinder children's natural development. Moreover, in seeking to solve nonexistent problems, it distracts teachers from focusing on their true mission—to educate children and to prepare them to be effective adults. Commenting on Ravitch's findings, Jonathan Yardley, columnist and book critic at the *Washington Post*, wrote, "A child with a rare disease may have to be put in a bubble, but putting the entire American system of elementary and secondary education into one borders on insanity."[25]

Many American teachers seem to believe children must be spared even the mildest criticism. Kevin Miller, a professor of psychology at the University of Illinois at Urbana-Champaign, has studied differences between Chinese and American pedagogy. In one of his videotapes, a group of children in a math class in China are learning about place values. The teacher asks a boy to make the number 14 using one bundle of ten sticks along with some single sticks, and the child uses only the bundle. The teacher then asks the class, in a calm, noncensorious tone, "Who can tell me what is wrong with this?" When Miller shows the video to American teachers, they are taken aback. They find it surprising to see an instructor being so openly critical of a student's performance. "Most of the teachers in training we've shown this to express the worry that this could be damaging to children's self-esteem," Miller reports.[26] Even the minority of American student teachers who don't disapprove of the practice agree that the practice of giving students explicit feedback in public "contravenes what we do in the U.S."

Rossella Santagata, a research psychologist at LessonLab in Santa Monica, California, has studied how American and Italian teachers differ in their reactions to students' mistakes. Italian teachers are very direct: they have no qualms about telling students their answer is wrong. In so doing, they violate all of the sensitivity standards that prevail in the United States. Santagata has a videotape of a typical exchange between an American math teacher and a student. An eighth grader named Steve is supposed to give the prime factors of the number 34; instead he lists all the factors. It is not easy for the teacher to be affirmative about Steve's answer. But she finds a way, "Okay. Now Steve you're exactly right that those are all *factors*. *Prime* factorization means that you *only* list the numbers that are *prime*. So can you modify your answer to make it all only prime numbers?" (Emphasis in original.)[27]

Santagata told us that when she shows this exchange to audiences of Italian researchers, they find the teachers strained response ("exactly right") hysterically funny. By contrast, American researchers see nothing unusual or amusing—because, as Santagata says, "Such reactions are normal."[28]

Even college students are not exempt from this new solicitude. Students in universities like Columbia, Duke, the University of Wisconsin, the University of Kansas, and the University of Buffalo can visit "stress-free zones" or attend "stress buster" workshops that include activities and palliatives once limited to young children or mental patients.[29] Wisconsin offers anxious undergraduates a safe space during finals where they can partake in a "napping event," get a backrub, or draw pictures with a box of crayolas.[30] Alas, not all students take the mental health offerings in the right spirit. Duke University provides massage therapy to tense undergraduates; but the facilitator found it necessary to post a warning on the Web site: "No 'hooking up' with a partner at the program."[31]

The Kids are All Right. Get Used to It

One reason there is so much concern over the mental health of the nation's young people is that some well-respected and widely read psychologists claim to have convincing evidence of a general malaise. In *Reviving Ophelia*, Pipher described girls as "crashing and burning" and warned that adults fail to appreciate "how universal and extreme the suffering is."[32] Nearly ten years later, in a 2003 interview on the Web site WebMD, Pipher reported that the situation had worsened—and not only for girls: "Whether we look at incidence rates for suicide, drug and alcohol abuse, children on prescribed medication, and children involved in antisocial behaviors, all of those show children are having a much more difficult time today than even 10 years ago."[33]

In his 1999 book *Real Boys*, William Pollack claimed that the rates of depression and suicide among boys were "frighteningly on the rise."[34] In a follow-up book in 2002, *Real Boys' Voices*, Pollack warned that "our nation is home to millions of boys who . . . are cast out to sea in separate lifeboats, and feel they are drowning in isolation, depression, loneliness, and despair."[35]

If the youth of America were truly suffering psychological meltdown from stress, anxiety, anger, and depression, then, perhaps, from the earliest age we should be doing our best to calm them down and to bolster their self-esteem. Perhaps then it might make sense to consider eliminating all games with losers and winners and to take special care not to expose children to teachers who correct students by telling them in front of the whole class that the answers they have given are wrong. We might then also be grateful to the Girl Scouts for distributing merit badges to stress-free girls and to colleges for providing "napping events" for anxious undergraduates.

In fact, none of the assumptions about young people's vulnerabilities and infirmities withstands the light of day. The vast majority of American children is mentally sound and will remain so. Contrary to the claims of Pipher, Pollack and other alarmists, the empirical evidence indicates that the prevalence of depression among children and adolescents has not significantly changed in the past thirty years. In fact, one highly respected, large-scale study of college freshman, carried out by the Higher Education Research Institute at the University of California at Los Angeles, reports that "rates of depression are on the decline." In 2003 (the fifth consecutive year showing a decline) it found that a "record low" number of students (7.4 percent) reported being frequently depressed, an impressive improvement from the record high (10.6 percent) in 1988.[36] As for suicide, in June 2004, the Centers for Disease Control reported that in the past decade, suicide among persons aged ten to nineteen years decreased by 25 percent.[37] To be sure, an unchanging small percentage of youth, some 5 percent, have severe mental problems, and an additional 6 percent have serious ones, according to the U.S. Surgeon General. An additional 10 percent have some kind of moderate or mild affliction that may or may not require clinical attention.[38] But this still means that at least 80 percent are psychologically fit, and do not appear to inhabit the stark and desolate inner world that Pipher and Pollack so poignantly describe.

Daniel Offer, professor of psychiatry at Northwestern, has referred to a "new generation of studies" that finds that most teenagers are normal and well-adjusted.[39] The Survey Research Center at the University of Michigan (in 2000) polled a scientifically selected sample of three thousand high school seniors on the question: "Taking all things together, how would you say things are these days—would you say you're very happy, pretty happy, or not too happy?" Slightly more than 87 percent of students responded that they were "pretty happy" or "very happy."[40]

Of course, if as many as 6 percent of American children have significant psychological problems, and another 15 percent are mildly or moderately disturbed, this adds up to a large number of children who may benefit from some clinical attention. Promising new therapies and drugs might spare such children and their families much suffering. It is true that we need better mental health screening in pediatric clinics and in schools. On the other hand, young people who are in genuine need of attention could easily get lost in an environment where a majority of children are regarded as infirm. If nearly everyone is crashing and burning, no one is.

Each year, the Federal Interagency Forum on Child and Family Statistics publishes a compendium of data on the status of the nation's children entitled *America's Children: Key National Indicators of Well-Being.* This survey is a synthesis of data from twenty federal agencies and it is considered a state-of-the-art profile. According to the survey, in the past few years there has been marked, indeed remarkable, improvement in the lives of American children. "One of the striking things is how many of these indicators are 'best evers,'" said Duane Alexander, the primary author of the study and director of the National Institute of Child Health and Human Development.[41]

Child poverty is down significantly from its recent high in 1994.[42] Birth rates for teens are at a record low for recent decades. According to the 2003 *Monitoring the Future* survey, the government's annual survey of high school students, there have been declines in the use of alcohol and most drugs since the mid-nineties (offset, unfortunately, by a steady gain in nonmedical use of painkillers over the last decade).[43]

Most unexpected is the dramatic drop in juvenile crime. In its December 2003 *Juvenile Justice Bulletin*, the U.S. Justice Department reported "Juvenile arrests for violence in 2001 were the lowest since 1988."[44] According to the same report, "Juvenile arrests for property crimes in 2001 were the lowest in at least three decades."

The Horatio Alger Association, a fifty-year-old organization devoted to promoting and affirming individual initiative and "the American Dream," found no evidence of pervasive misery in its annual teen survey in 2002–2003.[45] On the contrary, in its commissioned poll on teen attitudes it found widespread optimism. The poll looked carefully at young people's confidence about the future, particularly after the events of September 11. A significant majority of teens (73 percent) were "hopeful and optimistic in thinking about the future."[46] Family members (mostly their own parents) topped their list of role models.[47] Child doomsayers depict teens as lonely and isolated, but only 8 percent of those polled "felt lonely or left out."[48] These results reinforce the positive findings of Northwestern's Offer, the University of Michigan study, and the Federal Interagency Report.

In the spring of 2002, two new girl-crisis books appeared. Rachel Simmons's *Odd Girl Out: The Hidden Culture of Aggression in Girls* and Rosalind Wiseman's *Queen Bees and Wannabes* claimed that our daughters are struggling with a cutthroat, hypercompetitive, viciously cruel, appearance-obsessed girl culture.[49] To its credit, *Newsweek* challenged the myth of the girls' cult of cruelty. But that magazine was the exception.[50] The *Oprah Winfrey Show*, NBC'S *Today*, and National Public Radio took the alleged crisis seriously.[51] Even on ABC's *Nightline*, the usually skeptical Ted Koppel told his audience, "Girls, it seems, have developed the evolution of social nastiness into an art form, to a point at which it is almost dangerous."[52]

Unlike *Newsweek*, no one from *Nightline* thought to seek out the evidence-based expertise of someone like William Damon, director of the Stanford Center on the Study of Adolescence. Damon told us that there are no grounds for saying girls are more cruel today than in the past: "Whenever teenagers congregate in same-sex groups, there is and always has been a certain amount of cliquishness, teasing, and unfriendly in-group/out-group behavior."[53]

So why are we so quick to accept alarmist findings? Perhaps

it is because of a legitimate concern over the high levels of obscenity and violence in popular entertainment. Sadistic video games, lurid rap songs and grotesquely violent movies are everywhere available—even to very young children. This debased popular culture may be creating an epidemic of incivility and insensitivity. But there is no evidence of a psychological breakdown described by the child alarmists. On the contrary, the relative soundness and balance of today's kids could be taken as testament to their good sense and resilience.

Coach Fitz

Some parents, apprehensive about their children's self-esteem and anxious to spare them any hurt feelings, have lost the sense of their children's vital need for character development. A recent controversy involving an old-fashioned and "tough" high school athletic coach is a case in point.

Billy Fitzgerald—"Fitz"—has been the baseball coach for more than thirty years at Isidore Newman School, a private secondary school in New Orleans. Fitz's coaching style is not unlike that of the proverbial boot camp sergeant. He pushes the students in his charge to their limits. He expects absolute dedication and when a player disappoints him, he lets him know it in ways that fall far short of "sensitive." Nevertheless, generations of boys have flourished under his guidance and they never forget the life lessons he taught them.

Writer Michael Lewis interviewed twenty Isidore Newman alumni who had been coached by Fitzgerald. In a moving article in the *New York Times Magazine*, he summarized their collective reaction in these words: "Fitz changed my life."[54] Lewis himself had attended Newman in the late seventies and he credits the coach with miracles. "In the three years before I met Coach Fitz, the only task for which I exhibited any enthusiasm was sneaking out of the house at two in the morning to rip hood ornaments off cars. . . . Now this fantastically persuasive man was insisting, however improbably, that I might be some other kind of person. A hero."[55]

Fitzgerald's philosophy could not be more remote from therapism. Fitz is not interested in protecting his players from hurt feelings or from stress. He is concerned with their lack of youthful passion. He worries that they have been overindulged and insufficiently challenged; he deplores their tendency to blame others for their own inadequacies and failings, which he feels inevitably confines them to lives of mediocrity. Lewis, the former student, paints a portrait of a coach who is somehow able to enter the minds of undersocialized, disengaged adolescent males and to persuade them that there might be some greatness in them.

That someone like Fitzgerald can still be found in schools suggests that "the triumph of the therapeutic" is not yet complete. But while the alumni of Isidore Newman High School are looking for ways to honor Coach Fitzgerald, a vocal group of parents whose children are currently on the school team are actively working to get him fired. Why? They think he is too strict, too uncompromising. And they accuse him of being unacceptably insensitive.

"Fitz called my kid fat," complained one parent to the school. The coach had not called him fat, but had reminded the boy that he had agreed to lose fifteen pounds but instead had gained ten.[56] When several members of the team broke rules prohibiting drinking and then lied about it, Fitzgerald told them: "I'm going to run you until you hate me." Complaining phone calls followed from worried parents. One mother said that it was not fair that her son should have to run laps—he had only "one sip of a daiquiri."[57]

It's an open secret among school officials and teachers that if they hold students to high standards, punish them for bad behavior, or even disappoint them in some mild way, there will be visits from parents who will accuse the school of being unfair to Junior. The headmaster of the Isidore Newman School, Scott

McCleod, told Lewis, "The parents' willingness to intercede on the kids' behalf, to take the kids' side, to protect the kid, in a not healthy way—there's much more of that each year. . . . It's true in sports, it's true in the classroom. And it's only going to get worse."[58]

Overprotected children are denied essential life lessons. Healthy young people are shortchanged, even endangered, when the adults in their lives take the view that what is most important is to keep them free of stress, free of self-doubt, and happy in the conviction that they should be judged by no one's standards but their own.

The Homework "Crisis"

In December 2002, *CBS Evening News* broadcast a story about frazzled children overwhelmed by their homework. "In every town in America, parents . . . are watching their kids struggle," said reporter Jim Axelrod. He spoke of "the end of childhood." In one of his interviews, a sixth-grade girl named Cindy told him that on a bad day she worked as long as two and a half hours. Cindy recalled an earlier time when she could bike to the store for an ice cream, "but now I can't." Said Axelrod of her workload, "She's literally swallowed up by it." As proof that Cindy's plight was typical, Axelrod cited a statistic: "Studies show . . . since 1981 . . . homework for six- to nine-year-olds [has] tripled."[59]

But what does that mean? Researchers at the University of Michigan reported in 2000 that in the early eighties, only about one third of children aged six to eight had any homework at all; by the late nineties, about half did.[60] In 1981, those six to eight-year-olds who had homework spent an average of seven minutes per night doing it; by 1997, this had increased to eighteen minutes—not exactly drudgery.[61]

The fact is American students, on average and across all grade levels, do less than one hour of homework per night.[62]

Only about 10 percent do more; and even these children may not be doing work that appreciably improves their academic skills. It is now the fashion for teachers to assign "creative projects." Students spend their evenings struggling with inane assignments: write a suicide note from Lady Macbeth to her husband; use bread dough and other common kitchen staples to make a map of Italy—parents have heard it all.[63]

The CBS report presented a conventional but misleading picture of overworked, overburdened children at risk of being cheated out of their carefree childhoods. A 2003 Brookings Institution study debunking the homework overload myth ("Do Students Have Too Much Homework?") reports that "Since 2001, feature stories about onerous homework have appeared in the *New York Times, Washington Post, Chicago Sun-Times, Los Angeles Times*," and others.[64] According to Brookings education scholar Tom Loveless, "The stories are misleading. They do not reflect the experience of a majority—or even a significant minority—of American schoolchildren."[65]

The Public Agenda is a distinguished education research organization founded by Daniel Yankelovich (sometimes called the "founding father of public opinion research") and Cyrus Vance (Secretary of State under Jimmy Carter). In 1997, it published the results of its survey of teen attitudes toward school.[66] Among its findings: "Students from across the country repeatedly said that they could 'earn' acceptable grades, pass their courses, and receive a diploma, all while investing minimal effort in their school work."[67] It reported, "Half say their schools don't challenge them to do their best."[68] Students were not suffering from an intensely demanding or stressful academic environment. The report concluded, "They hunger for structure, discipline, and more rigorous standards. They complain bitterly about lax instructors and unenforced rules."[69] Many educators, however, do not see structure, discipline, or standards as pressing educational needs, and this applies especially to many professors of education who train the nation's teachers.

The Heart and Mind of a Therapistic Educator

Dr. Denise Clark Pope, an education scholar at Stanford University, recently published a critically acclaimed book entitled *Doing School: How We Are Creating a Generation of Stressed Out, Materialistic, and Miseducated Kids.*[70] The former education editor of the *New York Times*, Edward B. Fiske, praised it as a book that "should inform any discussion of what it means to be an educated person in the twenty-first century."[71]

It is worth taking a careful look at Pope's credo, because many education professors—a clear majority, according to a study we shall cite—share her convictions. Pope says, "In the American capitalist system, students learn to compete; the goal is to win, 'to beat the others,' . . . even if this means acting in ways that are personally frustrating and dissatisfying. . . . One may ask, is it worth it?"[72] Pope, herself, is convinced it is not worth it and calls for a "new vision of what it means to be successful in school and what it means to be successful in America."[73]

Pope rejects the focus on grades, test scores, and honors. These, she says, "ignite feelings of competition." She recommends that students be judged by standards that are less frustrating and upsetting. In preference to traditional measures of success, she endorses "mastery exhibitions" where students "choose to perform a dramatic piece, write a report, field questions from teachers and peers, complete a project, or create other 'exhibits.' "[74] In this way, all students have a chance to "feel as 'smart' as [their] peers."[75]

Pope bases many of her recommendations on her yearlong observations and interviews with five high-achieving students in a Northern California high school. These kids appear to be exemplary: they get high grades, take part in extracurricular activities and community service, and win awards and honors. However, behind the achievement, Pope sees unhappiness, emotional tumult, and compromised integrity. The students' quest for academic glory—perfect grades, high SAT scores, admission to elite colleges—makes them anxious, frustrated, and subject to "undue stress," even nauseous and fearful. Pope asks: "Are we fostering an environment that promotes intellectual curiosity, cooperation, and integrity, or are our schools breeding anxiety, deception, and frustration?"[76]

For Pope the answer is decidedly grim. She believes kids today are just "doing school" as a means to material success. They are captive to an "ideology of achievement." She reports, "Passion and engagement were rare, and the daily grind of the school took its toll on their 'health and happiness.' "[77] In her opinion, success in school has become a dog-eat-dog contest where "academic success for some must necessarily be accompanied by academic failure for others."[78]

In condemning competition in the schools, Pope has a lot of company. In 1997, Public Agenda polled a random sample of nine hundred professors of education about their educational philosophy—focusing on their views of academic hierarchies and competition. The results, released under the title *Different Drummers: How Teachers of Teachers View Public Education,* found that "64 percent [of education professors] think schools should avoid competition."[79] Almost half preferred a system where grades go to teams of students for group effort rather than to individuals.[80] (One wonders how these same professors would react if their individual salary increases were based on "group effort.")

In any case, it is not at all clear that the public wants the celebratory, standard-free style of education Pope and her colleagues favor. The idea of grades for "group effort" will strike many as bizarre: it ignores the students in the Public Agenda Survey who were asking for traditional standards and structure. Pope urges adults to listen to students' "voices." But she never explains why the voices of the five anxious students who were the focus of her study should be taken as representative of millions of American schoolchildren.

Where Pope and Her Colleagues Go Wrong

Pope and like-minded educators wish to spare students the emotional stresses that come from competing. Yet the desire to achieve—to be among the best and the first—is part of human nature. Competition fuels achievement in academics as in sports. Pope does report high levels of cheating among today's students, and she is right to be alarmed. But the solution is for adults to teach children the value of honesty and to hold them firmly to its standards. Within the constraints of morality and law, competition is a powerfully creative and animating force that drives the advancement of knowledge, art, and invention. Also, it can be fun.

E. D. Hirsch Jr., professor of English at the University of Virginia and president of the Core Knowledge Foundation, a non-profit organization devoted to educational reform, opposes the drive to do away with competition and rewards. Hirsch wisely says, "Instead of trying fruitlessly to abolish competition as an element of human nature, we should try to guide it into educationally productive channels."[81]

Parents and teachers must work hard to instill a code of ethics in children. But extinguishing the drive to compete and achieve is not the way to do it, not if we wish to prepare them for the real world. Pope speaks disapprovingly of "the American capitalist system [where] students learn to compete." But the responsible teacher must prepare her students to cope with this reality. No one, not the parents nor the state, has given educators a mandate to abandon their mission of educating children for the world in which they will actually live.

In 2000, Suzanne Hidi and Judith Harackiewicz, psychologists at the Universities of Toronto and Wisconsin, respectively, published an article in the *Review of Educational Research* (2000) summarizing the accumulating literature on the value of competing for academic prizes.[82] Children, they say, may undertake a new scholastic activity simply to get good grades, or to outshine friends, but in the course of pursuing these external goals, they often become competent, interested, and eventually, internally motivated.[83]

These conclusions will probably seem self-evident to anyone who has not been trained at a school of education. Common sense also tells us that in competing and striving to succeed, students learn self-discipline, concentration, and good work habits. But the response to the Hidi and Harackiewicz article from some professional educators was horror. In one published reaction, two education scholars questioned the ethical orientation of researchers who would even entertain the idea that "besting others and extrinsic rewards are worthy and valued purposes."[84] Harackiewicz was taken aback by the criticism of her research. When we talked to her she told us that she was "just doing science." These critics, she said, "want to change the world."[85]

It is ironic that the movement in the lower and secondary schools to eliminate competition is thriving at the very time that the competitive battle for admission to elite colleges is fiercer than ever. But that battle is limited to an extremely small number of superior students. These high achievers should not be confused with typical high school seniors—one third of whom do not go to college at all.[86] The Public Agenda study of student attitudes and prospects noted that among high school seniors, "Only a quarter will obtain an undergraduate degree. The rest are likely to be disappointed, and . . . genuinely 'clueless' about how to organize their futures."[87]

The anticompetition movement will do nothing to narrow the gap between low and high achievers. Unmotivated students and underperforming students can now be complacent about not entering the fray; by contrast, ambitious students do not for one moment let up in the pursuit of prizes.

The Myth of High Self-Esteem

The crusade against games with winners and losers, the sensitivity monitoring of classroom textbooks, the antipathy to competition, are all part of a national effort to enhance the self-confidence of American children. Yet, it has never been shown that "high self-esteem" is an essential trait for students to possess.

High school dropouts, shoplifters, burglars, car thieves, and even murderers are just as likely to have high self-esteem as Rhodes Scholars or winners of the Congressional Medal of Honor. As a 2001 article in *Scientific American* pointed out, "Saddam Hussein is not known as a modest, cautious, self-doubting individual."[88] Hopeful Americans continue to buy thousands of books each year with titles like *The Self-Esteem Companion* and *Hypnosis for Self-Confidence and Self-Esteem*. Still, no one seems to know how to define it, how to measure it, or whether it can be taught. Now, several studies suggest that inflated self-esteem may even be dangerous.[89]

In May 2003, four prominent academic psychologists published the first comprehensive review of the supposed benefits of self-esteem in a journal published by the American Psychological Society called *Psychological Science in the Public Interest*. Roy F. Baumeister of Case Western Reserve University and his colleagues looked at all the existing studies on self-esteem and found no significant connection between feelings of high self-worth and academic achievement, interpersonal relationships, or healthy lifestyles.[90]

On the contrary, high self-regard is very often found in people who are narcissistic and have an inflated sense of popularity and likeability. Such self-aggrandizing beliefs, said the authors, exist "mainly in their own minds."[91] Furthermore, those with exaggerated estimates of self-worth often become hostile when others criticize or reject them. "People who have elevated or inflated views of themselves tend to alienate others," the authors concluded.[92]

If high self-esteem does not improve academic performance, if it does not make people kinder or less likely to engage in self-destructive behavior, then why encourage it at all? The review article did find one significant advantage that seems, at first glance, highly attractive. People with high self-esteem are happier. According to Baumeister's team, "People with high self-esteem are significantly, substantially happier than other people. They are also less likely to be depressed."[93]

Baumeister and colleagues were careful to say that further research is needed to establish the positive link. Nor do researchers know precisely how to determine that someone is happy or in which direction the causal story goes (that is, happiness may lead to high self-esteem, not vice versa). For the moment, self-reports ("I'm happy. I feel great.") are the only source. But self-reports from those with very high self-regard are suspect. It is well-established that persons with inflated self-confidence tend to exaggerate their own positive qualities; they may well be overstating their levels of happiness.[94]

But suppose we were somehow able to establish that high self-esteem promotes happiness. What parent or teacher would not want to confer such felicity on a child? This finding alone would appear to justify the self-esteem movement. Or would it?

For one thing, what it is that makes us happy matters greatly. As we already noted, bullies and sociopaths often score very high on self-esteem tests and claim that they are very happy. Happiness, without a foundation in ethics, can characterize a smug, unfeeling person, and such people are often exploitive and dangerous. As the great nineteenth-century philosopher John Stuart Mill famously said:

No intelligent human being would consent to be a fool, no instructed person would be an ignoramus, no person of feeling
and conscience would be selfish and base, even though they
should be persuaded that the fool, the dunce, or the rascal is
better satisfied with his lot than they are with theirs . . . better
to be Socrates dissatisfied than a fool satisfied.[95]

Those who encourage children to "feel good about themselves" may be cheating them, unwittingly, out of becoming
the kind of conscientious, humane, and enlightened persons
Mill had in mind.

The American philosopher and psychologist William James,
a contemporary of Mill, noted that there is little or no connection between a man's self-esteem and his objective merits: "[A]
very meanly-conditioned man may abound in unfaltering con-
ceit, and one whose success in life is secure and who is esteemed
by all may remain diffident of his powers to the end."[96]

What should schools be doing about self-esteem? They
should not be addressing it directly at all. Self-esteem comes to
some of us when we have an objective record of accomplishment
in which we take pride. Even then, as the example of many
other wonderful humble people teaches us, there is no guarantee it will come at all. If so, we must make do without it.

Self Esteem and the Violation of Privacy

John Hewitt, a University of Massachusetts sociologist, has
examined the morality of the self-esteem movement from a
different direction. In his 1998 book, *The Myth of Self-Esteem*,
he points to the ethical hazards of using the classroom for
therapeutic purposes.[97] In a typical classroom self-esteem exercise, students complete sentences beginning "I love myself
because . . ." or "Yes, I love myself even though I sometimes . . ."[98] Hewitt explains that children interpret these assignments as *demands* for self-revelation. They feel pressed to

"correctly" complete the sentences in ways the teacher finds satisfactory.

As Hewitt observes:

> Teachers . . . no doubt regard the exercises as being in the best interest of their students. . . . Yet from a more skeptical perspective, these exercises are subtle instruments of social control. The child *must* be taught to like himself or herself. . . . The child *must* confess self-doubt or self-loathing, bringing into light the feelings that he or she might well prefer to keep private. [Emphasis in original.][99]

Teaching children to moderate their emotions is helpful to them. Forcing them to obsess over feelings and to share them with others, on the other hand, is meddling. Recall the exercise extolled by Daniel Goleman where, during roll call, children identify their current emotional state rather than saying "here." Suppose some of the children have serious problems at home—a depressed mother or alcoholic father? Should they feel compelled to disclose their true feelings? Or, alternatively, to present a false picture of themselves?

The roll call exercise was developed by "Self Science," a program started in 1978 by education researchers at the Neuva Learning Center in Hillsborough, California. Goleman's support and praise infused it with new life and in 1998 a second edition of the center's curriculum was published, entitled *Self-Science: The Emotional Intelligence Curriculum.*[100] The text, as befits a "scientific" treatise, is full of charts and graphs with names like "confluence models," "sequence spirals," and "affective education index." The course includes sixty-two lessons and requires children to meet for forty-five minutes, twice a week for an entire school year. It is intended for children in grades 1–8 and can be incorporated into social studies, language arts, and even math classes. One typical activity is the "Hot Potato Feeling Experiment."[101] It instructs schoolchildren in the art of "inventorying their feelings." Students, called "learners," toss a bean bag back and forth, and when they catch this "hot potato" they shout out their current emotion. Later, in a group or in their journals, they answer these questions:

"How does it feel to say what you are feeling?"
"How do you feel when you can't say anything?"
"Is there anything you would like to have said but censored instead? What?"[102]

The participants have to promise to keep everything said in the self-science sessions a secret. Parents are not allowed to be present. The book explains, "Confidentiality is important to the children."[103] The authors of the curriculum are unfazed by student resistance. Opposition only proves the program is working! As they say:

Somewhere during all this, there is a point where members need to rebel and test. (This testing is called 'storming' in the group development process of 'forming, norming, storming, performing.') Be listening for expressions of hostility . . . it's your clue that the process is working.[104]

What would it take to persuade the self-scientists that their process isn't working? Hostility could be regarded as a sign that students find the program absurd, tedious, intrusive, or just a waste of time. They may be "rebelling" because they resent the requirement that they must bare their feelings or suspect that their classmates will not respect the secrecy pledge. Goleman and other self-scientists who are in the business of promoting self-esteem education need to consider the possibility that their pedagogy is based on a false assumption. They take it for granted that open, emotional self-expression is necessarily a good thing for children. But what if it is not?

In a report called "Is Repression Adaptive?" a team of

psychologists studied a group of high school students, dividing them into three types: repressors (those who suppress unsettling thoughts); sensitizers (those keenly aware of their emotional states); and intermediates.[105]

The students were then asked to evaluate themselves and others using these distinctions; so were their teachers. The repressors were rated as more successful academically and socially. "In their day-to-day behavior it may be good not to be so emotional," said the researchers. "The moods of repressed people may be more balanced."

Though these data do not establish a cause-and-effect relationship between repression and success, they suggest that efforts to turn healthy repressors into nervous sensitizers may be injurious to them. School officials should be leery of "feelings" exercises, and curricula that demand that students bare their souls. Indeed, they should consider dispensing with them altogether.

Pushing Children Deeply into Their Own Experiences

In 2003, New York City adopted a self-focused, city-wide literacy program developed by Lucy Calkins, an education researcher from Columbia University. The *New York Times Magazine* writer James Traub, in a lengthy article about Calkins's curriculum, described her as a "leading guru" in New York City literacy instruction who pushes children "deeply into their experience."[106]

Calkins believes that "Young people need to be invited to put themselves on the line, to bring themselves into the classroom."[107] In her writing workshops, she shows teachers how to encourage personal revelation. The day Traub observed her, she asked participants to disclose their happiest and least happy memory of writing. One teacher reported that her least happy experience was writing a term paper in college; the most happy was keeping a journal when her father was dying. An exhilarated Calkins seized on this comment, "What works for us is writing that is personal." She then told several poignant stories about how children trained in her program had written about their deepest feelings and yearnings. "It does not have to be a book report. It doesn't have to be about Ancient Greece."[108]

Perhaps New York City's Mayor Bloomberg and Joel Klein, the chancellor of the New York City school system, should have taken a closer look at Calkins's influential book *The Writing Workshop: A World of Difference* and the video that goes along with it.[109] Both make clear the philosophy of education she is promoting in New York City schools.

Calkins says in the video, "Most of all, we write to make sense out of our lives." The camera then pans to a twelve-year-old boy, Jesse, who says, as if on cue, "When I write, I get a lot of madness out of me."[110] But it is Erica who is the star of the film, offering proof to Calkins that her workshops are making a "world of difference." In a final, highly emotional scene, we see this eleven-year-old girl reading aloud from her essay about her great-grandfather's funeral. Near tears, she describes her shame at having never told him how much she loved him:

> I was ashamed because I was afraid of him . . . I loved him so much but I didn't have the courage to tell him . . . Let me tell you something. Never lose your courage to tell someone you love them because if you do you're making the same mistake I did. I love you, Great-Grandfather, I really love you.[111]

Erica's story is moving, but why should teachers be encouraging such intense personal revelation from eleven-year-olds in an English class? It is quite possible that Erica felt subtle pressure to make extravagant disclosures. In this case, the scene she describes is highly improbable. For we learn that she was only two years old when her great-grandfather died and that she hardly knew him.

Has it occurred to Calkins that asking children to probe their deepest emotions is invasive? Or that such intrusion inevitably invites some children to prevaricate, invent, and dramatize? Why should young people who are in school to learn skills and become knowledgeable be asked to "put themselves on the line?" Reading and writing about ancient Greece is exactly the sort of thing they should be doing.

Calkins says, "Most of all we write to make sense of our lives." But how can young people make sense of their lives without at least a tenuous grasp of things outside themselves? In a letter reacting to Traub's article, a teacher from Staten Island, New York, pointed out that the new curriculum encourages children to be narrowly self-preoccupied: "Children who learn to read and write by reflecting on their friends, their pets, and their trips to Disney World can rapidly come to assume that their own experiences are much more valid and interesting than anyone else's."[112]

A classroom is where children should be getting out of themselves as they learn about the great world that surrounds them. The purpose of education is not to find yourself, but to lose yourself.

Happy Talk History

Even the study of history, and especially American history, has been radically transformed by the requirement that school materials should help children find themselves and feel good about themselves. In too many classrooms historical content is sacrificed for therapeutic goals: the primary emphasis is on feeling, personal growth, and validation.

The State of California, for example, requires that all instructional materials used in its classrooms "contribute to a positive educational experience for all students."[113] It therefore subjects prospective textbooks to a "social content review" to determine whether or not they "promote individual development and self-esteem" and "instill in each child a sense of pride in his or her heritage [and] develop a feeling of self-worth."[114] Because California is one of the largest markets in the country, textbook publishers marketing to other states tailor their books to its specifications. As Diane Ravitch abundantly shows, it is not just California. Sensitivity committees are everywhere.

What happens when social studies textbooks aim at boosting self-esteem and providing the student with a "positive experience?" Gilbert Sewall, director of the American Textbook Council, an organization dedicated to improving history and civics education, aptly sums up the effects: "Students and teachers alike are sedated by textbook happy talk."[115]

Publishers and educators now take great care to avoid giving the impression that the United States is in any way exceptional or superior to other societies; to single it out for praise could hurt the feelings of children born in other countries. According to the special logic of the sensitivity monitors, immigrant youth might feel diminished or marginalized by readings that extol American traditions. A fact-based history curriculum that highlights the founding doctrines, the great wars, and the traditional heroes of American history might valorize America at the expense of other nations and cultures.

Martin Rochester, Distinguished Teaching Professor of Political Science at the University of Missouri–St. Louis, points out that history education now requires teachers to be "sensitive to student emotions and feelings, and that [their] role is that of psychologist and problem solver as much as purveyor of knowledge and comprehension."[116] Rochester says that today's history curriculum has become "nonhierarchical, nonjudgmental, [and] nonacademic." The net result is something unprecedented. Young people, by design, are kept ignorant of much of their own history and of the virtues of its unique institutions.

There is in fact no evidence that immigrant children or their parents would feel in any way insulted or diminished by reading texts praising the nation's democratic tradition and its heroes. What we do know suggests the very opposite. An important study by Public Agenda, carried out with the support of the two largest teacher's unions, the National Education

Association and the American Federation of Teachers, finds that "parents of all demographic groups—white, black, or Hispanic, immigrant or U.S.-born—clearly and resoundingly want the schools to teach children the traditional ideals and stories of what it means to be an American."[117] Two-thirds of them feel strongly that schools should "teach kids to be patriotic and loyal toward the nation."[118]

Benjamin Barber, a political scientist at the University of Maryland, notes that historical knowledge is the ground of patriotic sentiment:

[We] derive our sense of national identity [from] the Declaration of Independence, the Constitution and the Bill of Rights, the inaugural addresses of our presidents, Lincoln's Gettysburg Address, and Martin Luther King's ["I Have a Dream"] sermon at the 1963 March on Washington—not so much the documents themselves as the felt sentiments tying us to them.[119]

This feeling of national identity presupposes familiarity with these documents—a presumption that is not generally warranted. Many young Americans today draw a blank when asked elementary questions about history. In 1995, when the Department of Education released the dismaying results of its National History Assessment, Lewis Lapham, editor of *Harper's Magazine*, spoke of the low scores as a "coroner's report." Students, he said, are in a "state of mortal danger." He noted, "More than 50 percent of all high school seniors were unaware of the Cold War. Nearly six in ten were bereft of even a primitive understanding of where America came from."[120] The results of the 2001 history assessment were no better.[121] Fifty-seven percent of twelfth graders scored "below basic" in their knowledge of U.S. history.[122]

In 2002, the American Council of Trustees and Alumni commissioned a Roper Survey measuring the historical knowledge of seniors from fifty elite colleges and universities.[123] Among the findings: "College seniors could not identify Valley Forge, words from the Gettysburg Address, or even basic principles of the U.S. Constitution."[124] The report corroborated the findings of the Department of Education. The Council's survey concludes, "Given high-school-level questions, 81 percent of the [college] seniors would have received a D or F."[125]

Students in the past may have been ignorant of the fine points of American history, but they carried around in their heads a crude outline of our national story. Their history textbooks showed them that they were part of a highly unusual culture of liberty, and they were acquainted with and took pride in the heroes of the Revolutionary and Civil Wars. That prideful perspective is fast becoming obsolete. Today's textbook writers take pains not to give students the impression that there is anything especially admirable or virtuous about the American experiment. Stanford's William Damon has written about the adverse effects on young Americans:

> Students are not learning much of what they need to know . . . there's another problem that may be even closer to the heart of the matter. This has to do with the capacity for positive feelings towards one's society, with a sense of attachment, a sense of affiliation, a sense of love for noble purposes larger than oneself, and a sense of inspiration fostered by one's role as citizen . . . since the time of the ancient Greeks, [this sentiment] has been known as patriotism.[126]

The very mention of the word *patriotism*, says Damon, provokes an argument: "If you think it's hard to talk about morality and values in the schools, try talking about patriotism."

How Therapism and Multiculturalism Circumvent Morality

One effect of the ignorance and confusion is that many students are reluctant or unable to condemn atrocities committed by other cultures no matter how heinous. In many world history classes, it is now the fashion to present all cultures and civilizations as morally equivalent.[127] To do otherwise is deemed intolerant and demeaning to "the Other." In one typical high school text, *American Odyssey: The United States in the Twentieth Century*, the Anasazi Indians, who inhabited large regions of the Southwest between A.D. 900 and 1300, are praised for their "egalitarian culture in which people functioned as equals."[128] Students do not learn about recent evidence that strongly suggests that Anasazi "egalitarians" were cannibals. A 1997 newsletter from the Archeological Institute of America reports on an Anasazi burial ground:

> The remains of 12 people were discovered at the site . . . but only five were from burials. The other seven appear to have been systematically dismembered, defleshed, their bones battered, and in some cases burned or stewed, leaving them in the same condition as bones of animals used for food. . . . Patterns of burning indicate that many were exposed to flame while still covered with flesh, which is what would be expected after cooking over a fire.[129]

Such information is routinely suppressed in K–12 textbooks and classrooms because revealing it would be disrespectful of the Anasazi and because a discussion of cannibalism might distress some students. It would inevitably raise questions about the moral status of another society, possibly implying that our own modern society might be superior. As Ravitch has pointed out, no hint of any such suggestion would ever get past the sensitivity police.

In California, the Department of Education explicitly requires that "when ethnic or cultural groups are portrayed, portrayals must not depict differences in customs or lifestyles as undesirable and must not reflect adversely on such differences."[130] The state of Connecticut requires that all classroom materials "present the rights, goals, and needs of all groups as worthwhile and authentic."[131]

A doggedly uncritical attitude to cultures other than our own demands a great deal of forgiveness on the part of the student. Inevitably, it requires that they approach exotic cruelties and barbarisms in a spirit of tolerance and forbearing. In a 2000 commencement address, the president of Wake Forest College, Dr. Thomas K. Hearn Jr., reported visiting a Wake Forest class whose students were "reluctant to denounce Hitler as a monster." One student defended Hitler as "a man of his own time. We cannot judge him by our different standards."[132]

Today, such no-fault history is common in American classrooms. Robert Simon, a professor of philosophy at Hamilton College, finds increasing numbers of students telling him "they accept the reality of the Holocaust, but they believe themselves unable morally to condemn it, or indeed to make any moral judgments whatsoever." Simon calls their moral paralysis and relativistic stance "absolutophobia."[133]

Phobias that inhibit moral judgment have found their way into all subjects, including English classes. Professor Kay Haugaard, a creative writing teacher at Pasadena City College, wrote in the *Chronicle of Higher Education* about her class's reaction to Shirley Jackson's story "The Lottery." This story describes a village that holds an annual lottery that all are obliged to enter. Each year the loser of the lottery is stoned to death. The villagers, who are otherwise moral and decent people, continue this practice because they sincerely believe it brings good fortune to the community as a whole.

Haugaard's students did not condemn the villagers. Instead they strained to understand them, to defend them and, in the end, to exculpate them. Haugaard sought in vain to find even one student who would react with moral indignation to the villagers' grisly custom of stoning an innocent person, but she failed. "At this point I gave up. No one in the whole class of more than twenty ostensibly intelligent individuals would go out on a limb and take a stand against human sacrifice."[134]

What can explain the moral timidity of today's students?

Students equate adverse moral judgment with intolerance and insensitivity. And though some professors are dismayed by their students' no-fault ethic, few appear to be doing anything to discourage it. On the other hand, not a few endorse and foster just this kind of moral agnosticism.

In July 2002, Zogby International released the results of a poll on moral education on the American campus. In a survey of four hundred randomly selected college seniors, Zogby found the overwhelming majority (97 percent) said that they expected to be ethical in their future undertakings. However, 73 percent said they had learned from their professors that "what is right and wrong depends on differences in individual values and cultural diversity."[135]

Professors, teachers, and textbook writers who promote relativism and nonjudgmentalism are, no doubt, sincerely and earnestly trying to instill in their students a tolerant and empathetic understanding of exotic societies. Paradoxically, such efforts can also undermine a student's capacity for empathy.

An Immense Human Idea

Pluralism is an American tradition, but moral relativism is not. In the Declaration of Independence, Thomas Jefferson asserts the universal right to life, liberty, and the pursuit of happiness. He does not add, "At least that is how many of us feel about it here." The assertions of Abraham Lincoln, Elizabeth Cady Stanton, and Martin Luther King are in that same spirit: they affirm transcendent moral ideals true for all mankind.

To be sure, the idea of "moral truth"—to say nothing of self-evident moral truth—is controversial, indeed. The theoretical debate over the ultimate status of moral judgments goes back to the very beginnings of philosophy in ancient Greece, when Plato (a moral absolutist) first challenged the Sophists (the upstart relativists). However fascinating and contentious the philosophical debate may be, we do not have the luxury of waiting to see which side finally prevails before we teach our children about right and wrong and good and evil. We must live in this world here and now where there is no choice but to take a committed stand on basic moral questions.

It is no great achievement for a teacher or textbook publisher to induce skepticism in American students about the truth or legitimacy of Jefferson's assertions. After all, many parts of the world today, and certainly, most societies in history, do not take it as self-evident that human beings possess basic inalienable rights.

What American students badly need to understand is how fortunate they are that the nation's founders had such unusual ideas about personal liberty and individual rights, and how blessed we are to live in a society that takes them as self-evident and incorporates them into its constitution and strives to live by them.

The Nobel Laureate author V. S. Naipaul is struck by the originality, power, and sheer beauty of America's founding ideals. He is particularly enraptured by the right of each individual to pursue his happiness:

The pursuit of happiness is . . . an elastic idea; it fits all men. . . . So much is contained in it: the idea of the individual, responsibility, choice, the life of the intellect, the idea of vocation and perfectibility and achievement. It is an immense human idea. It cannot be reduced to a fixed system. It cannot generate fanaticism. But it is known to exist; and because of that, other more rigid systems in the end blow away.[136]

American students need to appreciate and to cherish this "immense human idea." They must understand what it is they have inherited—especially at a time when free societies are under assault. Naipaul, who wrote before September 11, 2001, is confident the formidable influences opposed to democratic ideals will wither away, because he never doubts that democracies will confidently defend their principles of freedom. Such confidence assumes a lot. In particular, it assumes that children today are being educated to take pride in their country's way of life. But it ignores the effects of therapism.

As long as censorship and misguided sensitivities are allowed to constrain how and what our children are taught, civic education in America will fall short of its mission. For too many young people, the fear of being judgmental, categorical, and insensitive is paralyzing and quite literally demoralizing.

After several decades of therapeutic relativism, many of our young people are unable to speak with confidence in support of the moral ideals that have made their own way of life possible. Too many have been rendered incapable of standing up for the moral ideals that ground our constitutional democracy. Liberty? What of it? Some may not be sure whether our way of life is especially worth defending.

Then and Now

Several months after the Japanese bombed Pearl Harbor in 1941, the National Education Association published a slim volume titled *The Education of Free Men in American Democracy*.[137] Written by Columbia Teachers College Professor George S. Counts, the book discussed the role of teachers in the war effort. Here is how he described our enemies:

> Today the threat to democracy comes from a barbaric banditry, marked by cynical duplicity and outrageous violation of the ordinary rules of human decency. . . . This new threat to freedom comes from ruthless men of force who care nothing for civil liberties and who mock at all appeals to humanity.[138]

Counts saw teachers as frontline defense in the centuries-old battle against tyranny and injustice. Their job was to imbue students with a sense of history and a philosophical understanding of the principles of American democracy. According to Counts, students must be made fully familiar with "the long struggle to liberate the human mind and civilize the human heart."[139] To that end, the public schools "should fashion an education frankly and systematically designed to give to the rising generation the loyalties, the knowledge, the discipline of free men."[140]

September 11, 2001, has evoked comparison with Pearl Harbor Day. But today's National Education Association no longer publishes books like *The Education of Free Men in American Democracy*. Indeed, its policies and educational philosophy are in many ways antithetical to the idea that education should "frankly and systematically . . . give the rising generation the loyalties, the knowledge, the discipline of free men." On the first anniversary of the terrorist attack, the NEA produced a special Web site advisory titled "Remember September 11."[141]

The NEA saw the attack mainly in terms of the threat it posed to children's mental health. In one typical lesson, the guide suggests that teachers, "Have students draw a picture of the tragic event using colors they have chosen that represent the way they feel."[142] Children could also construct a "moving memorial" by expressing their feelings through movement, or send "patriotically-themed stuffed bears across the nation" along with a letter relating the class's feelings about September 11.[143] High school students were invited to join a "circle of feelings" where they "discuss and have validated their feelings about the events of September 11 in a nonjudgmental discussion circle."[144] They could also soothe themselves with recordings of rushing water and rustling trees. Parents and teachers were encouraged to provide students with "a low-key day" and, if possible, to "integrate healthy snacks." When Chester Finn, former Assistant Secretary of Education, examined it he said, "As one browsed its recommended lessons and background guidance for teachers, the dominant impression was one of psychotherapy via the Internet."[145]

The NEA materials were designed to help the nation's

schoolchildren cope with what the authors of "Remember September 11" called the "anniversary effect." However, apart from those directly victimized by the attack, there is no evidence that children en masse needed psychological comforting one year later. On the other hand, almost all children needed to understand the political and ethical significance of September 11. That kind of orientation, so natural to educators of yesteryear, is altogether unnatural to educators steeped in the therapism of today.

The current NEA was not alone in viewing the anniversary of September 11 as an opportunity for therapeutic healing and self-discovery. The Families and Work Institute, a nonprofit research organization that focuses on family, community, and the workforce produced a curriculum called "9/11 As History." According to its president, Ellen Galinsky, entire school districts, including Dallas and Phoenix, have used it.[146]

The sponsors of the curriculum could not be more mainstream. Corporate supporters of The Families and Work Institute include General Electric, IBM, Johnson & Johnson, and AT&T. CNN's senior correspondent Judy Woodruff and Pulitzer Prize–winning journalist/novelist Anna Quindlen are on its board. Philanthropies like the Red Cross and The Anti-Defamation League, joined by leading educators, made substantial contributions to the anniversary curriculum. Bank One was the Institute's partner in launching the "9/11 As History" Web site.[147]

The stated goal of "9/11 As History" is admirable: "To help children understand what would be lost if American values were lost to the world."[148] Jamie Dimon, president and chief executive officer of Bank One, wrote the foreword to a 2003 book summarizing and celebrating the sixteen lesson plans. He speaks of the importance of making children "more committed than ever to the values that make this country great."[149] According to Galinsky, "We decided that the most important lessons to impart should focus on teaching the skills of DEMOCRACY." (Emphasis in original.)[150] So far, at least programmatically, these sentiments are not very different from those of George Counts.

But there the comparison abruptly ends. Little in the curriculum would lead children to believe there is anything unique or precious about American ideals; nor do children learn much about how these ideals are threatened or under attack. The actual purpose of "9/11 As History" is not to enlighten or inspire children, but to improve their emotional self-awareness and to help them like themselves more.

The first lesson, "All Kinds of Feelings," developed by the Anti-Defamation League, is intended for children in prekindergarten through second grade. Soon after school opened in September 2002, teachers were to ask children a series of questions: "How did you feel about meeting new children in your class this year? How did you feel about already knowing some of the children in your class? How did you feel about having a new teacher? How did you feel about already knowing some of the teachers you have this year? How did you feel coming to a new place for school?" And so on. There are no direct inquires about the terrorist attack. But, out of nowhere, the teachers are supposed to ask: "How do you feel if someone knocks down the block tower you just built? What might you do?"[151]

The answers the children give to these questions are listed on the chalkboard and serve as the basis for a class "feelings collage." The collage, in turn, is to serve as a catalyst for a "feelings dance." If time allows, the guides suggests a "feelings book" and "feelings masks."[152]

The "feelings" drumbeat is unceasing. The authors of the curriculum never explain how such emphasis on children's emotions will help them understand and commemorate September 11. They do not tell us why children as young as three or four need special lessons and activities in the first place. Nor do they make a case for the need for a schoolwide program. No doubt, there were some young people who were distressed on the anniversary of the attack. But they were very much in the minority and could have been helped individually by parents or school counselors.

The teachers themselves are not spared the therapeutic ministrations. The "All Kinds of Feelings" lesson plan includes a warning: "NOTE TO TEACHERS: During the discussions about feelings . . . prepare yourself to handle comments about feelings that children may raise about September 11. Before you are able to help children, you will need to assist yourself with coming to terms with your own feelings."[153] To this end, the Families and Work Institute offers a workbook, "Helping People Who Work with Kids Prepare for the 9/11 Anniversary," written by two trauma experts from Morristown, New Jersey. The workbook takes teachers through the process of "Reconstructing Life Assumptions." It acknowledges that this may be the "the last thing" teachers wish to do over their summer vacation. All the same it reminds them, "Adults can't help kids with their reactions until we've first been helped with our own."[154]

Once the students have completed the "All Kinds of Feelings" unit and the teachers, presumably, have successfully restructured their life assumptions, the class is ready for Lesson 2, on "Everyday Heroes." Developed by the PBS literacy program *Reading Rainbow*, this lesson was designed to help children understand heroism "within themselves and others." Students are prompted to see heroism in "people who raise money for causes" or in "a tree planter who makes a home for birds." If a child defines a hero in a "negative" way—an example is "a soldier who kills bad people"—she should be encouraged to find a more affirmative characterization.[155]

Conspicuously absent from the parade of heroes are such figures as George Washington (himself a soldier who killed bad people), Abraham Lincoln, Martin Luther King, and others who helped make America the "land of the free."[156] Children in K–2 are fully capable of understanding, enjoying and being morally instructed by examples of such stock national heroes, yet they are never mentioned.

The Families and Work Institute has reduced September 11 to an occasion for self-preoccupation. After exploring their feelings and learning how to be their own heroes, the children are ready for "What's Special About Me?" Teachers are supposed to tell the class:

> Last year, as we watched the events of September 11th, one of the things most people felt very good about were all the people who helped in the rescue and recovery. We saw the police and the firemen, and we liked them because they were so brave. One of the things we don't often pay much attention to, though, is liking *ourselves*. [Emphasis in original.][157]

The teacher then draws a large outline of herself on the board, and says, "So today we're all going to take some time to think about what we like about who we are. . . . I'm going to draw all the things on this picture of me that I like about myself." And each student in the class is expected to follow suit. The idea behind the lesson plan, assumed but never proved, is that students who really like themselves will cope better with stress and trauma.[158]

"Building Strength Through Knowledge" is the title of Lesson 10. It was developed for children in junior high school by a professor at the University of Oklahoma Health Science Center. Here, finally, is a lesson with intellectual substance—or so the title of the lesson would lead us to expect. In fact, by "knowledge" the professor does not mean information about the world, but rather the students' "knowledge" of—what else?—their own feelings. "Explain that you are going to be discussing emotions or feelings." The guide informs teachers that students need to recognize "there are no rights or wrongs when it comes to feelings and opinions."[159]

One of the explicit central aims of "9/11 As History" is "helping children become critical thinkers."[160] In practice, however, the curriculum indiscriminately celebrates all differences of opinions and points of view, thereby discouraging all and any critical evaluations. In Lesson 10, the child continues to confront the large, vacuous, happy face of therapeutic pedagogy.

Not all of the sixteen lesson plans are about feelings. Lesson 15 discusses some historical antecedents of September 11; another looks at some of the new civil liberties dilemmas we now face. But, with few exceptions, the curriculum has no intellectual content. It is full of gimmicks and amateur psychology and in no way does it fulfill its stated promise to help children understand "what would be lost if American values were lost to the world."

Only one of the curricula has a clear patriotic slant. In Lesson 11, students study the American flag, design a community banner, and are asked to complete the phrase, "Being an American today means . . ." But the authors of "9/11 As History" seem very uncomfortable with this topic, and so they post a warning to teachers: "Discussing the events of 9/11, *as well as themes of being 'American,'* may raise emotions and uncomfortable questions. . . . You may also wish to consider inviting a guidance counselor or other trained professional to take part in the discussion and activity." (Emphasis added.)[161]

This is just one curriculum guide. However, those who would dismiss these lessons as marginal and atypical need to explain why, after an event like September 11, leading educators, school administrators, child development experts, and major corporations and philanthropies are offering lesson plans like "9/11 As History" to American children. Why, in a nation that has been attacked by implacable and ideologically hostile forces of terror, are school systems like Phoenix and Dallas teaching that "there are no right or wrong when it comes to feelings and opinions" and *not* teaching lessons that incorporate the perspectives of educators like George S. Counts? With the generous help of Jamie Dimon and Bank One, "9/11 As History" has been published as a book so it can be used for further anniversaries and commemorations.

During the Second World War, the focus was not on "validating feelings" but on teaching students about the moral dimensions of the fight in which all, including children, were engaged. A book about American children during World War II (*Children of the World War II Home Front*, by Sylvia Whitman) quotes a man looking back at his wartime childhood: "We saw ourselves as good guys who were united against the bad."[162] That simple and necessary perspective is lost in a nonjudgmental pedagogy that is preoccupied with feelings.

American children badly need moral clarity. But our education establishment is too uneasy about the idea of moral judgment to meet this elementary need. Feelings of helplessness and disorientation are thoroughly, even compulsively, canvassed, elicited, discussed, and promoted; by contrast, feelings of moral indignation and condemnation are deflected and downplayed. This leaves children defenseless, clueless and unprepared to meet real and grave threats to their own and the nation's future.

There are many who believe that therapism in the schools is a benign, constructive influence that comforts children, calming their fears and enhancing their feelings of self-acceptance. The evidence, however, does not bear this out. On the contrary, the therapeutic regime pathologizes healthy young people. It encourages remedial measures for nonexistent vulnerabilities, wastes students' time, and impedes their academic and moral development. American students are, with few exceptions, mentally and emotionally sound; they are resilient. They need more, not less, homework. They can cope with dodgeball.

2

Esteem Thyself

In the spring of 2003, a group of high school seniors from a Jewish day school outside Washington, D.C., spent a month in Israel. While camping in the Negev Desert, a counselor from a progressive-socialist kibbutz joined the group and led the students through a sensitivity exercise. The teens were told to walk into the desert until they were completely alone. The counselor, who was American-born, supplied them with a pencil, paper, matches, and a candle and instructed them to absorb the quiet calm of the desert, to record their feelings, and to "find themselves."

The students scattered into the desert, but several of them quickly became bored and sought one another's company. They threw the pencils and paper into a pile, and used the candles and matches to start a little bonfire. The kids enjoyed it; the sensitivity counselor was horrified. Later in the evening, the students sat in a circle to share their reflections. When one of them talked about the "haunting loneliness" of the desert; others could barely suppress laughter, causing further distress to the trainer.

What was the counselor trying to accomplish? Perhaps he just wanted them to experience the beauty and mystery of the desert. That is a commendable goal, and had he said that, the campers might have cooperated. It is likely however that he alienated them when he asked them to record their emotions and to "find themselves."

Daniel Goleman endorses these kinds of sensitivity exercises. Recall his enthusiasm for the self-science curriculum where students learn to "inventory their feelings." Goleman sees the art of feelings identification as a modern way to observe the ancient directive to be self-aware. " 'Know Thyself,' " says Goleman, "speaks to this keystone of emotional intelligence: awareness of one's own feelings as they occur."[1]

The authors of the self-science curriculum also invoke the Socratic tradition. For them, the injunction is really an imperative to *find* oneself, and, more important, to let others in on the discovery. "Know Yourself," they say, "includes naming and communicating emotions, understanding the way emotion and cognition interrelate, recognizing your own patterns, and identifying your needs."[2] These self-scientists urge children to "Know Yourself, Choose Yourself, and Give Yourself."

The words "Know Thyself" were inscribed on the Temple of Apollo at Delphi in ancient Greece. They are often associated with Socrates' maxim "the unexamined life is not worth living." But it is doubtful that either Socrates or the unknown author of "Know Thyself" was urging his countrymen to name and communicate emotions. Socrates cared about the good life, which he believed required an intense focus on the great questions of moral philosophy: the meaning of justice, wisdom, courage, temperance, and the essence of good and evil.

In *The Apology* Socrates says, "I say that this is the greatest good for a human being, every day to discuss goodness and other topics on which you've heard me conversing and examining myself and others, and that life without examination is not worth a man's living."[3] Nowhere does the great philosopher say anything about being aware of our feelings—or expressing them, trusting them, or living by them.

In truth, the ideas and ideals of self-scientists have their

sources in philosophies far more recent than those of ancient Greece. They are inspired by the popular psychologies
that pervaded American culture after the Second World
War—Freudian psychoanalysis and its successor known as
"the human potential movement."

According to the philosophy of human potential, self-
knowledge and personal salvation were to be attainable not, as
the Greeks had taught, through intellectual and moral discipline; nor, as the Judeo-Christian religions had taught, through
grace, devotion, and the performance of worthy deeds; but
rather through a regimen of self-preoccupation, self-expression,
and psychic release. The modern therapeutic era is marked by
this shift from an ethical imperative—"Know Thyself"—to the
clinical imperatives: "Express thyself," "Accept thyself," and
"Esteem thyself."

From Vienna to Santa Monica

Freud's writings were voluminous and obscure, and the versions of his theories that made their way into the popular culture were far from faithful to his views. Freud firmly believed in
the necessity and value of *suppressing* feelings.[4] He applied his
rule of "say anything that comes to mind" in the consulting
room only, not out in public. Nor was he an apostle of self-
preoccupation. As Freud never tired of repeating, the health of
society depends on finding ways to contain, control, and inhibit
impulse and desire. We must live with the resulting frustrations; to be civilized is to be discontented.

Freudian psychoanalysis as it was practiced in America
turned out to be something quite different. Dubbed the "talking cure," and for good reason, it promised psychological health
and happiness for everyone. In three or four weekly sessions,
over a period of many years, patients were expected to say ab-
solutely anything that occurred to them about their dreams,
thoughts, feelings, memories, and fantasies (even, or perhaps

especially, when they concerned the analyst himself).[5] Deliberate self-censorship and resistance to certain ideas and emotions were topics for intensive exploration.

In practice, Freudian psychoanalysis was too time-consuming and expensive to be an option for any but the affluent. Nevertheless, this therapeutic enterprise ushered in a new conception of knowing oneself, and in America it took on the urgency of a modern moral imperative. Even those who had no pressing personal problems felt an obligation to get in touch with themselves. Philosopher William Barrett, a former editor of the *Partisan Review*, describes the powerful appeal of psychoanalysis to writers and scholars in the middle of the twentieth century, "We . . . faced the matter of psychoanalysis with intellectual solemnity. If you could dig up the money, you had a moral duty to face yourself in psychoanalysis, and you were shirking if you didn't."[6]

During the late 1960s psychoanalysis began to lose ground. Its reputation was tarnished by the absence of evidence that it worked. By the 1970s, an increasing number of psychiatrists had turned to medication as an important means for treating illnesses such as depression and anxiety. A biological conception of mental illness was slowly displacing psychodynamic notions. By the 1980s, insurance companies were balking at the exorbitant cost of analysis and managed care emphasized brief psychotherapy and use of Prozac-like drugs. Psychoanalysis became the exception, not the rule, for treating low-grade depression and other psychological problems.

As psychoanalysis began its decline in the sixties, a new generation of therapists stepped in to fill the expanding void. These "humanist" psychologists were dissatisfied with Freudianism because of its exclusive focus on human psychopathology; they offered psychic health and personal deliverance more quickly and for far less money than one-on-one psychoanalysis. And they promised a kind of self-fulfillment that Freud was wary of offering. In the words of one of its founders, Abraham Maslow, humanist psychology focused on the "fully evolved and authentic self and its ways of being."[7] The humanists rejected Freud's bleak vision of human nature in favor of a celebratory view. The goal was to liberate human urges, not to inhibit them.

David Frum's history of the 1970s, *How We Got Here*, contrasts old-fashioned Freudianism with the later, sunnier, humanistic "California" model. Freud believed it was the job of therapy to subdue the dark impulses that lurked in the unconscious mind and to reassert the supremacy of reason and self-control in the person being treated. That harsh perspective, Frum notes, was quintessentially Central European:

> Freudianism originated in the lands of Kafka and Wagner, of the Brothers Grimm and the Thirty Years' War. Whatever their other failings, strict Freudians were in no danger of being conned into an excessively optimistic view of human nature. But as psychotherapy was Americanized—and even more, Californianized—all those dark Central European anxieties were dismissed as outdated gloom. The mind did not resemble Dracula's castle, with horrors unimaginable chained in its dungeons; it was like a Santa Monica sea house whose windows had become a little grimy. Polish them up, let the outside in and the inside out, and the owners will once again enjoy the sunlight, the ocean zephyrs, and the aroma of orange blossoms.[8]

Several prominent psychologists contributed to the humanistic turn in psychology, among them Wilhelm Reich, Erich Fromm, and Albert Ellis. But it was two men in particular, Abraham Maslow and Carl Rogers, who are generally regarded as the leading theorists of the movement.

Indeed, it is impossible to understand therapism without an appreciation of the kind of psychology that Rogers and Maslow were promoting. Both Rogers and Maslow served as president of the American Psychological Association. Both saw in human beings limitless possibilities for creativity, personal development, and happiness. How to "actualize" this potential was the central quest of the "human potential movement." Though Maslow and Rogers led more or less conventional personal lives, they attracted unconventional followers. Almost anyone who remembers the popular culture of the late sixties and seventies can recite the human potential experiments that are part of that colorful psychedelic period: the drug induced "peak-experiences," the encounter groups that elicited shocking personal revelations, the communes and the new personal "lifestyles" that often outraged or affronted conventional ethics.

The 1960s and 1970s were a time of unprecedented social and personal experimentation, much of which brought beneficial social change: a galvanized civil rights and women's movement, a healthy questioning of previously unchallenged authority. A motley collection of rebels, seekers, and activists—the "counterculture" was to have an invigorating and transforming effect on the "establishment," which, ironically, most of them would eventually join.

Of course, that period had a dark side as well. The late sixties and seventies were noted for a flourishing drug culture and a dramatic increase in crime. What is less known is that a dubious social science helped to provide cover for bizarre antisocial behavior, and promoted theories of the self that would later be used to justify the intrusion of therapism into all corners of American society.

Maslow and the Higher Life Within

Abraham Maslow taught psychology at Brandeis University from 1951 to 1969. In one sense, he was a traditional moralist. In the midfifties, when a colleague asked him about the focus of his research, Maslow said that he was writing on human values and the "higher life within," to which his colleague jokingly replied, "Plato already wrote that book, Abe." Maslow answered, with a smile, "Yes, but I know more than Plato did."[9]

A few months later, in a speech at the University of Ne-
braska, Maslow explained his ambitious project:

> I am also very definitely interested and concerned with man's
> fate. . . . I hope to help teach him how to be brotherly, cooper-
> ative, peaceful, courageous, and just. . . . I consider psychology
> most important to this end. Indeed, I sometimes think that the
> world will either be saved by psychologists—in the very broad-
> est sense—or else it will not be saved at all.[10]

From the beginning, Maslow's aim was to displace moral
philosophy and religion with a science of man. Traditional religion, in his judgment, had proved inadequate. He proposed a
"religion-surrogate."[11] He said, "Throughout history [human-
ity] has looked for guiding values, for principles of right and
wrong outside of [itself], to a God, to some sort of sacred book,
perhaps, or to a ruling class."[12] Maslow believed that he had
found the basis for ethics and personal fulfillment in human nature itself.

The approach was not new. As Maslow's colleague said,
Plato had already written that book. What was new, however,
was Maslow's assertion that the psychological theories had the
status of a revolutionary new *science*. In his 1968 bestseller, *Toward A Psychology of Being*, Maslow claimed that humanistic
psychology had caused a paradigm shift in human thinking: "I
must confess," he said, "that I have come to think of this humanist trend in psychology as a revolution in the truest, oldest
sense of the word."[13] He places the discoveries made by the new
psychology on a par with the breakthroughs of geniuses such as
Galileo, Darwin, and Einstein.

Maslow proposed a theory of human motivation that grew
out of his early research on primates. He called it "the hierarchy of needs." To flourish, he said, human beings must first sat-
isfy their basic physical needs for food, water, shelter, and
safety. As soon as these basic needs are met, a new set emerges:

"belonging needs" and "esteem needs." Maslow classified self-esteem as an essential human need and he called for institutions where the "core of the person is fundamentally accepted, loved, and respected by others and by himself."[14] Individuals who felt safe, loved, and confident, his theory went, could then move on to a higher state of creative or ethical being that Maslow called "self-actualization."

The self-actualized individual realizes his creative potential; he does what he is uniquely fitted to do. "A musician must make music, an artist must paint, a poet must write, if he is to be ultimately at peace with himself. What a man *can* be, he *must* be. This need we may call self-actualization."[15]

Maslow claimed that only a small percentage of human beings, no more than 2 percent, manage to reach this higher stage of being. In developing strategies for actualizing our potential, he recommended that psychology should focus on "man at his best." As he explained, "If we want to know the possibilities for spiritual growth, value growth, or moral development in human beings, then I maintain that we can learn most by studying our most moral, ethical, or saintly people."[16]

In one influential early paper entitled "Self-Actualizing People" (1950), Maslow looked at the lives of several towering figures, including Thomas Jefferson, Abraham Lincoln, Frederick Douglass, Mahatma Gandhi, and Albert Einstein. He identified several characteristics, including self-acceptance, autonomy, spontaneity, commitment to a cause, good-natured humor, and frequent "mystic-like" experiences—moments of rapture and ecstasy that Maslow dubbed "peak-experiences." (Maslow's view that the ability to have peak-experiences was a feature of the highly actualized, along with his theory of self-esteem, would be counted as one of his main contributions to humanistic psychology.)

Maslow was convinced that neurotic behavior and antisocial emotions (rage, jealousy, fear) have their origin in the frustrated needs (physical and emotional) of early life. "If this essential core of the person is denied or suppressed, he gets sick."[17] What we call "evil" or "immoral" behavior is caused by the frustration of healthy desires. In Maslow's words, "Sick people are made by a sick culture."[18]

Maslow, of course, is not alone in identifying "the culture" as the cause of widespread psychological sickness. On this view, a majority of human beings are frustrated, unhappy, unrealized beings trapped by their own neediness. But, a special group of confident, creative, nonauthoritarian, spontaneous individuals, with a capacity for peak-experiences, are fulfilled, happy, and free. This metaphysical/psychological theory was eagerly embraced by an emerging counterculture.

Maslow acknowledged that his conclusions were not based on conventional social science. As if to apologize for this omission, he said: "I consider the problem of psychological health to be so pressing that *any* leads, *any* suggestions, *any* bits of data, however moot, are endowed with a certain temporary value."[19] According to Edward Hoffman, Maslow's biographer, "Maslow felt sure that he was intuitively correct and that new research methods would eventually validate his ideas."[20]

But his optimism was ill-founded from the start. Maslow's intuition that self-esteem is essential for healthy development—a notion still widely held—would prove highly resistant to empirical verification. Moreover, Maslow's theory of a "hierarchy of needs" predicted that materially comfortable individuals whose need for "belongingness" and personal esteem were satisfied, would be the most self-actualized—the most creative, intensely engaged, and ethical. But experience and history belie such assertions. Starving artists, insecure geniuses, imperiled saints are everywhere. And, perhaps more to the point, so are well-educated, materially comfortable, self-confident villains.

It was not that Maslow eschewed the scientific approach. In fact, he had more than once tried to get empirical corroboration for his theories, but had failed. As early as 1945 he carried out experiments on students with negative results. To his surprise and disappointment, "many high-security scorers are just the opposite of [actualized]." He found his subjects "smug, self-satisfied, 'lumpish' in the sense of just not wanting or doing much, almost torpid."[21] On the other hand, subjects that he judged to be neurotic and insecure seemed to him to have far more promise for creativity and other "good developments." Maslow also worried that his definition of "self-actualized" was rather subjective: he found that he judged attractive female students to be more evolved than any other group.[22]

Throughout his career, Maslow would confront such troubling inconsistencies. His students at Brandeis University in the midsixties, for example, came from privileged backgrounds where all their basic needs were met. Yet Maslow sensed their lives were less "actualized" than those of their parents, who had suffered through the Depression and the Second World War.[23]

In his main theoretical collection, *Toward a Psychology of Being* (1968), Maslow continued to express confidence in his insights but had still not produced the promised research that would supply empirical backing for his claims. Again, he justified publishing his theories by explaining that exciting ideas cannot always wait to be confirmed by evidence:

> There is now emerging over the horizon a new conception of human sickness and of human health, a psychology that I find so thrilling and so full of wonderful possibilities that I yield to the temptation to present it publicly even before it is checked and confirmed, and before it can be called reliable scientific knowledge.[24]

By the end of his life, Maslow's ideas had become increasingly arcane and impressionistic. He still talked of "science or pre-science," but he no longer pretended that his own work was scientific. Today, his influence in the field of academic psychology is minimal, but his influence on popular culture is profound. Three Maslovian ideas still resonate deeply:

1. That emotional security and high self-esteem are essential for creativity and moral development.
2. That social science can provide the road map to self-fulfillment.
3. Societal or cultural repression of the authentic self is the primary source of human misery, immorality, and mental illness.

Maslow was a thoroughly decent man and a cultivated, imaginative, and serious thinker. Unfortunately, he left his ideas unprotected from eccentric followers who applied them in ways he privately deplored. He hoped to inspire individuals to intellectual, artistic, and ethical greatness. His "eupsychian" (utopian) communities of the future were supposed to be full of great-souled, autonomous beings modeled on Jefferson, Douglass, Lincoln, and Einstein. Instead, Maslow's best-known acolytes were Abbie Hoffman, Timothy Leary, and an assortment of searchers, seekers, and encounter-group facilitators, who thought themselves more evolved, more free, and more actualized than their fellow citizens.

Maslow's Apostles

It may not be fair to blame a scholar for the failings of his disciples. But, even when he could, Maslow did little to discourage the misapplication of his ideas. Abbie Hoffman was a student of Maslow's at Brandeis in the early 1960s. He regarded himself as a disciple. In his autobiography, Hoffman wrote, "Most of all, I loved Professor Abe Maslow. I took every class he gave and spent long evenings with him and his family. . . . [H]is teachings became my personal code. . . . I've found everything Maslow wrote applicable to modern revolutionary struggle in America."[25]

Hoffman was a "Yippie" prankster who took prodigious quantities of LSD and staged "happenings" around the country protesting the American capitalist system. These included an exorcism at the Pentagon, a violent protest at the 1968 Democratic Convention in Chicago, and a mock presidential convention in which a pig called Pigasus was nominated. Hoffman was a colorful character, but he was unstable and a sad travesty of Maslow's ideal. He was arrested for selling cocaine in 1973, and he committed suicide in 1989.

Maslow himself was politically conservative with little sympathy for radicalism. But his ideas were well-suited to the anti-establishment sixties and to personalities like Hoffman. As we have seen, the humanist psychologists had by now parted company with the Freudians on the crucial question of human nature. Where the Freudians had insisted that human beings need the civilizing constraints of tradition and culture, thinkers like Maslow sided with Rousseau. Man was born free but is everywhere in chains. Human nature is essentially benign or neutral and must be liberated in order to achieve ideal development. Society stands in the way of self-actualization, and so society must change. Maslow and others in the human potential movement were turning Freudian doctrine on its head.

This teaching was a siren song to Abbie Hoffman and thousands of other rebels in the growing counterculture. They found in Maslow an intellectually respectable beacon whose prestige gave scientific cachet to their antics. Maslow never actually advocated defying conventional morality as part of the process of achieving self-actualization. On the other hand, he never publicly reprimanded those who took that road to liberation. In his journals he described Hoffman as a clown and a "psychopathic personality."[26] But never once did he publicly dissociate himself from any of Hoffman's actions.

In Timothy Leary, Harvard psychologist and counterculture hero, Maslow found another devoted and energetic follower. In the early sixties they met often for lunch to discuss creativity and peak-experiences—which, for Leary, were usually brought on by LSD. In matters of lifestyle, Leary and Maslow were on altogether different wavelengths. Writer Joyce Milton, author of *The Road to Malpsychia: Humanistic Psychology and Our Discontents*, describes a chance encounter between Maslow and Leary

at Logan Airport in Boston in the spring of 1962. Leary was accompanied by two striking young women when the three
bumped into Maslow. He introduced Maslow as the man who
had coined the term "peak-experience." One of the women said,
"That's what we're going to have tonight." Maslow politely
declined her invitation to join them.[27]

For a generation of drug users the word "peaking" specifically referred to the intense moments of an LSD trip. Maslow
himself avoided drugs. "It's too easy," he told Leary. "To have
a peak-experience, you have to sweat."[28] Maslow believed that
hard work and intense focus precede moments of genius or rapture; such moments come only with effort and self-discipline.
He regarded intoxication as a cheap imitation of the kind of experience that comes to the genuinely self-actualized person. But
again, Maslow held back; he did not openly dissociate himself
from Leary's popularization of artificially induced "peak-
experiences."[29]

Maslow's relationship to institutions that were promoting
their own dubious versions of self-acceptance was similarly
ambiguous. In January 1966, Maslow paid a visit to the Esalen
Institute, a "personal growth center" and therapeutic retreat
in Big Sur, California, that would become emblematic of the
cultural revolution of the sixties. He gave lectures on self-
actualization and peak-experiences to groups of strangers
brought together at Esalen for intense, uncensored "encounters." The goal, in the words of a *Life* magazine writer, was for
participants to "risk revealing their unmasked, vulnerable
selves." There was a lot of crying, hugging, and, according to
one participant, a lot of "out-and-out ecstatic experience."[30]

Maslow complained to the director about the lack of a library and the general contempt for scholarship and disciplined
thought. He chastised the Esalen staff: "If you don't use your
brain, you're not fulfilling your potential."[31] At the same time,
his biographer Edward Hoffman says that Maslow "regarded
Esalen as potentially the most important educational experi-

ment in the world."[32] Esalen staff returned the compliment by naming their main hall the "Maslow" room. Moreover, although he himself was distressed to find Esalen so anti-intellectual, he grew deeply hostile to his colleagues in academic psychology who criticized it.[33]

Maslow was also enthusiastic about an experiment in alternative living called Synanon. Begun as a residential treatment program for drug addicts in Santa Monica, California, it was founded in 1958 by a charismatic former alcoholic, Charles Dederich Sr.[34] Initially, Synanon sought to use the peer groups to induce disciplined behavior change and improve self-awareness in drug abusers. Inculcating a work ethic was a key aspect of the program.

During the 1960s, however, Synanon metamorphosed from a drug treatment facility into a utopian reform movement that attracted hundreds of nonaddicts who wanted to transform themselves and society. By the seventies it had degenerated into an authoritarian cult that Dederich declared a religion in 1975. The institution began a steep decline in 1978, after Dederich pleaded no contest to charges of arranging to have a diamondback rattlesnake placed in the mailbox of a lawyer who had sued him.[35] When Maslow visited Synanon in 1967, he was favorably impressed. He saw Synanon as a kind of protoeupsychian community. Maslow did have some faint suspicions about Dederich's character and intelligence. Nevertheless, he wrote in his journal, "I'll back him up whenever I can."[36]

The sixties, it should be said, was a time when a great many mainstream scholars were taken in by the early promise of people like Timothy Leary and personalities like Dederich. Harvard supported Leary's research on the therapeutic effects of LSD (then legal) and other hallucinogens for a few years in the early sixties. Maslow was flattered by the respect accorded him by the Learys, the Dederichs, and the staffers at Esalen and Synanon. Perhaps that is why he stood by them and did so little to protect his theory of the self from their grotesque distortions and trivializations.

But it is also true that Maslow's ideas lent themselves to distortion. If they were false, Maslow never told us how we could prove they were. His theories were never formulated with sufficient precision to allow for critical experiments that could confirm or disconfirm them. Highly subjective and seductive, Maslow's notions invited charlatans and sensation seekers to claim they were on the royal road to personal flourishing.

Carl Rogers on How to "Become a Person"

Carl Rogers is often cited as the grandfather of the self-esteem movement.[37] His role in the development of humanistic psychology matches Maslow's; but where Maslow formed his ideas by reflecting on the humanities and philosophy and on his early work on primates, Rogers derived his from his vast experience as a clinical psychologist. Rogers taught psychology at the University of Chicago and the University of Wisconsin. In 1964, he moved to La Jolla, California, where he established the Center for the Study of the Person. The spirit of Rogerian therapy is captured in the question, "How do you feel about that?" (The seventies television hit *The Bob Newhart Show* was based on Rogerian therapy.)

For Rogers, the key to personal growth is "psychological safety," and the best way to achieve it is to grow up in a caring social milieu. Ideally, parents, teachers, therapists, and others "with a facilitating function" should offer children unconditional positive regard.[38] Such regard and acceptance from others permits them to become their authentic, genuine, uninhibited selves. Of course, most of us have never enjoyed that kind of psychological protection. The good news, said Rogers, is that a sympathetic therapist or a nurturing classroom can provide it.

Rogers believed we all possess a healthy but fragile inner self that we are afraid to show the world:

The spontaneous feelings of a child, his real attitudes, have so often been disapproved of by parents and others that he has come to introject this same attitude himself, and to feel that his spontaneous reactions and the self he truly is constitute a person whom no one could love.[39]

One way to retrieve this self and give it a chance to grow without impediment and discouragement is by participating in a therapy that provides a safe environment. The graduate of well-managed group therapy is on the way to self-realization: "He recognizes that it rests within himself to choose; that the only question which matters is, 'Am I living in a way which is deeply satisfying to me, and which truly expresses me?' "[40]

In his book *Freedom to Learn* (1969), Rogers proposed that schools become "personal growth" centers. Traditional schools, he said, were repressive institutions. An enlightened classroom would adopt the methods of group therapy: it would nurture children's self-esteem in an accepting, nonjudgmental setting. He imagined the ecstatic reaction of a student who found himself in such a caring environment: "At last someone understands how it feels and seems to be *me* without wanting to analyze me or judge me. Now I can blossom and grow and learn" [emphasis in original].[41]

Not all students appreciated Rogers's pedagogy. In *Freedom to Learn*, Rogers reported the experience of a high school geometry teacher who replaced conventional math problem worksheets with creative "projects." According to Rogers, "The students complained that [the old] worksheets would better prepare them for the college tests. The teacher responded that the projects they selected may better prepare them for life."[42] Rogers reacted by explaining why students were resisting his nostrums: person-centered education is threatening.

As we noted in chapter 1, many educators today are engaged in the mission of realizing Rogers's vision of a nurturing, therapy-based, esteem-building curriculum. The fundamental value of high self-regard and the importance of nonjudgmentalism have become unquestioned dogmas in American education and, indeed, in many quarters of American society as a whole.

Rogerian therapy practices "total acceptance" of the patient. Rogers called for radical empathy. He believed the patient would "grow and change" when the therapist viewed him with "deep respect and full acceptance . . . suffused with a sufficient warmth . . . [and] the most profound type of liking or affection for the core of the person."[43] Sometimes Rogers appeared to carry the practice of deep respect and total acceptance too far. Here, for example, is his account of a group therapy session with institutionalized adolescents. A young man has just revealed "an important aspect of himself," and finds that some in the group are hesitant to approve of his behavior:

GEORGE: This is the thing. I've got too many problems at home—um, I think some of you know why I'm here, what I was charged with.

MARY: I don't.

FACILITATOR: Do you want to tell us?

GEORGE: Well—uh—it's sort of embarrassing.

CAROL: Come on. It won't be so bad.

GEORGE: Well, I raped my sister. That's the only problem I have at home and I've overcome that, I think.

FREDA: Ooh, that's weird!

MARY: People have problems Freda, I mean ya know—

FREDA: Yeah, I know, but *yeOUW!!!*

FACILITATOR: (to Freda) You know about these problems, but they are still weird to you.

GEORGE: You see what I mean; it's embarrassing to talk about it.

MARY: Yeah, but it's OK.

GEORGE: It *hurts* to talk about it, but I know I've got to so I won't be guilt-ridden for the rest of my life.[44]

Rogers commended Mary for "showing a deep acceptance" and George for "taking a risk." He did not hesitate to censure Freda for her judgmentalism, "Clearly Freda is completely shutting him out psychologically."[45]

When Rogers's colleagues found fault with his innovative therapeutic practices, Rogers fought back, claiming his work was "a deep threat to many of their most cherished and unquestioned principles."[46] He was especially harsh to those who politically disagreed with him, calling them zealots, "right-wingers," and implying they were fascists. Rogers warned, "If there is a dictatorial takeover in this country—and it becomes frighteningly clearer that it might happen here—then the whole trend toward the intensive group experience would be one of the first developments to be crushed and obliterated."[47] Both professionally and politically, Rogers betrayed some obvious inconsistencies. On the one hand, he advocated a non-judgmentalism that countenances odd and conventionally outrageous behavior. On the other hand, he was censorious of anyone who challenged his eccentric principles and practices.

The Glorious Future

Maslow and Rogers believed that society corrupts and demoralizes people, imposing codes of conduct that foster self-loathing, fear, aggression, and sickness. As Rogers assured us, "[T]he basic nature of the human being, when functioning freely, is constructive and trustworthy."[48] Nevertheless, as one critic, Frank Furedi, sociologist and author of *Therapy Culture*, has observed, these psychologists' view of human nature is far from optimistic.[49]

Both Maslow and Rogers believed that the "realized self" could emerge only under highly specialized circumstances. Pending such change, we are all "unactualized," deeply alienated, and in serious need of therapeutic help. Rogers describes

the rampant "loneliness" of Americans, and the "dehumaniza-
tion of our culture, where the person does not count—only his
IBM card or Social Security number."[50] Group therapy, on the
other hand, if led by a caring facilitator, could be redemptive.
According to Furedi, "The very fact that the realisation of the
self is predicated on a relationship of dependence on therapeu-
tics, calls into question the quality and meaning of individual
autonomy."[51]

Maslow too held a gloomy view of his compatriots. In his
judgment, most people are bland, pale, unrealized beings whose
inner nature has been "warped, suppressed, or denied" by a
stultifying and silly world.[52] The contrast to people who have
achieved "authentic" selfhood is dramatic. In his 1964 *Religions,
Values, and Peak-Experiences*, Maslow writes:

> My studies of "self-actualizing people" . . . make it clear that
> human beings at their best are far more admirable (godlike,
> heroic, great, divine, awe-inspiring, lovable, etc.), than ever be-
> fore conceived.[53]

Unfortunately, few human beings are "at their best." Indeed,
from the beginning, there were indications that those on the
path of self-actualization were, in fact, far from being godlike,
awe-inspiring, or even likeable.

In January 1968, *Life* magazine sent writer Jane Howard to
Esalen to take part in a five-day encounter group. In one typical
exercise, group members were supposed to approach one another from across the room and then react emotionally, but non-
verbally, upon meeting. The standard reaction was hugging and
weeping; but when Howard took part in the exercise, the young
man she "encountered" did not hug her, he hurled her violently
across the room. This caused her to cry. The young man had authentically shown his anger, and Howard had displayed genuine
distress. The group considered the event a great success.[54]

That same year, George Leonard, a senior editor at *Look* magazine and an Esalen vice president, published *Education and Ec-stasy*. It became a bestseller. Leonard passionately defended the use of encounter group therapy.[55] He describes one multiracial group that he co-directed with an African-American psychiatrist. The encounters were designed to "get past superficial niceties" and to achieve a group catharsis that would remove racial hostilities. During one session, a black man named Chuck boasted that he could "take" any of the women in the room any time he felt like it. Pam, whom Leonard described as a "beautiful young white schoolteacher," replied: "You'd never take me. I wouldn't let you *touch* me. *Ever.*" Then, a "good-looking Negro housewife" added, "You could never take me, and I'm going to tell you why—because you're just a dirty little black nigger." This caused Chuck to leap from his chair and loosen "his hidden fury in a savage and frightening tirade." Eventually everyone calmed down. By the end of the day, says Leonard, "we rose and moved, without a word, to the center of the room in a mass, moist-eyed embrace."[56]

Telling a group of women you can "take" them, delivering savage tirades, humiliating others with vicious racial slurs are not generally considered to be within the bounds of acceptable behavior. Yet all this was tolerated, even encouraged, because the post-Freudian therapies of the late 1960s deliberately promoted emotional self-expression (however hurtful to others) and acceptance (however unnatural or galling) above all else.

Today, Esalen's Leonard concedes that the benefits of a "single cathartic" weekend were short-lived. He also says that he has come to understand that emotional expressiveness, without wisdom and kindness, "can be trivializing and in its own way destructive."[57]

Nevertheless, he speaks nostalgically of the heady exhilaration that characterized those "cathartic" weekends at Esalen. Psychologist Jean Huston, a prominent practitioner of techniques for achieving inner growth, told *Newsweek* in 1976: "We were the first to put a man into outer space. Now we have the opportunity of launching the first psychenauts into inner space."[58] (Ms. Huston would later achieve brief notoriety when she arranged conversations between then First Lady Hillary Clinton and the long-dead former First Lady Eleanor Roosevelt.)

More orthodox academics were less sanguine about the wholesome benefits of exploring one's "inner space." When Cambridge University intellectual historian George Steiner gave a talk at Esalen in the late sixties, he must have irritated his audience by telling them that "no great innovative thinkers have *ever* sat on the floor" (emphasis in original).[59] What he said about "self-discovery" is worth repeating:

> What's the point of self-discovery if there's nothing, or very little, there to discover? Having [people] go even deeper inside themselves only shows them what bores they are. It would be better if they would memorize poetry, or learn a language, or play chess, or listen to music, or study butterflies.[60]

Outside the universities and the therapeutic retreats, Americans were having mixed reactions to the philosophies of liberation. The latent conservatism of many Americans had not been exorcised. In 1966, the citizens of California elected Ronald Reagan governor. Two years later, voters put Richard Nixon in the White House by one of the widest margins of victory in United States history.

By the second half of the seventies, films like *Semi-Tough* (1977) and *The Big Fix* (1978) were irreverently parodying the human potential movement. Hard-hitting exposés appeared, such as R. D. Rosen's amusing *Psychobabble* (1977) and Martin Gross's astute and prescient *The Psychological Society* (1978).[61] Maslow and Rogers are no longer taken seriously in the world of academic psychology. Richard McNally, who teaches graduate students in psychology at Harvard, tells us they are "warm, fuzzy, and unread." Only three decades after its heyday, the hu-

man potential movement is little more than a footnote in the
history of clinical psychology.

In the face of increasing derision from skeptical scholars and
popular satirists, one might have expected the human potential
movement to quietly fade away. But that is not what happened.
True, the more bizarre expressive therapies, with names like
Primal Scream, Attack Therapy, Nude Encounter, and Rolfing,
have gone the way of the Nehru jacket and love beads. But the
human potential movement of Rogers and Maslow, dead now in
most of the academy, remains very much alive in the hearts and
minds of vast numbers of Americans. It lives on in the applied
psychologies of the various helping professions, much of whose
personnel work with norms that are markedly less rigorous and
evidence-based than the norms of academic psychologists. The
Maslow-Rogers view of human nature has serious practical and
conceptual failings, but it has a passionate and committed following among educators and mental health counselors.

It's not hard to see why the ideas of Maslow and Rogers remain attractive and beguiling. Both psychologists were persuaded that self-esteem is the mainspring of a healthy life. Both
proffered fulfillment and personal happiness—especially to
children. More than that, Maslow and Rogers had a solution to
the problem of moral evil. Recall Maslow's admonition, "If the
essential core of a person is denied or suppressed, he gets sick."
What most of us would call "evil" or "immoral" behavior is as-
cribed to the frustration of healthy desires.

Throughout history various prophets and assorted millenar-
ians have promised redemption from evil. Rogers and Maslow
were the first salvationists to serve as presidents of the American Psychological Association. This gave their assurances the
backing and cachet of a universal human science. Americans
were naturally impressed.

Their program for self-actualization was especially attractive to those who looked to psychology for self-discovery. The
ancient injunction to "Know Thyself," particularly Socrates'

interpretation, called for prodigious mental effort and discipline. To know oneself, to examine one's life—meant learning what it is to be a good human being. It entailed knowledge of science, moral philosophy, literature, and history. The human potential movement offered a far less strenuous path. You could know yourself without ever going to the library. According to Rogers, your ideal self was already there within you, buried under a lot of wreckage put there by a judgmental, emotionally withholding, unforgiving, and oppressive society. Personal redemption would come to those who had the courage to discover their true feelings and genuine attitudes—and to accept what they found. In this quest for self-knowledge and self-actualization, families and schools were to play a liberating "facilitating function."

In this chapter, we have tried to show that therapism, in its various versions, does not live up to its promises. Many of its basic assumptions turn out to be wrong: self-esteem is not the solution Maslow and Rogers took it to be; children do not blossom when schools follow Rogers's suggestion to become personal growth centers. George Steiner was right to ask "What's the point of self-discovery if there's nothing, or very little, there to discover?"

The human potential movement may not have delivered salvation, but its influence has not waned. It lives on in the form of therapism. It appears to be deeply compassionate, and that explains its abiding appeal. Maslow and Rogers developed a philosophy of life based on the ideal of mutual understanding. Its central injunctions are to grant one another "total acceptance," to withhold censorious judgment, and to meet each and everyone's "belonging needs." It asks us to be tolerant and "nice." One might well ask: What could possibly be wrong with that? That question we now consider.

3

Sin to Syndrome

Canadian journalist Mark Steyn coined the term "sensitivity coma" to characterize the mental state of helping professionals who have lost all common sense in their concern to be supportive, nurturing, and nice. Steyn applied it to an official in the United States Department of Agriculture who had an encounter with none other than Mohammed Atta, the terrorist in charge of the September 11 attack.[1]

In May 2000, Atta visited this woman's office in Homestead, Florida, demanding a $650,000 loan to buy a crop duster. When she told him the application would have to be processed, Atta became incensed. As the woman recounted in an interview with ABC's *World News Tonight*, "He asked me what would prevent him going behind my desk and cutting my throat and making off with the millions of dollars of cash in that safe."[2] The official responded to the threat by politely and gently explaining that there was no cash in the safe.

In the course of their encounter, Atta tried to buy an aerial photograph on her wall that showed all of the major monuments in Washington, D.C. When she refused to sell it, Atta assailed her again. "How would America like it if another country destroyed the city and some of the monuments in it?"[3] He then asked her about security around the World Trade Center and other landmarks.

What did this federal official make of Atta's threat to slit her throat, his interest in buying a chemical crop duster, his questions about monuments and security around the World Trade Center? "I felt that he was trying to make the cultural leap from the country that he came from. I was attempting, in every manner I could, to help him make his relocation into our country as easy for him as I could." Steyn draws this lesson from the encounter: "[Atta's] one great insight into Western culture was his assumption that he could get a government grant to take out the Pentagon."[4]

As for the well-meaning government official, her desire to understand Atta and attend to his inner needs rendered her incapable of recognizing a wolf even when he was wearing wolf's clothing. There are some grounds for thinking this official is typical of large numbers of Americans.

Nice Americans

With the help of the *New York Times*, Boston College political science professor Alan Wolfe did a survey of American values in 2000 and reported his findings in the *New York Times Magazine* (March 18, 2001) as well as in a book entitled *Moral Freedom* (2001).[5] In addition to the interviews Wolfe conducted with a sample of citizens from eight U.S. communities (ranging from the culturally liberal Castro district of San Francisco to the more conservative farm town of Tipton, Iowa), the *Times* commissioned a scientific poll (1,003 adults from all fifty states) measuring values and attitudes. Both Wolfe's anecdotes and his data capture the new nonjudgmentalism.

Quite a few of those Wolfe interviewed for his survey were loath to make any meaningful moral judgment about any behavior, no matter how criminal or depraved. Cheryl of Fall River, Massachusetts, was opposed to penalizing priests who molest children: "Everybody makes mistakes . . . 'they're no different than anyone else.' Certainly what they did was wrong, but not forgiving them would also be wrong."[6] A woman in San Francisco denied that Jeffrey Dahmer, the Milwaukee serial killer, was evil: "I just thought he was very sick, and I felt sorry for him."[7]

Most of Wolfe's subjects also took a medicalized perspective on drug and alcohol abuse. According to Kelly from Fall River, referring to gamblers, alcoholics, and drug addicts, "I think there's an internal something within them that's drawing them to it. I don't think that a person's character is weak or anything."[8] Rosalyn, a kindergarten teacher, expressed what Wolfe characterizes as the conventional wisdom: "If you have ten people that are exposed at age twenty-one to drinking, a certain number of them will become alcoholics because it was already part of their system."[9]

Wolfe is ambivalent about his findings. He worries that Americans are naïve and lack a "tragic sense of life." But he sees a bright side: "Their unwillingness to point the finger of shame at others . . . can also signify the virtue of humility. If we judge too much and too often, we turn harsh and hypocritical."[10]

Wolfe reminds us that the new nonjudgmentalism has its source in such commendable American traits as our optimism about human possibility, our desire to be caring, and our eagerness to be "nice." Wolfe asks rhetorically, "Would America really be better off if its citizens were meaner?"[11]

But meanness is not the only alternative to niceness. Common sense, fair-mindedness, and ethical sensitivity must also enter the moral equation. And these entail a capacity for appropriate moral indignation and a willingness to censure irresponsible and destructive behavior.

Sins of the Fathers

The child abuse scandal in the Catholic Church is a sobering example of what can happen when the therapeutic perspective displaces a judgmental moral point of view. One year after the

Wolfe/*Times* study was published, stories of Catholic priests taking sexual advantage of teenagers and children began to appear everywhere in the press. It soon became evident that even the Catholic Church, a stronghold of traditional moral teaching, had been seriously affected by therapism.

In the 1970s, it was the fashion among mental health professionals to view pedophilia as a treatable form of psychological immaturity. The pedophile, so the theory went, was sexually attracted to children because, emotionally, he was a child himself. Talk therapy and other transformative treatments would help him understand himself better and move beyond his arrested state of development. Tragically, the church accepted this theory and sent predatory priests to mental health clinics to be cured.

The idea that pedophilia is curable is no longer taken seriously by most clinicians. The only recourse is strict control, primarily by imprisoning the perpetrators and, after their release, by denying them unsupervised access to children. But as Dr. Fred Berlin, director of the National Institute for the Study, Prevention, and Treatment of Sexual Trauma at Johns Hopkins University School of Medicine, says, "Years back, the Church, very sadly, was misled by mental health professionals."[12] For their part, therapists who treated the priests now blame the church for rushing priests back into service against their advice.[13]

Church officials sent errant priests to various centers where they received counseling, group therapy, psychodrama, role-playing therapy, and, according to a report in *The Economist*, "holistic medicine [and] Christian forgiveness."[14] Once "cured," many were permitted to resume their duties. The following case of Father David L. Bentley is not atypical.

In 1973, Curtis Oathout was ten years old, living in Albany, New York, when Bentley began to abuse him sexually. The molestation continued until the boy was 16.[15] Bentley was treated by a church therapist in 1978 and then returned to service. Church higher-ups became aware of Bentley's abuses in 1986, but it was not until April 2002, after the nationwide scandal had broken, that Bentley was removed from service at a parish in New Mexico.

In April of 2003, Oathout, then forty years old, conducted a taped interview with his abuser. Here is how Father Bentley, by then sixty years old, tried to explain himself to his victim: "[W]hat I've learned in my therapy is that I suffer from very immature sexual development, and that goes back to when I was a kid. Nothing happened to me, but my sexual development was arrested in terms of probably when I was seven, eight years old." His victim replied, "[I was] a little boy. Who needed his innocence, who needed to be left alone. Who was vulnerable, who needed a friend, who only needed a friend."[16]

It seems that thirty years have barely taken the edge off Curtis Oathout's anguish and shame. As for Father Bentley, he seems to be excited by having "learned" that his actions were the product of an arrested development whose effects he considers to have been beyond his capacities to control. Here the Father appears to ride roughshod over the crucial distinction between acknowledging an explanation for an action and excusing that action.

The more famous case of Father John Geoghan again illustrates how the church lost its moral bearings and medicalized the abuses.[17] As early as 1984, church officials in the Boston Archdiocese knew that Geoghan was a child molester. The priest's predatory behavior was sinful, criminal, and the cause of great and enduring suffering. But again and again, Geoghan's superiors referred him for remedial therapy. In 1989, for example, they sent him to a luxurious mental health clinic in Hartford, Connecticut called the "Institute of Living" that specialized in treating "impaired" clergy. According to *The New Yorker*, he also took classes in human development and assertiveness training. When he was discharged a few months later, he was "left with instructions for stress reduction and 'leisure-skills management.'"[18] Geoghan's therapist eventually declared him "fit for pastoral work in general including children."[19] Before long, he

was assigned to a parish and put in charge of children. New ac-
cusations followed.

In July 2001, Cardinal Bernard Law explained in *The Pilot*, a
newspaper of the Boston Archdiocese, that just as society has been
on a "learning curve" with regard to the sexual abuse of minors,
"the Church, too, has been on a learning curve."[20]

The cardinal did not explain why the Church so uncritically
relied on psychotherapy to deal with what it regards as a mortal
sin. A *learning curve* on how to react to someone who is molest-
ing children—not to mention violating his vow of chastity and
betraying the trust of his parishioners?

Father Richard Neuhaus, editor of the religious/political
magazine *First Things*, is an acute and sympathetic observer of
his Church. In a 2002 article defending, but not exculpating
Cardinal Law, Neuhaus wrote:

> [T]he medicalizing of gross wrongdoing too often lets ever-
> changing psychological theory trump commonsense judg-
> ments about sin and its consequences . . . Cardinal Law has
> confessed that . . . he has made "tragic mistakes." It is not
> possible to disagree. The word bishop is derived from the
> Greek *episcopos*, which means "overseer," and there would
> seem to be no doubt that there have been grave deficiencies in
> the *moral* oversight of some of the clergy of Boston. [Emphasis
> added.][21]

Philip Jenkins, professor of religious studies at Pennsylvania
State University, sees to the heart of the problem the Church
faces when it compromises its episcopal mission and yields to
the therapistic ethos:

> During the 1970s and 1980s, psychological values and assump-
> tions permeated the religious world no less than the secular
> culture. . . . But an intellectual chasm separates the assumptions

of traditional churches from those of mainstream therapy and psychology. The medicalization of wrongdoing sharply circumscribes the areas in which clergy can appropriately exercise their professional jurisdiction, and this loss of acknowledged expertise to therapists and medical authorities at once symbolizes and accelerates a substantial decline in the professional status of priests and ministers.[22]

Eventually, Cardinal Law himself came to see that his leniency had betrayed Church traditions. The cardinal, who resigned in 2003, was a beloved figure in the Boston community, well-known for his kindness. Tragically, he had extended his goodwill without getting the full picture of the harm that had been inflicted on the abused. As the scandal was exploding all around him, the cardinal consented to meet with some victims. As one of the group explained to the *Globe*, "He has to see the devastation and peripheral fallout that sex abuse has caused."[23] Close to tears, the Cardinal asked for forgiveness. "I did assign priests who had committed sexual abuse. . . . I acknowledge my own responsibly for decisions which led to intense suffering. While that suffering was never intended, it could have been avoided, had I acted differently."[24]

Charles Krauthammer, *Washington Post* columnist and psychiatrist, wondered, "Why didn't the Church call the cops?"[25] In his column, he told about an event that transpired in Hobart, Australia, forty years ago. A rapist ran into a church seeking asylum from the police. The priest let him in, heard what he had to say, then promptly punched him in the nose and called the police. Krauthammer wrote, "Upon hearing this story, one can only imagine in what different shape American Catholicism would be if just one bishop had done the same thing to just one priest seeking counseling and sanctuary for his molestation of children."[26]

Krauthammer said that by choosing to view the priests' behavior as primarily a psychological disorder and not a crime, and therefore treating it as a strictly internal matter, the church "violates the most elementary notions of civil society."[27] To us, what is most significant about the failure of the Catholic leaders is not their uncivic attitude, but their uncharacteristic abandonment of traditional moral teaching.

The extraordinary reaction of the prelates to the sinful acts of the errant priests horrified many traditional Catholics. William Donohue, president of a Catholic antidefamation organization, lamented the church leaders' "tolerance . . . for intolerable behavior."[28] The problem with therapism is that it licenses tolerance of the intolerable. Its medicalized perspective on wrongdoers enabled Catholic officials to regard the criminal priests as victims, in need of compassion, care, understanding, and treatment. Even as late as 1996, Cardinal Law, by then fully aware of Geoghan's history of child abuse, wrote him a sympathetic letter, in which he used the amoral, pseudoscientific language of pathology and not the vocabulary of sin or vice or disobedience that are the hallmark of his Church. "Yours has been an effective life of ministry," he wrote, "sadly impaired by illness."[29]

Here the cardinal sounds very much like one of Alan Wolfe's nonjudgmental subjects. And here we see how the all-is-forgiven ethos of therapism leads not to "niceness," but to cruelty. Of course, the pedophile priests are human beings, and in the eyes of the Church they remain subject to redemption and forgiveness. But there can be no forgiveness before repentance—and, in the case of criminal behavior, legal punishment.

The church's descent into therapism illustrates how powerfully tempting it is to replace ethical judgments with psychological diagnoses. It also shows how the real victims are disregarded. When sin becomes syndrome, ethically inexcusable behavior is granted absolution and innocents suffer.

The Real Me

When Father Geoghan was given a clean bill of health after treatment for pedophilia in 1981, he reacted like someone who had been cured of bacterial pneumonia. "Thank God for modern medicine and good doctors." He was a new man. As he put it, "I feel like a newly ordained priest!"[30]

Geoghan had a vested interest in the no-fault theory of the self that is a feature of therapism. Baldly stated, the theory says that immoral acts are not the result of personal failings or malevolence, but manifestations of an illness, or brain disorder, requiring the attention of "good doctors."

Consider how Daniel Goleman graphically describes a murder in *Emotional Intelligence*.[31] On August 8, 1963, Richard Robles killed two young women in their Upper East Side apartment in New York City. Robles clubbed them unconscious with a soda bottle and then slashed them repeatedly with a kitchen knife. Robles, a former drug addict who had already committed more than one hundred robberies, was eventually arrested and convicted for what came to be known as the "Career Girl Murders."

Goleman reports that Robles told him that he had "panicked" when one of the girls said she would remember his face and help the police find him. Goleman calls what then happened to Robles a "neural hijacking":

> At those moments, evidence suggests, a center in the limbic brain proclaims an emergency, recruiting the rest of the brain to its urgent agenda. The hijacking occurs in an instant, triggering this reaction crucial moments before the neocortex, the thinking brain, has had a chance to glimpse fully what is happening, let alone decide if it is a good idea. The hallmark of such a hijack is that once the moment passes, those so possessed have the sense of not knowing what came over them.[32]

Whether or not he intends to, Goleman leaves readers with the distinct impression that Robles was himself a casualty of the attack. While the girls ended up dead, Robles ended up with a life sentence—yet another victim of "what happened." He was taken over, commandeered, by an irresistible force— his own nervous system. His brain was hijacked. Robles was possessed. As Goleman tells it, the real Robles had little or nothing to do with the killings. When Robles says, "I just went bananas. . . . My head just exploded," Goleman hears a man reporting some kind of cerebral pathology.

Let us consider for a moment the notion of powerlessness in the commission of violence. Statistically speaking, having epilepsy or low intelligence is correlated with violence, but the vast majority of people with these conditions are not violent. Some moral or prudential constraint keeps them from harming others. Neuropsychiatrists have yet to identify any type of seizure disorder, tumor, or lesion—congenital or acquired— that actually causes someone to commit purposeful violence. Violent acts committed by people with damage to the prefrontal cortex are impulsive in nature; that is because the prefrontal cortex is the region necessary for reflection and premeditation.

Goleman seems to accept the perpetrator's assertion that he has little idea of "what came over him." Typically however, someone with prefrontal damage and an intact moral sense is authentically humiliated and remorseful after an outburst, especially if he has hurt anyone. Furthermore, a person aware of his own trip-wire temper might try to avoid situations that could set him off. This was not the case with Robles, who refused to admit his crime until more than a decade later. He did not notify police of their error when they were convinced they had found the killer, a nineteen-year-old man named George Whitmore Jr. In any case, Goleman presents no evidence that Robles's prefrontal cortex was damaged. Instead, Goleman's circular reasoning—the killings themselves prove the murderer's cortex was impaired—quite baselessly absolves Robles of responsibility. Surely Robles's character, which he formed over many years, should crucially figure in any assessment of what he did.

The influence of character is in fact the view of Anthony Daniels, a psychiatrist whose work in British prisons places him in daily contact with men like Robles. He hears excuses like "my head just exploded" all the time:

> That criminals often shift the locus of responsibility for their acts elsewhere is illustrated by some of the expressions they use most frequently in their consultations with me. Describing, for example, their habitual loss of temper, which leads them to assault whomever displeases them sufficiently, they say, "My head goes," or "My head just went."[33]

Where Goleman credits the criminal's own description of how he came to do what he did, Daniels rejects it. He says that by using phrases like "My head just went," criminals absolve themselves of responsibility, attributing their criminal act to a neural event over which they had no control. The responsibility for what happened, and may happen again, is now the doctor's. According to Daniels, "They mean that they consider themselves to suffer from a form of epilepsy or other cerebral pathology whose only manifestation is involuntary rage, of which it is the doctor's duty to cure them."[34]

Daniels finds that many of the convicts he counsels hold a distinctive and original theory of the self. He calls it the doctrine of the "Real Me."[35] The Real Me has little or nothing to do with the self who breaks into houses, uses drugs and alcohol, and beats his wife and children. "No, the 'Real Me' is an immaculate conception, untouched by human conduct: it is the unassailable core of virtue that enables me to retain my self-respect whatever I do."[36]

The doctrine of the Real Me lies at the heart of therapism. Filling in the neurological details, Goleman's account of Robles's crime takes the murderer's self-exculpation seriously; the criminal's Real Me has indeed been hijacked. It is now up to us to get beyond his criminal behavior to understand his true self.

Daniels buys none of this. He insists that one's actions are the best guide to the "Real Me." A burglar, fully committed to the no-fault ethic of therapism, asked Daniels to help him find the deeper reasons for his antisocial behavior. "But something must make me do it!" he told Daniels. Upon which the doctor suggested, "How about greed, laziness, and a thirst for excitement?"[37] Of course something "made" the burglar commit the crime. But when it is greed (joined to a reluctance to work honestly for pay), or a thirst for excitement that "made" him do it, then *that's* the "Real Me" that should be held responsible for the damage caused and the pain inflicted.

Excuses

On January 27, 2001, two young men from Vermont, sixteen-year-old James Parker and seventeen-year-old Robert Tulloch, crossed the border into New Hampshire, entered the house of Dartmouth professors Susanne and Half Zantop, and hacked them to death with twelve-inch-long combat knives. They stole Half Zantop's wallet and then fled after burning their own bloody clothes. Parker and Tulloch were arrested in Indiana at a truck stop and brought back to New Hampshire for trial.

Initially, Tulloch's lawyer planned to use an insanity defense. He claimed that the young man was afflicted with a "severe mental defect or disease."[38] The younger boy, Parker, decided to plead guilty to a lesser charge and testify against Tulloch. In a press release, Parker's lawyer said "[Parker] has made the decision to accept responsibility for his actions, and is hopeful that his plea will enable his family and that of the Zantops to begin the healing process."[39] Parker was sentenced to twenty-five years to life; Tulloch (whose lawyer abandoned the insanity plea) was given a mandatory sentence of life in prison.

The town was of course horrified by the crime. Nothing like it had happened before. But in March of 2002, *The Atlantic Monthly* ran a story about the murders entitled, "The Apocalypse of Adolescence," in which the author, journalist Ron Powers, portrayed Tulloch and Parker as " 'ordinary' teenagers" from " 'ordinary' communities" who were "consumed by the dictates of some private murderous fantasy."[40]

Powers placed the killings in the context of an "explosion" of serious juvenile crime in Vermont, reporting that "data gathered by the Vermont Department of Corrections in 1999 revealed that the number of jail inmates aged sixteen to twenty-one had jumped by more than 77 percent in three years."[41] But Powers did not disclose the absolute numbers. In 1999, out of a population of more than 45,000 Vermont teenagers aged sixteen to twenty, a total of 167 were incarcerated. That was indeed up from 90 in 1996, and 111 in 1995.[42] Shifting gears, Powers noted in passing that Vermont enjoys one of the lowest crime rates in the country—then went on to explain that "ordinary teenagers from ordinary communities" have ordinary adolescent brains, which are dangerous.

Powers's article included a lesson on the neurology of teenage crime. The "emerging research," he reported, "demonstrat[es] that the brains of children and adolescents are not yet fully formed—not yet equipped to make precisely the sort of emotional and rational decisions necessary to restrain impulses in certain situations that can lead to antisocial and criminal behavior."[43] But this grossly overstates what current brain research is able to tell us. Most children, even children as young as six or seven, are sufficiently rational and moral to know that butchering other human beings is wrong. As for typical sixteen- or seventeen-year-olds, they know right from wrong as well as most adults. The Zantop killings cannot be explained by a general reference to adolescent problems with impulse control.

It turned out, in fact, that impulse had nothing to do with the Zantop murders. Soon after Powers's *Atlantic* article appeared, state prosecutors released the indictment, which revealed that the boys had spent months planning the attack. Before invading the Zantop house, they had made four failed attempts at other addresses. Their plan was to kill the residents and steal their ATM cards. Far from being "without obvious motivation" (Powers's phrase), their crime was calculated with a clear incentive: money.[44]

To be sure, Powers's argument, like Goleman's, has some support among neuroscientists. Dr. Deborah Yurgelin-Todd at Harvard Medical School, for example, says, "Adult brains use the frontal lobe to rationalize or apply brakes to emotional responses. Adolescent brains are just beginning to develop that ability."[45] Daniel Weinberger, Director of Clinical Brain Disorders Laboratory at the National Institutes of Health, went further in a *New York Times* op-ed in which he discussed the brains of violent youths. "I doubt that most school shooters intend to kill, in the adult sense of permanently ending a life. . . . Such intention would require a fully developed prefrontal cortex. . . . The often reported lack of apparent remorse illustrates how unreal the reality is to these teenagers."[46]

Weinberger adds, "This brief lesson in brain development is not meant to absolve criminal behavior."[47] But whatever his intention, Weinberger's "brief lesson" does, indeed, absolve teen criminals. We do not blame very young children for crimes precisely because they are mentally incapable of understanding right and wrong. Weinberger would extend this exculpation to adolescents. His science, however, is too soft to supply firm ground for his conclusions. He posits a connection between adolescent immaturity of the prefrontal lobe and overt criminal behavior. But even if we accept that almost all teenagers have relatively immature brains, Weinberger needs to explain why so few engage in impulsive criminality and why impulsive criminality is found in adults.

In his most recent book, *The Blank Slate: The Modern Denial of Human Nature*, Steven Pinker, a cognitive psychologist at

Harvard, supplies a welcome antidote to the many experts who explain criminal behavior by citing "new research" in neuroscience.[48] Pinker warns of the temptation—not to say the absurdity—of using biology as "the perfect alibi, the get-out-of-jail-free card, the ultimate doctor's excuse note."[49] He asks, "Is this the bright future promised by the sciences of human nature—it wasn't me, it was my amygdala? Darwin made me do it? The genes ate my homework?"[50]

The Metaphysics of Responsibility

Moral philosophers such as Socrates, Aristotle, St. Thomas Aquinas, David Hume, Immanuel Kant, and John Stuart Mill, down to the existentialists in the middle of the twentieth century, attribute unacceptable conduct to flawed character, weakness of will, failure of conscience, or bad faith. By contrast, those who profess therapism tend to regard personal shortcomings in terms of maladies, syndromes, disorders, pathologies needing treatment, and suppressed emotions.

Shakespeare, in a celebrated passage in *King Lear*, chides those who blame astrology for their personal failings and their tragic consequences:

> This is the excellent foppery of the world, that . . . we make guilty of our disasters the sun, the moon, and the stars: as if we were villains on necessity; fools by heavenly compulsion; knaves, thieves, and treachers, by spherical predominance; drunkards, liars, and adulterers, by an enforced obedience of planetary influence; and all that we are evil in, by a divine thrusting on: An admirable evasion of whoremaster man, to lay his goatish disposition to the charge of a star![51]

Today's excellent foppery is of a different order. Our admirable evasion no longer locates the causes of "all that we are evil in" in external, planetary influence, but in low self-esteem, presumed neurological impairments and malfunctions, and arrested development—all equally deemed outside our control. What the older moralists spoke of as irresponsible behavior due to bad character, the new champions of therapism—an array of helping professionals, journalists, and educators—speak of as ailment, dysfunction, and brain disease. The range of behavior that therapism subjects to moral censure is now sharply curtailed and in some instances has vanished altogether.

But is it really just foppery to replace sin with syndrome? Much here appears to turn on the age-old philosophical debate over free will and determinism. Traditional moralists believe that human beings initiate actions and shape their destinies. They deserve praise or blame for who they are and reward or punishment for what they do. Proponents of therapism, on the other hand, are uncomfortable with the notion of personal responsibility.

Many of Alan Wolfe's subjects, as well as members of the helping professions, sincerely believe that the choices we make are outside our control. We inherit a set of genetic predispositions and are born into an environment that give us our values and shape our characters. According to those who deny free will, the idea of an autonomous self that initiates action for which it is morally responsible is incoherent. In their view, a person is no more responsible for his character and preferences than for the color of his skin.

Who is winning the free will vs. determinism debate these days? If the opponents of free will have the better arguments that would seem to strengthen the case for nonjudgmentalism. If, however, the free will camp has the upper hand in this classic metaphysical dispute, then the doctrine of moral responsibility is vindicated. The stark fact is there is no resolution in sight. No headline will appear any time soon announcing which side of the free will dispute has won. What Samuel Johnson said in the eighteenth century remains true today: "All theory is against the freedom of the will; all experience for it."[52]

Because the notion of a free and independent "self" operating outside the laws of causation remains a metaphysical curiosity, free will deniers have the advantage of taking the scientific perspective. On the other hand, these skeptics face some problems themselves. The doctrine that we are not free directly contradicts a powerful intuition possessed by most human beings: that we choose freely and that we deserve praise or blame for the choices we make. Strong intuitions are not decisive, but philosophers rightly hesitate to dismiss our powerful sense of freedom as illusory. Free will skeptics have yet to offer adequate explanations for why we are so strongly convinced of our own inner freedom. Many philosophers are convinced that a world in which we lack free will is morally incoherent and somehow degraded. The philosopher Sidney Hook remarked, "One feels lessened as a human being if one's actions are always excused. . . . As bad as the priggishness of the self-righteous is the whine of the self-pitying."[53] Certainly many diminished and "excused" persons fostered by a nonjudgmental therapism tempt us to parody. The comic strip *Non Sequitur* describes the directory of a mental health facility: "1st Floor: Mother's Fault. 2nd Floor, Father's Fault. 3rd Floor, Society's Fault."[54]

Fortunately for the purposes of this book, there is no urgent need to come down on one or the other side of the perennial debate over free will. As a theoretical issue, it remains unresolved. As to the policy questions that divide the friends of therapism from the friends of traditional ethics, they are altogether practical. For example, how should we deal with miscreants who break the law? Should we approach them as therapists dedicated to healing them, or as judges dedicated to assigning responsibility and meting out justice?

On practical grounds, an exclusively therapeutic approach is simply unworkable. Even philosophers whose conception of human nature leads them to the conclusion that we cannot fairly hold anyone morally responsible for his actions concede that every viable society imposes sanctions and rewards. We cannot exist in mutual association without a system of personal accountability that stigmatizes some actions and rewards others. Actions must be characterized as right or wrong, praiseworthy or blameworthy, good or evil. These notions and judgments may be challenged on theoretical grounds, but they are essential to the workings and survival of any society.

Those committed to therapism because it is a nicer and more sensitive philosophy of life should certainly reconsider construing criminals as medical patients in need of treatment. Again, cognitive psychologist Steven Pinker is a good example of someone who is sympathetic to scientific determinism, but remains strongly committed to personal responsibility as a pragmatic matter. As Pinker insists, "Whatever may be its inherent abstract worth, responsibility has an eminently practical function: deterring harmful behavior."[55] Pinker does not deny that neuroscience is helping us understand those parts of the brain that trigger dark passions such as envy and rage. At the same time, he notes that neuroscience is also teaching us about those parts of the brain that inhibit the destructive passions. The prefrontal cortex is the site of our awareness of the effects of our actions. In particular, it controls behavior by making us conscious that members of our community will blame us, castigate us, and perhaps punish us for antisocial acts. Pinker says:

> We are that community, and our major lever of influence consists in appealing to that inhibitory brain system. Why should we discard our lever on the system for inhibition just because we are coming to understand the system for temptation? If you believe we shouldn't, that is enough to hold people responsible for their actions—without appealing to a will, a soul, a self, or any other ghost in the machine.[56]

If Alan Wolfe's nonjudgmental, all-is-forgiven subjects really do typify a prevalent American ethic, that is grave cause for concern. There may be abstract philosophical reasons for denying the kind of free will that we ascribe to people in blaming or praising them for their choices; but there are overriding practical reasons for assuming that people are morally responsible and for stigmatizing them when they choose to behave in ways that we find morally reprehensible. One such reason is that only a society that treats its members as ethically responsible and personally accountable can achieve and sustain a democratic civil order.

The Abuse Excuse

When Dan White brutally murdered San Francisco Mayor George Moscone and Supervisor Harvey Milk in 1978, his attorneys argued that he suffered from "diminished capacity" syndrome. Defense lawyers claimed that Damien Williams and his cohorts, who nearly beat Reginald Denny to death in the 1991 Los Angeles riot, were victims of "mob frenzy." Some defenses come under what is called "the abuse excuse." The Menendez brothers, who in 1992 shot their parents to death in their Beverly Hills home, were alleged to have suffered from "Battered-Child Syndrome."

Harvard Law School professor Alan Dershowitz and political scientist James Q. Wilson both deplore the "abuse excuse" and similar strategies in contemporary courtrooms.[57] Both cite cases where a perpetrator, whose sanity is not in question, murders or maims someone, confesses to the crime, but pleads not guilty on the grounds that he was impelled to the act by some psychological condition. The absolving disability is colorfully characterized by one or more experts as a typical part of some "syndrome" that the defendant is said to have suffered or be suffering from and which caused him to do what he did. The list of potentially exculpating syndromes includes battered persons syndrome, Super Bowl Sunday syndrome, premenstrual stress syndrome, rape trauma syndrome, steroid defense, and urban survival syndrome.[58] Dershowitz calls all such descriptions and explanations of unlawful behavior "cop-outs, sob stories, and . . . evasions of responsibility."[59]

When understanding the psyche of the accused becomes the primary task of jurors, they are faced with evaluating competing "scientific" explanations for the defendant's behavior. Lawyers invite warring experts into the court: One side uses the explanation for the crime as an excuse and argues for the defendant's innocence. The other side seeks to discredit the explanation or the expert. In James Q. Wilson's words, "The stern task of judging the behavior of a defendant, based on a dispassionate review of objective evidence, has given way to explaining that behavior on the basis of conflicting theories presented by rival expert witnesses speaking psychobabble."[60]

Wilson, a famed expert on criminology, calls this phenomenon a "loosening of the criminal law" and he ascribes it to "the rise of a therapeutic ethic."[61] Wilson and Dershowitz acknowledge that abuse-excuse defenses only occasionally succeed in getting the defendant off or punished lightly. Nevertheless, both point out that these cases do real harm to the judicial system. Here is Dershowitz on how the "abuse excuse" undermines the rule of law:

On the surface, the abuse excuse affects only the few handfuls of defendants who raise it. . . . But at a deeper level, the abuse excuse is a symptom of a general abdication of responsibility by individuals, families, groups, and even nations. Its widespread acceptance is dangerous to the very tenets of democracy, which presupposes personal accountability for choices and actions.[62]

Personal accountability is at the center of our moral and legal system. Unless someone is mentally retarded, psychotic, or demented, the law holds him responsible for his actions. The abuse excuse is a direct challenge to this fundamental principle. A murderer can now claim: "I committed the crime; I knew it was wrong; I am not certifiably insane. Nevertheless, I should not be found guilty because I am not responsible for what I did." Jurors are invited to evaluate such a defendant's mental state at the time of the crime with the objective of discovering its determining causes.

Unfortunately, this is a nearly impossible task for mental health professionals, let alone jurors. Indeed, no expert—psychiatrist or psychologist—can know for sure, with the degree of certainty required by law, whether a particular mental syndrome caused a defendant to commit a crime. To simplify the task of meting out punishment, Wilson insists that the court concern itself with two mental states as the only legitimate grounds for avoiding criminal responsibility: madness and self-defense. Only the former calls for psychiatric expertise.

Consider the abused wife who stabs her sleeping spouse. If she acted in self-defense, the jury should be able to determine that using the evidence already at hand; there's no need for experts to testify that "battered woman syndrome" drove her to violence. After all, no single "battered woman" profile exists—and clearly, not all battered women attack their abusers. Thus such "expertise" serves only to mislead many a jury by imprecise explanations of behavior.

Similarly, the age-old excuse of drunkenness fails. Obviously, not every intoxicated man becomes violent. What's more, choices are involved. Some people deliberately take that first drink to embolden themselves to commit a crime. Others know from experience that they become violent while drunk, yet go on a binge anyway. If you excuse the drunken man, why not the enraged man or the person with attention deficit disorder. Pretty soon, Wilson notes, all murderers would have some condition that allegedly influenced their conduct. Even if a cause can be identified, the author asks, must it be considered an excuse? With so much at risk—"excusing failures of self-control will increase the frequency of such failures"[63]—we can't afford to dilute the moral power of the law.

Our legal system relies on juries to use common sense in applying the law to arrive at a judgment of the defendant's guilt or innocence. Common sense and a regard for fairness involve a careful consideration of mitigating circumstances as well as a keen appreciation of the defendant's responsibility to refrain from wrongdoing. It is to be expected that clever attorneys will exploit the jurists' desire to be fair by exaggerating the defendants' helplessness.

Proponents of the abuse excuse will reply that no judge or jury can fairly decide on the guilt or innocence of defendants without understanding the root causes of their actions. Just as juries listen to experts who claim that a defendant is legally insane, so they should listen to those who can explain their diminished capacity as moral agents in the grip of a syndrome. And they ask: What would possibly be wrong with jurors getting the aid of professional experts to help them reach a full understanding of why the defendant did what he did?

To this the reply is that psychology is at present not an exact science and no one has the expertise to give us an account of the root causes of any criminal act. Justice is subverted when juries are led to believe that an expert has offered them a scientific understanding of the deep causes behind a defendant's actions. The best an expert can do is provide information of clinical or statistical nature that would assist the jurors in their deliberations. Our entire legal and moral system depends on our willingness and readiness to make judgments about right and wrong and guilt and innocence based on limited (scientific) knowledge. No other course is humanly possible.

Human motivation is complex and obscure and actions are multidetermined. Most people have trouble gaining insight into even their own motivations. To ask a jury to fathom the precise causes of an act like murder is to ask too much. A detailed causal psychological account is typically introduced in evidence by those who believe that such an account, however fanciful, may persuade the jury that the perpetrator of a crime is not really responsible. In the present state of our knowledge of the causes of human behavior, the use of such "evidence" is all too often a subversion of common sense and common morality. We are, in any case, in no position to give a full explanation for any human action.

Medicalizing Addiction

In June 2003, the College for the Problems of Drug Dependence, a large professional organization for addiction researchers, hosted a panel discussion at its annual meeting: "Is Addiction a Brain Disease?" The huge lecture hall was packed to hear debate between the standard bearers and invited skeptics, Sally Satel among them, who would challenge the prevailing wisdom that drug addiction is indeed a "chronic and relapsing brain disease."

As the audience made clear during the Q-and-A period, two points were especially contentious. The first was the skeptics' insistence that addiction had an important voluntary dimension. The other was the belief that while we should offer treatment to addicted people, it is also perfectly natural and appropriate for society to stigmatize them when they abandon their responsibilities to family, job, or community.

A few weeks later, coverage of the college's meeting appeared in the *Journal of the American Medical Association*. Headlined "Addiction Poorly Understood By Clinicians," the story gave short shrift to the dissenters' views and focused on the frustration of many addiction experts at her defiance of their settled belief that addiction is a chronic and relapsing brain disease.[64] "It's something we have to keep selling," said Charles P. O'Brien of the University of Pennsylvania, a respected addiction expert.[65]

And sell they do. The National Institute on Drug Abuse (NIDA), part of the National Institutes of Health, endorses the brain disease model as its signature public health message. In the midnineties the institute waged an energetic campaign to spread the word. Officials from NIDA visited editorial board-rooms, town hall gatherings, and Capitol Hill briefings and hearings. Alan Leshner, the former head of NIDA who mounted the campaign, claims success. "The majority of the biomedical community now considers addiction, in its essence, to be a brain disease," he states.[66]

Indeed, world-renowned treatment centers such as Hazelden and the Betty Ford Center now assert that addiction is a brain disease.[67] The Institute of Medicine declares addiction a chronic and relapsing brain disease.[68] President George W. Bush's drug czar, John Walters, has stated that "drug addiction is a disease of the brain" (though in private Walters seems reluctant to use the vocabulary of disease and is vigilant about detracting from personal responsibility).[69] In the spring of 1998, the media personality Bill Moyers Sr. broadcast the brain disease concept into millions of living rooms with his five-part television special on addiction. The addict's "brain is literally hijacked" by drugs, Moyers announced in a promotional interview on *Meet the Press*.[70] These are the words of a loving father who was once at his wits' end over his son's drug and alcohol habit. But they are woefully misleading.

For one thing, a medicalized portrait of addiction is bound to confuse the public and politicians about the feasibility of holding drug addicts and alcoholics accountable. It reduces a complex human activity to a slice of damaged brain tissue. And it vastly underplays the reality that much of substance use behavior is actually voluntary. The truth is that the chronic drug abuser is capable of a large measure of self-control—a much more hopeful state of affairs than the inevitability of relapse implied by the chronic-and-relapsing-brain-disease model.

This is not to deny altogether the usefulness of the disease concept that infuses Americans' understanding of addiction to drugs and alcohol. On balance, Americans seem to endorse the idea that drug and alcohol problems should be viewed as diseases.[71] Many compulsive drinkers and drug users themselves seem to find the disease notion helpful—it convinces them of the gravity of their problem and persuades them to get help from a twelve-step fellowship, like Narcotics Anonymous, Smart Recovery, or formal therapy.

But a chronic-and-relapsing "hijacked brain" creates an understanding of disease distinctly different from that promoted by Alcoholics Anonymous. In twelve-step fellowship programs like AA, disease is used primarily as a metaphor for loss of control and self-centeredness. Thus, members might say, "I am unable to drink or take drugs because I have a disease that leads me to lose control when I do." In fact, when AA was in its infancy almost seventy years ago, its founders were leery of the word *disease* because they thought it discounted the moral dimension of addiction.[72] And even though AA teaches that the alcoholic's inability to stop drinking is somehow biologically driven, it does not allow this to overshadow its central belief that addiction is a symptom of something amiss within the person, not reducible to a disorder of his brain.

This is why twelve-step groups promote sobriety through the practice of honesty and humility. "Self-centeredness," says Alcoholics Anonymous, "is the root of our troubles."[73] Ultimately, those who help addicts—counselors in clinics, fellow twelve-step participants and sponsors, or faith-based program staff—recognize that despair and an unrestrained desire for immediate gratification are most often the reasons why people seek refuge in intoxicants. They appeal to the drug user's wish for a better life, his need to acquire skills and repair relationships, and form a concept of his future. In this regard, addiction is best thought of as a symptom of a troubled life, not a disease in itself.

The Hijacked Brain

When Bill Moyers Sr. describes the addict's brain as "hijacked" by drugs, he is referring to a much-cited 1997 article in *Science*,

"Addiction Is a Brain Disease, and It Matters."[74] Written by Alan Leshner during his tenure as director of NIDA, the piece explains that long-term exposure to drugs produces addiction—or, more precisely, the compulsion to take drugs—by causing changes in the central nervous system. Leshner acknowledges that people initiate drug use voluntarily, but as they use drugs repeatedly, he explains, the brain's pleasure centers are overtaken. Because these neurological changes are presumed to last indefinitely, the addict is at perpetual risk of relapse.

It is true that repeated drug use alters brain chemistry and function, at least temporarily. The question is whether these changes completely obliterate the addict's capacity to make choices. We realize that it would be nearly impossible for an addict in the throes of alcohol or heroin withdrawal, or in the midst of a cocaine binge, to reject available alcohol or drugs. It is during those periods that one could say the individual is in a "brain disease" state, his neuronal function so disrupted and his impulses so intense that drug-taking under such circumstances would be extremely difficult to stop.

But addicts spend only a fraction of their time in such states. A large percentage of them hold jobs, and all of them make scores of decisions throughout the day, influenced by what is at stake. Some of them decide to get detoxification and drug treatment, or even to stop cold turkey (not an uncommon phenomenon). Most addicts, furthermore, have episodes of clean time that last for weeks, months, or years. During these periods it is the individual's responsibility to make himself less vulnerable to drug craving and relapse.

As we said, drugs affect the brain. Why else would anyone take them? But does this mean the user inevitably loses control? Brain disease enthusiasts would say yes and point to PET scans of the brain as evidence.[75] These colorful pictures show parts of the brain, called reward centers, "lighting up" with increased metabolic activity when a drug is taken. One does not even have to take a drug. Merely showing pictures of people snorting lines of white powder to cocaine addicts causes their reward centers to light up, signifying the sensation of drug craving.

This has prompted talk of the "biology of desire."[76] And indeed, brain scans are dramatic, so striking that NIDA scientists routinely showcase them to politicians and the public. Yet biology is not destiny. In fact, the brain of an addict who is experiencing drug craving but fights it lights up like a Christmas tree, too—more brightly than the brain of a person who planned to obtain drugs to quell the craving. Resisting craving activates additional (inhibitory) centers in the brain—which also light up.[77] Furthermore, researchers have noted that self-reported craving does not necessarily correlate with a greater chance of actually using cocaine.[78] This is why, as one wise colleague says, "You can examine pictures of brains all day, but you'd never call anyone an addict unless he acted like one."[79]

Clearly, it is easy to read too much into brain scans. The neuropsychologist William R. Uttal, of Arizona State University, has written a cautionary book called *The New Phrenology: The Limits of Localizing Cognitive Processes in the Brain*.[80] Phrenology was the popular nineteenth-century practice of examining bumps and depressions on the head to decipher a person's abilities and character. Uttal of course acknowledges that today's brain-imaging techniques are triumphs of modern diagnostic medicine, not quackery. Even so, they almost never permit scientists to predict whether a person with a desire-activated brain will act on that desire. Nor can they distinguish between an impulse that is irresistible and an impulse that is not resisted.

Thus, it is misleading to call addiction a brain disease. But what about its alleged chronic and relapsing nature? This is an empirical question that should be explored. "It would be irresponsible to tell an addict that he or she had a chronic disease if in fact this was not true," writes the psychologist Gene Heyman, of McLean Hospital and Harvard Medical School.[81] As Heyman shows, the relapse rates of addicts who have been through treatment programs (on average, they relapse within a year after discharge) is much higher than the rates for addicts who have never sought treatment. Nonetheless, it is the program-seeking addicts that clinicians come to know—not the ones who quit on their own—and thus shape clinicians' perceptions of addiction as a commonly recurring problem, even though the pattern is far from universal.[82]

Oops?

"I've never come across a single person that was addicted that wanted to be addicted," said the psychiatrist Nora Volkow, named director of NIDA in 2003. "Something has happened in their brains that has led to that process"[83] According to the medicalized model of addiction, drug users just wake up one day and can no longer control themselves. The "oops phenomenon" is how Glen Hanson, a former acting director of NIDA, puts it. "[I]nexorable and undetected, destructive biochemical processes" are at work, Hanson says.[84]

True enough, it is doubtful that anyone sets out to become an addict. Nonetheless, countless red flags have shot up along the way to becoming one. Consider: Two people at a party decide they want to try cocaine for the first time, just to see what it feels like. One person snorts a line and feels nothing; the other snorts a line and loves it. From a scientific standpoint this is intriguing; our users' respective brain pleasure centers are hardwired to respond differently—the difference is in part based on genetics, leading one user to find the drug appealing and the other unimpressed by its allure. Now imagine two more people trying cocaine for the first time. One loves it and asks for more. The other also loves it but says, "Take this away," leaves the party immediately, and never touches cocaine again. The second person does not want even to risk addiction. This is not a matter of brain physiology.

Our cocaine-loving experimenter who asked for more keeps

snorting on a daily basis and ultimately becomes a compulsive user: "Something happened" in his brain, to borrow Volkow's words. But when we retrace the addict's steps, it is clear that the trajectory leading to compulsive use was marked by scores of small, deliberate choices, made many times a day: whom to spend time with, which neighborhoods to visit, whether to allow himself to become bored.

With each decision he made himself more vulnerable to continued use. These small decisions, then, are critical to becoming an addict—but the good news is that they are also critical to recovery. Which is why recovery programs universally stress the importance of learning to make safer choices, called "relapse prevention" therapy.

The author Jacob Sullum interviewed scores of drug users who became aware that they were sliding down the path to full-blown addiction—and then pulled themselves back. "It undermined their sense of themselves as individuals in control of their own destinies. And so they stopped," Sullum writes. "That doesn't mean that giving up cocaine might be harder for different people in different circumstances, but it does show that the chemical does not neutralize free will."[85]

Deceptive Analogies

Brain disease proponents insist that addiction is just like any other chronic and relapsing medical disease, such as asthma, diabetes, or high blood pressure. The analogy rests on two observations. First, drug addicts and asthmatics (or diabetics or hypertensives) have similar rates of noncompliance with treatment and therefore of relapse. Second, addiction and chronic medical diseases are equally likely to be passed down to offspring.

Let us first consider the matter of compliance. A much-cited 2000 *Journal of the American Medical Association* article, "Drug Dependence: A Chronic Medical Illness," spells out the relationship between noncompliance and relapse. The authors argue that: (1) relapse in long-term conditions such as asthma, diabetes, and high blood pressure is often due to the patient's poor compliance with prescribed diet, exercise, or medication; (2) an addict's relapse is a result of poor compliance; thus (3) addiction is like other medical diseases.[86]

But the parallel here is misleading. It is true that many chronic health problems have a large "behavioral component"—that is, patients can influence the course of these conditions by deciding to follow medical advice on diet, exercise, or medications. But when a person in recovery fails to comply with medical advice ("don't drink or use drugs"), his decision to act against the injunction to abstain is no mere *component* of his relapse, it is the sole cause.

Argument by analogy, moreover, can be turned on its head. For example, one could argue that antisocial behavior bears a close resemblance to addiction—after all, it runs in families to the same extent that addiction does, and the "afflicted" are just as likely to relapse to crime as addicts are to resume their use of substances.[87] Not surprisingly, brain disease enthusiasts never draw an analogy between addiction and antisocial behavior, perhaps because "treatment" for antisocial behavior is punitive, and thus treatment of addiction would, in keeping with the analogy, be punitive as well.

So why push the analogy between, say, asthma and addiction? Proponents believe that establishing a clinical equivalence between addiction and other medical conditions will yield social benefits. They hope to decrease stigma associated with addiction, to secure better financing for research and treatment, and expand insurance and disability coverage.[88] Others want to abolish criminal penalties for drug-related conduct.[89] We too favor funding quality research and treatment, but we recognize that effective treatment is aimed, foremost, at the patient's behavior and habits of thought, not his brain.[90]

Clinical experience makes this clear. Ironically, some of the most vocal promoters of the brain disease rhetoric have never treated patients with drug problems. Leshner and Hanson, for example, spent most of their careers in the laboratory. "As we relate to the public and policymakers," Hanson said, "[we must] help them understand that this is a disease process . . . rather than an issue of decision making."[91] Fortunately for addicts, the process of addiction largely is about decision making.[92]

Neither Moral nor Medical Alone

To say that the addict is capable of voluntary behavior, or choices, means that he can modify his actions in response to the short-term consequences those actions provoke. This has been amply demonstrated. Alcoholics can regulate the amount they consume depending on the cost and the effort required to obtain it.[93] Scores of studies demonstrate that even small monetary incentives or token gifts awarded for staying clean substantially increase the numbers of patients who become drug-free while in treatment.[94] Conversely, the imposition of certain and immediate sanctions for resumption of use, such as loss of a job or violation of parole or probation, is also effective.[95]

More than three decades ago Lee Robins, a professor of psychiatry at Washington University in St. Louis, conducted a study of returning Vietnam veterans.[96] Robins and her team found that only 12 percent of men who had become addicted to heroin in Vietnam resumed regular use back home. The major reasons for use in Vietnam—the fear of combat combined with the excruciating boredom of life at base camp—had disappeared. What's more, the culture surrounding heroin use back home, as well as the cost and fear of arrest, helped keep the men off the needle.

A person with a physical illness like asthma or cancer or a true brain disease such as multiple sclerosis or schizophrenia does not get well when threatened with arrest. It would be meaningless and cruel to promise him a reward in exchange for

remission of his disease or punishment if his condition worsened. Yet a public health message to the effect that addiction is
a chronic and relapsing brain disease implies as much and is in-
compatible with holding individuals accountable. As such it de-
tracts from the great promise of strategies that rely on
sanctions and rewards to develop self-control.

When the *New York Times* health writer Jane Brody writes
about "Addiction—A Brain Ailment, Not a Moral Lapse," she is
drawing a false distinction.[97] Both elements are involved in addiction; this is why treatment coupled with sanctions and rewards is more effective than treatment alone.[98] Drug courts are a
good example: they offer treatment instead of jail to minor drug
offenders, but poor performance in the program is dealt with
swiftly and surely. The criminal justice system is not the only
kind of leverage that helps a patient take recovery seriously—a
boss's warning that an employee must stay clean or be fired, or a
judge's refusal to restore parental rights until a mother main-
tains sobriety can motivate too. This is why understanding addiction as a *behavioral* condition—emphasizing that the person,
in the context of his environment, and not a disembodied brain,
is the instigator of his relapse and the agent of his recovery—is
far more practical than the brain disease model.

The behavioral perspective transcends the false dichotomy
Brody, Leshner, and the others put before us. Either we view
the addict as a bad person who deserves punishment, or we see
him as a chronic illness sufferer, the product of a brain disease
who deserves treatment.[99] Yet experience and research tell us
that the moral and medical models of addiction combined—that
is treatment programs that incorporate rewards and sanctions—
work synergistically, better than either alone.

Finally, what about stigma? Ameliorating the stigma associated with addiction—as if this were even possible—is high on
the agenda of brain disease proponents. But arguing that addiction is like diabetes or Huntington's disease will not remove
the taint. That is in the hands of the addict himself: Only he can

take advantage of treatment or quit by himself, harness his will to prevent relapse, become an example of hard work and responsibility.

This behavioral perspective does not overlook the fact that some people live in circumstances that make it hard to reject drugs—either because drugs are ubiquitous in the environment, or because they have less to lose if they use. Some feel desolate; after all, cocaine, heroin, and alcohol provide short-term relief for hopelessness, boredom, self-loathing, or fear. Doubtless, some people have predispositions, biological and otherwise, to addiction. And their struggle to relinquish drugs is what makes achieving recovery all the more ennobling.

To return to Wolfe's question, "Would America really be better off if its citizens were meaner?" Of course, the answer is no. We have, however, tried to show that the traditional, ethical, judgmental approach is, on the whole, more compassionate than the medical approach. The defense and protection of innocents must be our paramount concern.

There is an important place for a therapeutic perspective, for even the gravest misconduct, but it is secondary to the moral perspective. To condemn someone for harming others not only shows proper compassion, it also shows respect for the offender by holding him morally accountable and capable of doing better. There is nothing mean about a judgmental insistence that our fellow citizens are morally responsible to others and to themselves. Personal responsibility cannot be compromised without indignity and injustice for all.

4

Emotional Correctness

When the columnist Molly Ivins learned in 1999 that she had stage III inflammatory breast cancer, friends urged her to confront her feelings. Ivins tried it and found the experience "awful." As she wrote in *Time* magazine: "I am one of those people who are out of touch with their emotions. I tend to treat my emotions like unpleasant relatives—a long-distance call once or twice a year is more than enough. If I got in touch with them, they might come to stay."[1]

In an age when talking about one's feelings has become a mark of personal authenticity, Ivins's spirited refusal to open up is a breath of fresh air. Over the past thirty years or so, emotive outpouring has become routine on television and radio and in our leading news magazines. So powerful is this trend that Ivins's reluctance to dwell on her feelings about her cancer seems almost an affront. Merely suggesting to someone that she is talking too much about herself can be taken as "a form of abuse," observed Wendy Kaminer in her 1992 bestseller *I'm Dysfunctional, You're Dysfunctional*.[2] "What might have once been called whining is now exalted as a process of exerting selfhood," Kaminer continued, and "self-absorption is regarded as a form of self-expression."[3]

More than a decade after Kaminer's incisive exposé of confessional culture, the *New York Times Magazine* carried an article with the improbable title "Repress Yourself."[4] The author, psychologist Lauren Slater, sought to show that science was bearing out the value of self-restraint. "New research," she wrote, "shows that some traumatized people may be better off repressing the experience."[5] Slater cited recent studies showing that heart attack victims and bereaved spouses who "minimize, distract, and deny" felt far less anxious about their illness or loss months later.

Slater wasn't talking about everyone, of course. But she wanted to show that recounting one's anxieties (again and again) or pondering them (over and over) is not required for psychological health. It soon became clear that Slater had tapped a rich vein of rebellion against the still-pervasive idea that the well adjusted are those who focus attention on and talk about their feelings. Wrote one appreciative reader, "Maybe the talking cure would be helpful if you talked once, but most shrinks want the patient to go on and on, reducing you to only your horror story."[6] Another recalled Don Imus's remark "that in at least one of the early 'sessions' at the New Mexico ranch [for children with cancer], the children said, 'Send those psychologists home.'"[7]

By some definitions of "emotional intelligence" Slater and these readers are to be pitied. They are emotionally obtuse. Their reticence is supposed to put them at a disadvantage. But is this true?

About thirty years ago, a psychiatrist at the University of Wisconsin named John R. Marshall sought to confirm the already dominant view that openness was critical to mental health. In his essay "The Expression of Feelings," published in the *Archives of General Psychiatry*, Marshall noted that most mental health experts as well as the general public held the belief "that if a person can be convinced, allowed, or helped to express his feelings, he will in some way benefit from it."[8]

"Surely," Marshall postulated, "a concept so ubiquitous should be relatively easy to validate." But when he reviewed the literature for evidence of the benefits of sharing one's feelings, he found a confusing muddle of "ambiguous and contradictory studies."[9] The intervening years have produced a sizable and compelling body of research demonstrating that the expression of feelings is not a sure pathway to fulfillment. On the contrary, it often leads to unhappiness.

Consider anger. Charles Darwin was one of the first to observe that the verbal and physical expression of anger often begets anger. In *The Expression of the Emotions in Man and Animals*, published in 1872, he wrote that, "the free expression by outward signs of an emotion intensifies it" and that "he who gives way to violent gestures will increase his rage."[10] A century later, experimental studies were confirming Darwin's observations.[11] By 1973 the president of the American Psychological Association, Albert Bandura, was calling for a moratorium on the use of "venting" in therapy.[12] That same year the psychologist Leonard Berkowitz, renowned for his work on aggression, wrote an article in *Psychology Today* called "The Case for Bottling Up Rage" in which he criticized "ventilationist" therapists.[13]

Following these pronouncements, data have continued to spill out of journals confirming, with few exceptions, that physical and verbal expression of anger is usually self-reinforcing.[14] Nor does talking about negative experiences necessarily ameliorate the anxiety accompanying them. Despite the claims of Jon G. Allen, a psychologist and author of *Treatment Approaches to Coping with Trauma*, who states that "the universal prescription for trauma [is to] talk about it with any trusted person who will listen," a number of studies show that talking per se has little effect on emotional recovery.[15] For example, Yale psychiatrists found no relationship between the degree to which Gulf War veterans talked with family about their experiences and their ratings of residual war-related anxiety.[16] After the 1989 Loma Prieta earthquake in Northern California, a Stanford University psychologist found no difference in distress between college students who talked about their experiences and those who did not.[17] Other researchers found a similar lack of protective effect of so-called social sharing on symptoms of distress.[18]

What about self-absorption? Intense contemplation of one's inner landscape, especially during times of distress, has long been considered necessary for deeper self-knowledge and, ultimately, for mental well-being. But this, too, turns out to be psychological lore. An incident from the life of John Stuart Mill, the nineteenth-century philosopher and one of the founders of utilitarianism, is exemplary.

Happiness was a state that Mill deemed the greatest good and believed it came from the pleasurable fulfillment of human desire. Now one might think this philosophy favors therapism since it seems to demand that we all pay a great deal of attention to our feelings and desires. But Mill found otherwise. A section in his autobiography called "A Crisis In My Mental History" describes his painful discovery that self-preoccupation can be disastrous.

In the fall of 1826, at age twenty, Mill suffered a debilitating, long-lasting depression. Antidepressants were not available to him. Nor was talk therapy; it was thirty years before Freud was even born. Mill's depression persisted and deepened. Relief came only by accident. Mill happened to read a very moving story that caused him to forget about his own psyche for a brief spell—and the depression lifted. This experience had a profound effect on him, leading the philosopher to adopt what he called an "anti-self-consciousness" theory. Here is how Mill describes the lesson he learned:

> The experience of this period had [a] very marked effect on my opinions and character. . . . Those only are happy who have their minds fixed on some object other than their own happiness; on the happiness of others, on the improvement of mankind, even on some art or pursuit. . . . Aiming thus at something else, they find happiness by the way. . . . The only chance is to treat, not happiness, but some end external to it, as the purpose of life. Let your self-consciousness, your scrutiny,

your self-interrogation, exhaust themselves on [some external end].[19]

It is possible that Mill's depression was starting to fade before he found relief through literary distraction. In fact, an improvement in mood may be what gave him the capacity to be distracted in the first place; after all, a prominent symptom of major depression is the inability to focus on a task. In Mill's case, even if his depression were starting to melt as part of the natural cycle of remission, his ability to distract himself surely accelerated his recovery.[20] Ample research demonstrates that purposeful distraction can lift one's mood when depressed, just as ruminating about problems and the meaning of negative feelings can amplify them.

Now, two centuries after Mill and three decades after Marshall, despite a large body of research challenging the virtue of dwelling on and expressing one's emotions, those bedrock principles of therapism remain alive and well. We do not suggest that naturally passionate or voluble people should suppress their emotions or their desire to talk. But we caution against pressing, shaming, or subtly coercing anyone into trying to feel more deeply or be more expressive than befits his natural style.

The Cancer Studies

Many people believe that the unwillingness of patients with serious illnesses to explore the way they feel about their condition is unhealthy both mentally and physically. They believe such reticence could influence the progression of the disease. For years, cancer patients have been encouraged to join therapy groups—not simply for the emotional support such groups provide, but because "studies showed" that they could actually extend life. The genesis of this belief was a 1989 study by David Spiegel, a psychiatrist at Stanford.[21]

In the British journal *The Lancet*, Spiegel and colleagues reported that women with metastatic breast cancer lived longer if they attended group therapy than those who did not. Specifically, those randomly assigned to group therapy and who attended for one year lived 36.6 months past the point of diagnosis; those who were not assigned to attend lived only 18.9 months beyond the time of diagnosis. This was a dramatic finding: an apparent near-doubling of life expectancy. Spiegel's discovery quickly became medical lore. As a result, numerous self-help books tout the life-extending value of group therapy.[22]

In *When Hope Never Dies*, for example, we read:

> Studies have shown that women who are coping with breast cancer and join a support group live up to 2 years longer on average, than those who avoid such groups. Other researchers have demonstrated that support groups strengthen immune response. One of the essential parts of any healing program is support from others. Do not attempt to heal yourself on your own.[23]

Daniel Goleman, the former *New York Times* science writer, summarizes Spiegel's "powerful" findings in his bestseller *Emotional Intelligence*. With unreserved approval Goleman tells readers, "Dr. David Spiegel was himself stunned by the findings, as was the medical community."[24] Displaying little of the skepticism we expect from science writers, Goleman enthuses, "Indeed, if it had been a new drug that produced the extended life expectancy, pharmaceutical companies would be battling to produce it."[25]

Spiegel himself was more dispassionate about his study. He carefully warned that his results were inconclusive. In particular, he noted that the data had not been collected for the purpose of studying life expectancy, but to examine patients' psychological adjustment to having cancer. Only after the adjustment study was completed did Spiegel's research group return to the data and address the matter of longevity. This kind of retrospective analysis is accepted practice in medical research. However, as researchers readily acknowledge, it produces less trustworthy results than studies explicitly designed to answer the question at hand, so-called prospective studies. This is because prospective inquiries control more tightly for relevant characteristics (such as age, severity of illness, concurrent medical problems) that differ between the control and experimental groups.[26] Unless these characteristics are accounted for as carefully as possible, researchers cannot discern whether two groups differ in outcome because of the impact of the intervention itself or because the two groups differed at the beginning of the study and were thus prone to fare differently.

In their critique of Spiegel's study, Arnold Relman and Marcia Angell, both former editors of the *New England Journal of Medicine*, noted that it lacked data on possible between-group differences in lifestyle and type of treatment received.[27] Spiegel himself properly insisted that more rigorous, prospective, follow-up studies were needed. But in many quarters caveats so crucial to scientists fell on deaf ears—for Spiegel's findings resonated with popular beliefs about the therapeutic value of emotional disclosure.

In 2001, Pamela J. Goodwin, an oncologist at Mount Sinai Hospital in Toronto, answered Spiegel's call for more rigorous follow-up study.[28] Concerned that many cancer patients felt obligated to join therapy groups regardless of their desire to do so, Goodwin and her team undertook the largest prospective study to date. They assigned 235 breast cancer patients who were agreeable to being in group therapy to either ninety-minute weekly group therapy sessions or to no intervention. Every woman in the study was expected to survive at least three months. And the two groups were comparable in terms of many crucial characteristics, including age at diagnosis, time from first metastasis, marital status, duration of the disease, estimated survival, and tumor characteristics or type of cancer treatment at the time of the women's random assignment.[29]

Goodwin's team trained the group therapists in Spiegel's method and modeled the sessions on his, using the same number of patients per group, length, and frequency of meetings, and evaluating subjects with the same rating scales—all essential to replicating the earlier study. The therapy was intended to foster support and, Goodwin explained, "encourage the expression of emotions about cancer and its broad-ranging effects on their lives."[30] Patients participated for a year. The researchers rated them at several intervals. At one year's time, they found that women who had not been particularly distraught at the start of the study showed no change in mood after one year, whether or not they had been assigned to group therapy. However, women who had reported emotional distress and physical pain at the start did experience improvement in mood if they participated in group therapy.[31]

It is not surprising that social support, information exchange, and frank talk about existential issues were comforting to women who were distraught and in physical pain. Easing demoralization, sadness, and somatic pain is important and reason enough to join a therapy group.[32] Some studies have shown that patients assigned to groups become more conscientious about complying with their cancer care, and this itself may improve their survival.[33] But even that did not appear to be the case in the Goodwin study.[34] The most coveted potential benefit of group therapy—extra months or years of life—was not to be had. The women in group therapy lived nine days longer, on average, than those who received no group therapy. Thus, Goodwin concluded, "expressive group therapy does not prolong survival in women with metastatic breast cancer."

Goodwin was not the first to show that group therapy had no effect on survival in cancer patients, but her study was the largest and, crucially, the only one that replicated the methods used by Spiegel.[35] Therefore, her study attracted substantial media attention. According to Gina Kolata of the *New York Times*, "the study disputed a belief that has been stated so often it is almost considered a truism."[36] Her *Times* article quoted Harmon Eyer, the chief medical officer at the American Cancer

Society, who called the Goodwin study "quite conclusive." Dr. Eyer said that women who wish to join an expressive group should be encouraged to do so, but those who are disinclined "should not feel forced to put their time in." Among nonscientists, however, the widespread belief in the beneficial power of therapy is not so easily dissipated. According to a 2002 article in the *Journal of the National Cancer Institute*, "Patients have high expectations of psychological therapies: In one study, up to 25 percent of participants expected the psychological therapy to cure their cancer and 75–100 percent expected it to assist their traditional therapies."[37]

The *Complete Idiot's Guide to Living with Breast Cancer* tells women that they can't know "whether a support group works for you unless you check it out."[38] This is reasonable advice for a patient open to discussion of her problem, less so for one who prefers not to dwell on it. Indeed, a recent study of heart attack patients showed that those who were disinclined to talk about the emotions surrounding their illness fared *worse* when assigned by chance to treatment than if they had none.[39]

Jimmie Holland, chief of psychiatric oncology at Sloan-Kettering, was frustrated that so many of her patients had fallen prey to the "tyranny of support groups," as she called it.[40] So she wrote a book, *The Human Side of Cancer*, for her patients.[41] "There has been this ethos," Holland writes. "You have to think positively, you have to go to your group, you have to talk about your cancer. . . . People are criticized if they don't join one. . . . Groups are great for some people but terrible for others."[42] Not only is the insistence on self-expression potentially harmful in the case of patients temperamentally unsuited for it, but it can cause unnecessary guilt in surviving relatives. One anguished woman whose husband had died of lung cancer lamented to Holland: "I feel so guilty. I never made him go to one of those groups."[43]

The matter of guilt was a major reason Goodwin and her colleagues decided to undertake their study. "They were concerned," Kolata reported, "that many patients felt obligated to go to support groups, whether they wanted to or not, to fight their cancer."[44] Healthy skepticism about the life-extending benefits for cancer patients of emotional disclosure was long overdue.[45] Common sense alone should tell us that a one-size-fits-all psychological approach to anything as complicated and varied as human reaction to disease is deeply misguided.

But common sense is neither foolproof nor universal. By now, there is compelling evidence that neither psychological stress nor coping style nor optimism has much impact on whether a person develops cancer or how it progresses.[46] Group therapy, for those drawn to it, often provides major emotional benefits, but such sessions do not appear to prolong life or cure cancer. Goodwin's well-publicized findings, in particular, should help put to rest that unquestioned tenet of therapism that all cancer patients belong in "one of those groups."

The Perils of Overthinking

On October 17, 1989, the Oakland A's were in the middle of a World Series game against the San Francisco Giants when a severe earthquake rocked the San Francisco Area. The Loma Prieta earthquake, measuring 7.1 on the Richter scale, was the largest in the Bay Area since 1906. Sixty-two people were killed, and thousands were injured or left homeless.

Fortuitously, two weeks earlier, Susan Nolen-Hoeksema, a Stanford University psychologist and noted expert on bereavement and coping, had asked her students to complete a battery of questionnaires on their emotional health and coping style. This put her in an excellent position to study how they coped with disaster in real time.[47]

Nolen-Hoeksema was particularly interested in students with a ruminative coping style, a tendency to what she calls "overthinking"—in other words, a tendency to focus repetitively on one's distress and to ponder in an obsessive way the causes and implications of the mood. This phenomenon is separate from whether the ruminator talks about his preoccupations; some express, others won't.[48] Nolen-Hoeksema predicted that students with a ruminative style, no matter what their prequake emotional state, would experience more intense and longer-lived symptoms of distress than students who coped by distracting themselves through activities like exercise, schoolwork, or earthquake-relief efforts.

Ten days after the earthquake, Nolen-Hoeksema measured her students' moods and stress levels. She also asked students how much they thought about the disaster (e.g., "thought about the moment [it] happened," "thought about people who were killed," and so on) and how they coped (whether they "talked about the facts of the earthquake," "talked about their feelings," "tried to distract yourself," "avoided talking about it," and so on). Students rated the intensity of these thoughts and actions on a scale of 1 (none) to 5 (a great deal). Six weeks later the students were queried a third and final time.

Students with ruminative, self-preoccupied coping styles were more likely to be depressed at ten days and seven weeks following the earthquake. Conversely, those with a coping style that relied on distraction to ease their mood felt better, even if they had been in a depressed mood before the disaster. Nolen-Hoeksema concluded, "People who tend to focus on their symptoms and the possible causes and implications of them tend to remain symptomatic longer than those who do not."[49]

The Loma Prieta study joins a substantial body of evidence showing how the disposition to focus on one's internal state can backfire. Preoccupation with one's mood can intensify and extend the period of depressed mood.[50] Worrying about how your mood is affecting your job performance, or repeatedly asking yourself, "What's wrong with me?" heightens feelings of helplessness, and makes one more likely to grasp in desperation at the first solution to come along. Overall, it contributes to pessimism and demoralization.

What about purposeful repressors, the mirror image of ruminators? These individuals claim to be largely unaffected by negative events compared with ruminators.[51] They seem to be on an 'even keel,' rarely acknowledging negative events, and are more adept at shifting from an unpleasant thought to something more cheerful. They consider themselves more capable of coping with their distressing thoughts.[52] Repressors test better at solving problems, they are more popular with peers, and report better self-image than ruminators.[53]

A 2002 study led by Karni Ginzburg of Tel Aviv University in Israel found that heart attack victims with a repressive coping style enjoyed better psychological health immediately after the attack and seven months later.[54] The team studied 116 heart attack patients, one fourth of whom were judged to have a repressive coping style. Members of the repressor group were significantly less likely than their nonrepressor counterparts to report high levels of anxiety seven months later.

You might think that these differences between repressors and their more expressive counterparts simply meant that the repressors were medically healthier. But researchers found that the actual severity of cardiac condition as well as patients' perception of their health was similar between repressors and nonrepressors. "The findings of this study," Ginzburg concluded, "suggest that a repressive coping style may promote adjustment to the [stress of a heart attack], both in the short and longer term."[55]

Another study of heart attack victims suggested that repressive styles should not be tampered with. Researchers with the Montreal Heart Attack Readjustment Trial randomly assigned patients to a year-long program of monthly phone calls to monitor their "psychological distress."[56] Repressors who got the phone call program were more likely to be prescribed tranquilizers and to visit emergency rooms within the year than were repressors not assigned. The authors suggest that the program "may have increased distress in repressors."[57]

Experiments in Overthinking

Observations regarding rumination are intriguing, if counterintuitive. They tell us that deep involvement with one's emotional state is not always adaptive. Yet the question remains: Do ruminative habits of mind (or repressive ones, for that matter) actually *cause* particular mental states? It could well be, after all, that people who naturally dwell on their emotional states also happen to be the types who respond to trying situations with more agitation, anxiety, or hopelessness. This implies that some third factor may be at work and that one's style of coping does not by itself determine well-being.

The question of whether ruminating can actually *cause* a particular outcome can be answered only with experiments in which subjects are "made" to ruminate. Nolen-Hoeksema and colleagues induced depressed individuals to ruminate and compared them to similarly dejected subjects who were not so instructed. In order to encourage rumination, the researchers told the first set of subjects to focus on "what your feelings mean," "the physical sensations in your body," "what kind of person you are," and "why you react the way you do."

Their counterparts were instructed to think of neutral things like the "expression on the face of the Mona Lisa," and "the layout of the local post office." Next, all subjects were asked to describe their willingness to engage in activities they had earlier judged as being likely to cheer them up—such as going to a movie or dinner with a friend. Subjects induced to ruminate expressed less interest in engaging in these activities, even though they had considered them potentially uplifting.

In another experiment, depressed subjects were asked to make a list of memorable experiences. Those instructed to ruminate were more likely to recall negative memories, despite having earlier listed many happy ones. Those not encouraged to ruminate recalled a more balanced set of incidents from their lives.[58] The conclusion: people who ruminate while in a depressed mood are more likely to recall negative memories and use them in interpreting their current situation.[59]

These are only two studies in a substantial body of experimental work on rumination conducted with otherwise healthy people. The findings are consistent: sad or demoralized individuals will say that their mood lifts when they distract themselves, and that it declines when they ruminate. An effective therapeutic technique, called behavioral activation, employs repressive (or at least nonruminative) techniques to help clinically depressed patients.[60] The therapist asks the patient to pay less attention to what he is feeling and thinking and more to how he acts. The idea is to break out of a limited repertoire of passive, evasive, or ineffectual behaviors in order to find work and relationships more rewarding.[61]

Given the virtues of distraction, why do some choose to focus on their negative moods? When Sonya Lyubomirsky and Nolen-Hoeksema asked subjects about this they claimed they were gaining insight into their problems. They did not want to interrupt their self-exploration—despite acknowledging they would probably enjoy distracting activities.[62] Women in particular said that overthinking reflected their capacity for caring and concern.[63] Isn't it good to ponder deeply? the subjects asked. Shouldn't we try to illuminate the darkened recesses of our consciousness?[64]

Behind these questions is the common assumption that intense reflection on troubling thoughts and emotions is rewarded by a clearer vision. What Nolen-Hoeksema and others have repeatedly shown, however, is that overthinking tends to "impose a lens that shows a distorted, narrow view of our world."[65] Things that are wrong, not the solutions, are what come most sharply into view. "When you are sad," Nolen-Hoeksema explains, "your brain has greater access to sad thoughts and memories and you are more likely to interpret events in a sad way."[66] Neural connections between memories with similar emotional color are activated even when we think about depressing incidents that have no apparent relationship to those memories.[67]

As a result, pessimism snowballs, motivation flags, concentration suffers, and it becomes harder to make a decision. Negativity drives other people away, confirming our worst fears about our being unlikable or uninteresting. Problems seem overwhelming. These distortions often lead to bad decision making or verbal outbursts we later regret. Rumination, writes Nolen-Hoeksema, can "take you down paths to hopelessness, self-hate, and immobility."[68] In the end, rumination can engender perceptions of one's self and the world that are anything but objective and liberating.

Just a final word about therapy. Although no "rumination industry" exists as such, psychotherapy can sometimes engender obsessive self-involvement that is not especially productive for patients. Good therapists know this; in fact, they gently guide patients away from thinking in demoralizing circles about themselves. Instead, they encourage patients to engage in a rational evaluation of their emotions and circumstances.[69] There may be tears and consternation, of course, but the careful therapist rarely considers their expression an end in itself—save, perhaps, for the most inhibited of patients for whom constructive assertion of feelings is an explicit goal of the therapy. Usually, the aim of therapy is some combination of symptom amelioration, greater depth of understanding (typically, of the ways in which one sabotages one's self), and behavioral change.

Good Grief!

In 1988 Susan Cohen lost her only child when Pan Am Flight 103 exploded over Lockerbie, Scotland. The terrible hours following the tragedy were full of confusion, yet Cohen remembers clearly the grief counselor "assigned" to her and her husband. He showered them with clichés about hope and quizzed them about their daughter's hobbies. The couple insisted on their privacy, but this "ambulance chaser," as the Cohens came to call him, simply would not go away.[70]

A few days later, Mrs. Cohen encountered another grief therapist who was conducting a group for bereaved family members. The therapist, Mrs. Cohen said, was "worried about my anger, that I should open my heart, [but] . . . I didn't need clichés. Most of all, I didn't need anyone telling me there was something wrong with the enormous rage I was feeling."[71]

Susan Cohen was one of the first to go public with her exasperation over the intrusive methods of disaster-scene grief counseling. Some ten years later, when two students gunned down their classmates and a teacher at Columbine High School in Littleton, Colorado, a chorus of protest rang out against the procession of counselors converging on the school.

The *New Yorker* captured the cultural moment with a cartoon. Two cowboys survey the horizon from a mountaintop. Off in the distance is a cluster of black dots. "Hard to tell from here," says one cowboy to the other. "Could be buzzards, could be grief counselors."[72]

In his essay "The Grief Racket," Charles Krauthammer, a psychiatrist and *Washington Post* columnist, asked:

> Why were packs of practitioners sent off to Littleton without the slightest hesitation? Or skepticism? Because the grief counseling business lives off the universal modern dogma that venting and openness, talking it out and letting it out, is good for the soul. . . . They embrace—they demand—openness on the grounds of mental health: that show and display without taboo is healthy; that reticence and repression, whether societal or individual, is a breeding ground for pathology.[73]

Jonathan Yardley, also of the *Washington Post*, wrote a column called "Vultures Over Littleton" in which he described grief counselors as

> the self-appointed priests and priestesses of this New Age of self-awareness, unctuous parasites bearing portable confessionals who

swoop down wherever catastrophe strikes, chanting mantras of
pop psychology. . . . Surely there are few sights in the contemporary landscape more repellent than that of these leeches attaching
themselves to the stunned, bewildered survivors of affliction, demanding that they give vent to their "feelings."[74]

By exhorting victims to vent, counselors can cause more
harm than good.[75] Pushing traumatized people toward open
self-expression—especially when the press is swarming, the mi-
crophones are on, and the cameras are rolling—makes for sensa-
tional photos and footage of people sobbing hysterically, but it
violates a key ethical principle of therapy: the duty to protect
the client's dignity. Moreover, victims' relentless communication of intense sadness or distress can actually drive away their
loved ones, the very people upon whom they depend for solace
and support.[76] In a lighthearted reminder of this fact, a T-shirt
appeared on the streets of San Francisco after the 1987 Loma
Prieta earthquake that said, "Thank you for not sharing your
earthquake experience."[77]

In England, too, where grief counselors are popular, some are
fed up. One British commentator described them as "mostly
middle-aged women with dangly earrings and diplomas from
dubious institutions, speaking fluent psychobabble."[78] Frank
Furedi, a sociologist at the University of Kent and author of the
2003 book *Therapy Culture*, assails counselors for their very distortion of grieving. "Bereavement becomes not so much an act
of remembrance about the dead," he writes, "but a therapeutic
statement about the survivor."[79]

"Recovery Issues"

The grief industry survived its post-Columbine savaging. The
deployment of grief counselors to schools after the deaths of students, to accident sites, to scenes of suicide or illness is still de
rigueur. "Students will need to talk about what happened," says

the National Association of School Psychologists.[80] The U.S. Department of Education concurs: "Stress-management needs to be conducted for all students," says its 2003 school guide on crisis management.[81] School districts can apply for U.S. Department of Education grants to help them coordinate with mental health agencies that will assist them with "recovery issues."[82]

For on-the-job crises, deployment of grief counselors is now the standard response of employers. According to the Employees Assistance Professionals Association, the trade group for the nation's employee assistance programs, more than 90 percent of their five thousand members offer grief counseling.[83] After the Columbia space shuttle explosion in the winter of 2003, for example, counselors attended to workers at United Space Alliance, a company that had worked with NASA.[84] Surely many Alliance workers were devastated, but why import strangers to the workplace when colleagues, bosses, friends, and family can provide comfort?

All kinds of disappointments have become opportunities for the "grief brigade," as *Time* magazine has called it. When the Boston Public Library was flooded in 1998, grief counselors were called in to help librarians cope with the stress of ruined books. When the employees of Portland General Electric in Oregon took a rough hit on their 401(k) accounts, counselors were summoned.[85] "Our CEO likened the situation to grieving a death and going through all the shock and anger you have to deal with," a PGE spokesman explained to a *Smart Money* reporter.[86]

The commodification of grief also proceeds apace. There are "healing puppets," chat rooms, bereavement books, workshops, and certification programs.[87] It is through such programs that the grief industry perpetuates itself. Qualifications for becoming a counselor run the gamut. No wonder Jessica Mitford, author of *The American Way of Death* in 1963 and, almost forty years later, *The American Way of Death Revisited*, wrote, "Trying to pin down the meaning of [grief therapy] is like trying to pick up quicksilver with a fork."[88]

The Grief Recovery Institute in Sherman Oaks, California, for example, will award a certificate to "anyone with a genuine desire to help grieving people" (and who can pay $1,500 for the four-day course).[89] Or one could become a "degriefer." The degriefing technique uses massage to "unlock and remove grief from the body," says its developer, Lyn Prashant of San Anselmo, California.[90] A five-day course culminates in a National Degriefing Certification.

By contrast, the Association of Death Education and Counseling in Hartford, Connecticut, one of the best-known groups, with about two thousand members, has requirements.[91] Applicants must have at least a bachelor's degree plus two years of related experience and three hundred dollars for the examination, culminating in a "Certificate in Thanatology: Dying, Death, and Bereavement."[92] The American Academy of Grief Counseling in Warren, Ohio, trains health professionals, social workers, clergy, and funeral directors to become Certified Grief Counselors. At least eighty hours of courses in bereavement are required. Recertification every three years costs one hundred and fifty dollars.[93]

To be sure, grief counselors, as individuals, tend to be very caring and well-intentioned people. If they are simply available, if they refrain from pressuring the bereaved to engage with them, as the two therapists pressured Susan Cohen, and if their ministrations are humane and attuned to individuals with whom they are working, their efforts will probably be appreciated by the small minority who seek them out.

Myths of Coping with Loss

Grieving is a complex process that individuals manage in their own idiosyncratic ways. Some people are highly emotional and express their feelings. Some withhold their sentiments, and others find that the nature of their emotions and their desire to talk about them fluctuate over time. Yet to this day, observes George

Hagman, director of outpatient mental health services at the
Greater Bridgeport Community Mental Health Center in Connecticut, "In order to be considered normal, the bereaved person
must endure the additional stress of having to express grief and
sadness." Hagman continues:

> Most popular forms of bereavement counseling . . . prescribe
> that the therapist challenge the bereaved patient's "resistance"
> to mourning, compelling him to express sadness, in the belief
> that the [discharge] of suppressed feeling is at the core of suc-
> cessful treatment.[94]

There is now a formidable scholarly literature on bereavement
that reveals just how misguided this approach is. But the public
knows little about it. George Bonanno, a professor of psychology
at Columbia University who has studied bereavement patterns
and published widely on the topic, feels his work is dismissed because it contradicts so much of what is assumed to be true in the
field. "It frustrates me quite a bit," he said in an interview with
the *Baltimore Sun*.[95] Bonanno has found, for example, that many
mourners do not display a great deal of anguish after their loss, go
on with their lives, and seem happy again fairly quickly. Though
failing to display marked distress is commonly viewed as "maladaptive," Bonanno says, "there's no evidence for that."

Bonanno is one of the leaders of what journalist Emily Nussbaum calls "an academic countermovement."[96] The two camps
come out in force at annual meetings of the Association for Death
Education and Counseling. On one side are the empaths—grief
counselors who are guided by subjective emotion, anecdote, and
intuition. And on the other are the skeptical empiricists who
want to make the field more scientific by testing theories about
bereavement and studying the value of well-defined therapies.[97]

The social psychologists Camille Wortman of SUNY Stony
Brook and Roxane Cohen Silver of the University of California
at Irvine are also part of the "countermovement."[98] In 1989 they

rattled the bereavement field by pointedly challenging several deeply held notions—that grief unfolds in a particular sequence, that feelings of intense sadness are universal after a loss, and that we must "work through" grief. Their iconoclastic analysis, "The Myths of Coping With Loss," published in the *Journal of Consulting and Clinical Psychology*, is now routine reading in academic courses on bereavement. But much of it has not yet filtered down to the ranks of workshop-trained grief counselors and grief gurus who write self-help books and host Web sites.[99]

Myth of Inconsolable Sadness

A few years ago Brendan Maher, a research professor of psychology at Harvard, lost his beloved 105-year-old aunt. The woman had already made arrangements with a local funeral home in Denver. Maher attended her funeral and then flew back to Massachusetts. Days later he received a phone call from a young woman from the funeral home who wanted to schedule him for grief counseling:

WOMAN: I would like to arrange an appointment for the grief counseling.

MAHER: What are you talking about?

WOMAN: You are entitled to one hour of grief counseling after your aunt's death and we need to arrange a time to do this.

MAHER: Where are you calling from? Denver? Are you suggesting that I come out to Denver for you to counsel me?

WOMAN: Oh no! We usually counsel over the telephone, so we need to choose a time when this would be convenient.

MAHER: Let me explain. My aunt was a wonderful woman, and we always enjoyed being with her. But she was 105 years old and happy to be passing on. We shall miss her, but I have to say that I feel sadness but I do not feel what could honestly be called grief. Her time had come, and she was relieved by it. Incidentally, did you know my aunt personally?

WOMAN: No. We make a point not to know the loved one.

MAHER: And you don't know me, either.

WOMAN: That's right.

MAHER: So you, a complete stranger who does not know either my aunt or myself, are proposing to counsel me for a grief that I do not feel?

WOMAN: (silence) Perhaps I should explain. There is no cost—it has already been paid for as part of the funeral package that was pre-paid by your aunt.

MAHER: *(Click)*[100]

Maher's experience underscores two assumptions of the grief industry: (1) that unbidden strangers will be welcomed as comforters and (2) that the bereaved are always distraught to the point of needing specialized help to cope with a normal human experience, loss.

Like Maher, many bereaved subjects do not report feeling intense grief.[101] George Bonanno and colleagues found that "stable, low-level depression" was the most common emotional state in elderly bereaved spouses, characteristic of almost half.[102] Sidney Zisook of the University of California at San Diego and colleagues found an especially low occurrence of grief in elderly widows and widowers. Within two months of bereavement half of them claimed to experience no negative mood at all, and one-third had only intermediate levels of distress. A mere one-fifth was miserable and thus fit the stereotype.[103]

Furthermore, loss can engender some positive feelings mixed in with sorrow. Men who lost a partner to AIDS have felt they gained personal strength and wisdom during the loss. Many loved ones are relieved that the deceased was no longer suffering, or in the case of elderly spouses, that a relationship that had been chronically tense and unhappy has come to an end.[104]

As part of the University of Michigan's extensive project Changing Lives of Older Couples, Bonanno worked with a team that conducted in-depth interviews of more than 1,500 couples during the 1980s and 1990s.[105] During the course of the study, 205 of the participants were widowed. When the researchers examined the widows and widowers at six and eighteen months after their spouses died they found nearly half reported negligible distress after the loss. Members of this "resilient" group, as the researchers called them, tended to display a preloss acceptance of death and held an overall belief that the world was a just place. This is not to say, of course, that they did not occasionally yearn for their spouse, feel sad, or miss the tenderness of the marital relationship. It is simply a description of how most couples in the study coped with the loss of their longtime partners.

The researchers noted four other patterns. "Chronic grievers," representing about 16 percent, remained depressed for at least eighteen months. Notably, they were very dependent on their spouses. Another subgroup, comprising about 10 percent of the sample, experienced a pattern mood improvement after the loss; their marriages were judged by the researchers to be stressful. So-called "common grief," typical of about 10 percent, was marked by postloss sadness and depressive symptoms that peaked after about six months and then declined slowly. And, finally, around 8 percent of the sample of widows and widowers manifested prolonged deep depression ("chronic depressives"); they were likely to be chronically depressed even *before* their spouses died.

This long-range study of Detroit elderly was powerful in undermining the lore about the relationship of the nature of attachment to the spouse to a pattern of grieving. To recap, it showed that individuals who deeply loved their spouses were not destined to grieve intensely, and that widows and widowers who had conflicted or stressful marriages did not go on to develop clinical depression, as classical bereavement theory predicts. Finally, half of the bereaved subjects experienced minimal distress and disruption in normal function yet were rated, contrary to tenets of bereavement theory, as psychologically well-adjusted in a happy marriage prior to loss.[106]

To be sure, some of these findings seem counterintuitive. The idea that loss and deep depression are intimately linked has a long pedigree. It is expounded in exhaustive detail in Robert Burton's 1621 book *The Anatomy of Melancholie*, an encyclopedic sweep of the condition. Burton begins with earliest Greeks and ends with his contemporaries of the early 1600s.[107] In that century, "griefe" itself was considered a potential cause of death in parts of Europe. By the 1800s, Colonial-era psychiatrists advised "liberal doses of opium" to dull the pangs of grief. Freud's 1917 classic *Mourning and Melancholia* put forth the idea that severe depression develops when the bereaved person's love for the deceased is ambivalent. The empirical study of bereavement began with Eric Lindemann in 1942, who described "morbid grief" in survivors of the Coconut Grove nightclub fire in Boston.[108] It is important to remember, though, that such observations and theories derive from individuals whose grief did not resolve spontaneously or who were patients in clinical settings, not everyday subjects volunteering for a study.

Myth of Delayed Grief

Traditionally, the absence of crying, sad facial expression, and lamentation was taken as a worrisome sign that the bereaved person was only delaying the inevitable.[109] In her landmark 1937 paper, "The Absence of Grief," Freud's protégé Helene Deutsch argued that lack of intense distress—severe emotional pain, listlessness, and observable despondency—in the wake of loss was a portent of emotional problems to come.[110] Deutsch's insight drew on the classic Freudian idea that emotions and drives are internal forces that need to be discharged in order for psychic equilibrium to be maintained.

According to this theory, absent grief would ultimately trigger a delayed reaction that would be "as fresh and intense as if the loss just occurred."[111] Victims of delayed grief were believed to be developmentally immature, cold, narcissistic, or poorly attached to the spouse when living; therapy was needed to address their "unhealthy denial and repression of feeling."[112] In a 1993 survey, psychiatrist Warwick Middleton of the University of Queensland in Australia, found that more than three quarters of experts in the United States and elsewhere believed that delayed grief was a genuine phenomenon.[113]

But empirical support for delayed grief is lacking.[114] In their review of the published literature, Wortman and Silver found that delayed grief reactions were rare.[115] When Bonanno's team assessed bereaved spouses at six months after loss and five years later—one of the longer periods of observation ever documented—they did not find a single low-distress subject who went on to experience a "delayed" intense reaction at five years.[116] Following up their survey, Middleton and his colleagues interviewed bereaved spouses, children, and parents at intervals up to thirteen months. Their conclusion: "No evidence was found for . . . delayed grief."[117]

There is a difference, however, between not experiencing intense sadness and concealing feelings from one's self or others. Actively suppressing one's feelings can be unhealthy. For example, people who drink or use drugs to dull the pain of loss appear to suffer prolonged distress.[118] Also, bereaved individuals who deliberately hold back expressing their feelings out of a desire to "appear strong" for those around them may find that they inadvertently increase their own anguish.[119] This is not to say, however, that our emotional health should be the final arbiter of our actions. A divorcing parent, for example, who contains rage at her soon-to-be ex-husband for the sake of her children is reasonably putting her moral duty to protect them ahead of her own emotional needs.

Stages of Grief and "Grief Work"

Empirical observations show that bereavement does not unfold along predictable lines, but that it varies with a person's temperament and circumstances. Yet the well-worn stage theory of grief seems immune to repeal. Even the Federal Emergency Management Agency, which routinely responds to fatal disasters, lists shock, protest, disorganization, and reorganization as the steps in the grieving process. During the disorganization stage "the loss is only too real," says the agency's Web site. "You are likely to experience overwhelming feelings of bleakness, despair, apathy, anxiety, and confusion."[120]

The popular misconception that grief has a fixed course is a garbled legacy from the work of the late Elisabeth Kübler-Ross. A Swiss psychiatrist who immigrated to New York City, Kübler-Ross made a study of people who were dying. She distilled her observations in the classic *On Death and Dying*, published in 1969.[121] Here she described five "phases of dying"—denial, anger, depression, bargaining, and acceptance—some or all of which any given person might experience, in no fixed sequence. Although Kübler-Ross's "phases of dying" gained common currency as the "stages of grief," she was actually referring to the grief experienced by the person who was dying, not that of his survivors.

The late John Bowlby and Colin Murray Parkes, British psychiatrists, from St. Christopher's Hospice in London, also found themselves misinterpreted. In 1970 they described a pattern of grief that comprised (1) numbness, (2) yearning and searching, (3) disorganization and despair, and (4) reorganization. But thirty years later Parkes writes, "The sequence was never intended to be more than a rough guide, and it was recognized from the start that people would move back and forth . . . rather than follow a fixed passage."[122] Parkes laments how some therapists applied this model in a "rigid way to bereaved people . . . attempting to force them to fit a pattern with which they felt very uncomfortable."[123]

Parkes posits two reasons why the model was accepted with "enthusiasm" by some psychotherapists and counselors. First, it resembled stages they already knew about and endorsed—that is, Freud's classic stages (oral, anal, genital) of psychosocial development. According to this theory, adult neuroses resulted from fixation at one of the stages; the point of therapy was to help the patient move forward. It was a framework that led easily to the idea that clinical intervention could help those who got "stuck" at some point in the grieving process.

For such individuals, that prescription was "grief work"—a prolonged review of the emotional meaning of the loss, concentration on memories of the deceased and, finally, a withdrawal of emotional ties to the lost person. Indeed, according to the popular handbook *Grief Counseling and Grief Therapy*, used by trainees and practicing therapists, the purpose of grief therapy is to "facilitate the grieving process."[124]

Once again, however, research shows that popular notions are wrong: not everyone who suffers a significant loss is helped by talking about it.[125] In their article, "Does 'Grief Work' Work?" Margaret Stroebe and Wolfgang Stroebe, prominent bereavement researchers at the University of Utrecht, the Netherlands, compared widows who did not confront the loss—that is, widows who did not disclose their feelings to others and who avoided reminders of the deceased—with widows who did so. They found no differences between the groups in terms of depression, anxiety, sleep difficulties, and physical complaints.[126]

Among parents of children who died of Sudden Infant Death Syndrome, the ones who tried "working through" the loss—by trying to make sense of it, thinking of ways the death could have been avoided, and dwelling on the loss—showed more distress three weeks after the baby's death than those who did not. They also showed less "emotional resolution" eighteen months later.[127] Almost identical findings have been validated with one group of grieving people after another—Holocaust survivors, young women who had been abused, gay men who had lost their partners to AIDS.[128]

Thus, the failure to express distress even when one is feeling distress can be regarded as a valuable coping skill for some people, not something to be stigmatized as "denial." Indeed, it is tempting to interpret these observations as a lesson in the benefits of a restrained coping style. Unfortunately, we cannot really know whether a particular coping style actually *produces* an outcome, or whether styles are merely linked with a yet undiscovered common cause or set of causes. Does the downcast widow dwell on her loss because she is depressed, or is she depressed because she dwells on the loss? Like most social science research, the studies of bereavement deal only in correlations. What the foregoing observations of bereaved individuals *do* show, however, is that disclosing sadness or focusing on it is not a *necessary* part of healthy coping with loss. "Grief work" is not a prerequisite for healthy grieving.

Limits of Formal Therapy

We emphasized these points because subscribing to grief myths can lead to added heartache for the bereaved. Imagine the widow who braces for agony in the future because she does not care to talk about or dwell upon her loss now. Imagine the adult child who worries he is somehow abnormal or unloving because his distress over his mother's death does not seem deep enough. Now imagine the widow's relief to learn that some people simply prefer not to express their sadness, and do not suffer for it later. Imagine the son's relief when he learns that failure to experience persistent wrenching emotion after a loss does not in any way mean he did not love his mother with all of his heart.

Grief myths can claim other victims as well. An otherwise normal bereaved individual can find herself prodded into therapy by concerned friends who are worried by her failure to conform to popular notions of how a grieving person is supposed to behave and feel. She herself may subscribe to those standards, too, and fear she is not reacting to loss appropriately. She might answer an ad offering grief therapy or go out of her way to find a therapist specializing in bereavement. If she does this she will most likely confront the philosophy expressed by Therese Rando, a popular workshop leader. In Rando's 1991 book, *How To Go On Living When Someone You Love Dies*, the reader is told "you will have to give expression to *all* of your feelings . . . adequate rest and nutrition are important as your grief work requires enormous energy. . . . Many people need professional assistance to help them experience the natural grief processes."[129]

But do they? Evaluations show that intervention programs that recruit clients, through advertisements for example, or that visit families within hours of a loss are far more likely to have no effect or a negative one than programs that wait for the bereaved person to initiate contact.[130] In addition, grief therapists may fail to realize that for some patients real problems are tied to relations to the surviving family and that the immediate loss is only part of a larger set of difficulties.

When patients volunteer for the therapy, however, outcomes seem hardly better. A number of studies have reached the conclusion that grief therapies are relatively ineffective and even harmful to a minority.[131] A 2000 study by Robert Neimeyer of the University of Memphis reported that 38 percent of subjects receiving grief therapy actually fared worse than a matched group not receiving treatment.[132] Reviewing several studies, Neimeyer summarizes that "such interventions are typically ineffective, and perhaps even deleterious, at least for persons experiencing normal bereavement."[133] In particular, people with more avoidant coping styles, or those who prefer to "do" something, are more likely to respond poorly to traditional bereavement interventions which are emotion-focused, not problem-focused.[134]

Typically, grief is self-limiting and the vast majority of us do not need "experts" to guide us through mourning. Some people, of course, will become impaired by intense, unremitting grief. Among those at high risk are mothers who lose young children, and those whose loved ones die unexpectedly or violently.[135] Such so-called complicated, or traumatic, grief tends to be marked by a strong feeling of disbelief about the death, an inability to think of little else, and a detachment from loved ones; this may be accompanied by thoughts of suicide, excessive use of alcohol, or inability to function in daily life.[136] For this subgroup, roughly estimated to be between 10 and 15 percent of bereaved individuals, psychotherapy and medication have proved to be of great help.[137] A pressing topic in bereavement research today is identifying those at high risk for developing complicated grief, so that clinicians can engage them if their suffering does not diminish within a reasonable amount of time.[138]

At this point, let us consider that some readers may remain skeptical about the findings we presented. Perhaps they are reluctant, for example, to relinquish the popular wisdom that grief is played out in five stages—we understand. We, too, were surprised at the evidence and worried that perhaps we were missing other quality research that contradicted the summaries we have presented. So we contacted several of the leading bereavement researchers and asked them who their most vocal critics were, and whether there was scholarship that challenged their conclusions.

None could point to fellow researchers who discovered opposing findings. They did, however, say that their work had antagonized many so-called grief theorists. Such theorists remain wedded to concepts like grief work or the idea that counseling and therapy is almost inevitably a good thing. But their evidence is idiosyncratic, coming from case studies or their own impressions.

We were further reassured that we had surveyed the evidence fairly when the *Report on Bereavement and Grief Research* from the Washington D.C.–based nonprofit Center for Health Advancement was released in late 2003.[139] This three-year project was the collaborative product of twenty-three recognized bereavement researchers. They combed through the entire peer-reviewed literature on bereavement—hundreds of studies—and concluded that (1) "responses to loss vary widely and

that there is no clearly defined course or process of grieving,"
(2) most people do not experience problematic grief, (3) the
most effective support is likely to come from family, friends,
colleagues, religious institutions, and (4) grief counseling and
therapy "may not always be effective, and in some cases, may
be harmful."[140] Grief mythologizers take note.

Molly Ivins Was Right

As we have seen, the popular psychological imperatives to "get
it all out" and "feel it to heal it" do not always work. Cancer patients who talk about their ordeal in therapy groups do *not* live
longer. Mourners do not have to go through five stages of grieving, and healthy grieving does not require wrenching sadness.
Expressing anger does not invariably alleviate it; on the contrary, it can make one angrier. And when people are distraught,
ruminating about their pain may only intensify the pain: repression and distraction can be the best remedies.

John Stuart Mill urged us to pursue our own good in our own
way without imposing on others; his wisdom applies here as
well. Each of us, he writes, "is the proper guardian of his own
health, whether bodily, or mental and spiritual."[141] And so, for
Molly Ivins and all the other contented repressors who are not
joining the cathartic majority, if they do not wish to get in
touch with their feelings, they should be left alone.

5

From Pathos to Pathology

For fifty-seven consecutive days during World War II the city of London endured harrowing and relentless firebombing by German forces. All the while, Sigmund Freud's daughter, Anna, was operating nursery schools. She reported that only a handful of children in her so-called War Nurseries needed professional psychological help. Those who remained with their parents, even if bombed repeatedly and partly buried in debris, showed "no signs of traumatic shock . . . [and] little excitement and no undue disturbance," she observed.[1]

Many of today's mental health professionals would be stunned to hear this, certain that many of Freud's young charges suffered lifelong mental scarring.[2] Was Anna Freud in serious denial?

The social anthropologist Barbara Harrell-Bond found that people essentially respond to crisis in three ways: as threat, as loss, or as challenge.[3] For most trauma professionals the drama of threat and loss take center stage. Yet in her work with Ugandans fleeing the terror reign of dictator Idi Amin, Harrell-Bond saw people meet disaster as if rising to a challenge. Though heartbroken, many of the refugees were also hopeful that their ordeal, no matter how chaotic or seemingly bleak, could ultimately lead to improvements in their lives.

Naturally, we must be ready to care for those who are psychologically damaged by crisis, but it is folly to imagine that vast numbers of individuals and entire communities, if left to manage on their own, will inevitably be crippled by catastrophe. At issue is post-traumatic stress disorder, a disabling condition marked by intense reexperiencing of the horrific event. It is marked by relentless nightmares or unbidden waking images, and in many cases, crippling anxiety and phobias.

Fortunately, most people who experience sudden life-threatening or horrifying events do not develop reactions so severe as to qualify for PTSD. While over half of us have encountered such crises within our lifetimes, only a minority, between 2 and 10 percent, develop PTSD over the course of our lives.[4] Why, then, have so many mental health experts underestimated our inherent resilience and resourcefulness?[5] Why do they presume fragility in the face of powerful events?

Post-Vietnam Syndrome

The story of PTSD starts with the Vietnam veteran. In the waning days of the war, a band of psychiatrists set about formulating a new diagnosis to describe the psychological wounds veterans sustained in the Vietnam War. The effort was spearheaded by two New York City psychiatrists, both fervently opposed to the war: Robert Jay Lifton, well-known for his work on the psychological impact of Hiroshima on the Japanese, and Chaim Shatan.

They organized "rap" groups for veterans who felt socially and spiritually dislocated. These men, the psychiatrists warned, were the tip of an iceberg; hundreds of thousands, perhaps millions, of other traumatized veterans across the country suffered out of sight and in silence. Lifton and Shatan became their voice. "Out of kinship with the veterans [we] have moved

beyond therapy alone and toward advocacy; we have entered
actively into public affairs," Shatan said. He described his goal
as giving

> the widest possible publicity to the unique emotional experi-
> ences of these men. To do so, we go—together with the veter-
> ans—wherever we will be heard, conventions, war crimes
> hearings, churches, Congress, even abroad.[6]

Along with a handful of colleagues, Lifton and Shatan would
shape the image of the Vietnam veteran as walking time bombs,
subsequently immortalized by Hollywood in films like *Taxi
Driver*, *Coming Home*, *The Deer Hunter*, and *Rambo: First Blood*.[7]

In 1972 Shatan unveiled the Post-Vietnam Syndrome. He described it in a *New York Times* op-ed as a condition marked by
self-punishment, rage at being "duped and manipulated by society," and alienation from one's feelings.[8] Shatan acknowledged
that veterans of other wars wrestled with depression, alienation, and nightmares, but the Vietnam veteran suffered
uniquely because the military discouraged him from grieving
for his lost buddies. A hostile homecoming magnified feelings of
guilt—over having killed and over having survived—and made
it almost impossible for him to mourn.[9]

The result, as Shatan described it, was a "delayed massive
trauma" response that could manifest months or years later as
family discord, unemployment, and addiction. "He returns as a
tainted intruder in our own society," Lifton testified before the
Senate in 1970, with some "likely to seek continuing outlets for
a pattern of violence to which they have become habituated."[10]

Jerry Lembcke, a former member of Vietnam Veterans
Against the War and now a sociologist at Holy Cross College,
considers the May 6, 1972, publication of Shatan's *Times* op-ed a
turning point in the campaign to publicize the plight of the returning soldier. Lembcke described the scene at the Republican
convention three months later:

On the very day the Republican convention opened [in Miami] with over a thousand protesting veterans in the streets, the *Times* ran a major front page story on Post-Vietnam Syndrome. Entitled "Postwar Shock Is Found to Beset Veterans Returning From the War in Vietnam," the article alleged that 50 percent of Vietnam veterans needed "professional help to readjust." The association with mental illness was deepened in the text of the story that contained a liberal sprinkling of phrases like "psychiatric casualty," "emotionally disturbed," "mental breakdowns," and "men with damaged brains."[11]

The story provided no data to support the image of the dysfunctional veterans, Lembcke said; what it did provide "was a mode of discourse within which America's memory of the war and the veterans' coming-home experience would be constructed."

This mode of discourse set the Vietnam veteran apart from soldiers who came before him. It bore the "suggestion or outright assertion that Vietnam veterans have been unique in American history for their psychiatric problems," writes the historian Eric T. Dean Jr. in *Shook Over Hell—Post-Traumatic Stress, Vietnam, and the Civil War*.[12] Civil War soldiers also succumbed to mental breakdown, but because the Union soldiers' war is today perceived as a righteous crusade to save the Union and end slavery, it elicits images of heroes and prompts battle reenactments. World War II was a fight to protect our values against a foreign threat; soldiers' stories were those of courage and noble sacrifice.

Only an unjust conflict like Vietnam, Dean argues, could prime the cultural imagination to accept the idea of soldiers as psychiatric victims, misfits, and tormented losers. Soon the idea took hold that most people, not just veterans, who endured tragic ordeals, are damaged by their experience—not changed, as almost all would be, but damaged. Other axioms of therapism emerged on its heels: that most victims of traumatic experience need professional help to cope, and that they are passive recipients of tragedy, helpless to control their reactions to disaster and heartbreak.

PTSD: Part Politics, Part Pathology

In 1974 the American Psychiatric Association began planning a third edition of the *Diagnostic and Statistical Manual*, the association's taxonomy of mental disorders. As the image of the psychologically disabled veteran took root in the national consciousness the psychiatric profession debated the wisdom of giving him his own diagnosis. Soon, Lifton and Shatan—along with other activist clinicians, antiwar veterans, and religious groups—were lobbying the members of the manual task force to adopt Post-Vietnam Syndrome. The task force rejected the syndrome as vague and unscientific and turned its attention to a more systematic diagnosis called post-traumatic stress disorder.[13]

As a taxonomic category, PTSD was indeed more refined than Post-Vietnam Syndrome. It focused on specific symptoms, not social attitudes, and it applied to a wide variety of ghastly events, such as natural disasters, severe accidents, or confinement in a concentration camp. The women's movement greeted PTSD enthusiastically because it created a diagnostic niche for victims of rape, domestic violence, child abuse, and sexual assault.[14] Even so, some members of the task force remained doubtful about the wisdom of adopting PTSD. Symptoms such as recurrent images, avoidance, guilt, jumpiness, and irritability, they argued, were not distinctive and could be subsumed under variants of existing disorders such as depression or anxiety.[15]

In the end, PTSD became part of the psychiatric nomenclature with the publication of the third edition of the diagnostic manual in 1980. Its inclusion was certainly defensible. For example, it could help avert serious diagnostic errors—the kind reported in damning accounts from veterans' hospitals, where Vietnam veterans with flashbacks (vivid, lifelike replays of terrifying scenes) were mistaken for schizophrenic patients and wrongly treated with potent antipsychotic medications.[16] Clearer nomenclature made research more objective and replicable. In addition, the PTSD designation was helpful for patients who sought federal disability benefits for chronic war stress as the government required a diagnosis classifying them as a psychiatric casualty of war.[17]

Combat veteran and sociologist Wilbur Scott chronicles the roots of PTSD in his detailed 1993 account *The Politics of Readjustment: Vietnam Veterans Since the War*. "The placement of posttraumatic stress disorder in [the *Diagnostic and Statistical Manual*] allows us to see the politics of diagnosis and disease in an especially clear light," he writes. "PTSD is in [the manual] . . . because a core of psychiatrists and Vietnam veterans worked conscientiously and deliberately for years to put it there . . . at issue was the question of what constitutes a normal reaction or experience of soldiers to combat."[18]

Psychiatrists like Robert Jay Lifton clearly saw PTSD as the normal response. And, normal or not, veterans with the condition were indeed a boon to the antiwar agenda, touted as living proof that military aggression destroys minds and annihilates souls.[19] Thus, by the time PTSD was incorporated into the official psychiatric lexicon, it bore a hybrid legacy—part political artifact of the antiwar movement, part legitimate diagnosis.

A New Consciousness of Trauma

During the Civil War, breakdown in combat was called "irritable heart" or "nostalgia." In World War I "shell shock" was its name, and in World War II it was called "battle fatigue," "combat exhaustion," or "war stress." The shell-shocked soldiers of Britain and Germany in World War I were widely accused by military authorities, as well as by most army doctors and the public, of laziness, cowardliness, or of faking their condition.[20]

Military psychiatrists subscribed to a hereditary model of war stress. Men who succumbed were considered constitutionally inferior. In 1917, however, the British neuroanatomist Grafton Elliot Smith and the psychologist Tom Pear challenged this view. "Psychoneurosis may be produced in almost anyone if only his environment be made 'difficult' enough for him," they wrote in *Shell Shock and Its Lessons*.[21] This triggered a feisty nature-nurture debate within British military psychiatry, but eventually the two sides came to agree that both the soldier's predisposition to stress and his exposure to hostilities contributed to breakdown.

By World War II, then, military psychiatrists believed that even the bravest and fittest soldier could endure only so much. However, the threshold for breakdown, and especially for persistence of symptoms once the soldier was removed from the front, was lower in men with prewar difficulties.[22] This wisdom seemed to evaporate by the late 1970s when PTSD was being formulated. Instead, traumatic reactions were viewed almost exclusively as a function of exposure to trauma; predisposing traits of the victim were virtually ignored.

Moreover, PTSD was now assumed to be a normal and natural process of adaptation to extreme stress.[23] Thus, writes the British war historian Ben Shephard, "Vietnam helped to create a new consciousness of trauma in Western society."[24] It was a consciousness that saw the traumatic incident itself as the sole determinant of whether a victim developed PTSD.[25]

But if the pendulum swung too far, obliterating the role of an individual's own characteristics in the development of the condition, it served a political purpose. As British psychiatrist Derek Summerfield put it, the newly minted diagnosis of PTSD "was meant to shift the focus of attention from the details of a soldier's background and psyche to the fundamentally traumatogenic nature of war."[26]

Today, more than two decades after ratification of PTSD, we know that the condition is neither normal nor inevitable in the wake of catastrophe.[27] Although otherwise healthy people can develop PTSD, the risk is considerably greater for those with preexisting psychological vulnerabilities, such as depression, anxiety or personality disorders, or conduct problems in childhood.[28] Apostles of therapism, however, tend to give short shrift to these and other factors. Take intelligence and temperament.[29] Intelligence has been shown to be a protective factor.[30] After all, cognitive competence enables one to evaluate and adapt to new information and experiences. People who are sensation-seeking, impulsive, or poor at predicting the consequences of their actions are more likely to get in harm's way.

Psychologist Marilyn Bowman of Simon Fraser University has remarked upon the reluctance of some of her colleagues to acknowledge that a traumatic event alone is not sufficient to produce PTSD. She notes in her book *Individual Differences in Posttraumatic Response* that "clinical practice is based on an exaggerated idea of the power of life events, and a correspondingly significant inattention to preexisting factors."[31] Attention to those factors, in fact, should be a key aspect of treatment. If the clinician can help a patient modulate his baseline anxiety, depression, or impulsivity, chances are he will be less vulnerable to disruptive events in the future.

Not surprisingly, to ask what a person was like before he encountered catastrophe is to invite charges of insensitivity.[32] Yet acknowledging what a person was like before his exposure to trauma is hardly blaming the victim. "Discovering risk factors is essential for understanding PTSD just as it is for understanding heart disease," asserts Richard McNally, a clinical psychologist at Harvard. "The alternative is ignorance, and ignorance is an unreliable basis for treatment and prevention of any disorder, including PTSD."[33]

Post-Traumatic Stress Disorder Today

What is a normal response to traumatic events? The answer goes to the heart of one of the imperatives of therapism: to pathologize normal human response to tragedy.

In the immediate aftermath of disaster, most people feel

emotionally devastated, jittery, or perhaps even numb. These reactions fade over a few days or weeks, leaving a residue of painful memories that varies from person to person. When disturbing nightmares, anxiety, and phobias last longer than one month the individual may have PTSD. But this happens in a minority of victims; most people are not clinically traumatized by extreme events.

According to the current edition of the *Diagnostic and Statistical Manual of Mental Disorders* of the American Psychiatric Association, the fourth edition, text revision, published in 2000, PTSD (code 309.81) comprises the following symptoms:

1. intense reexperiencing of the event (often nightmares or intrusive waking images), severe anxiety and physical agitation upon confronting a reminder of the event;
2. efforts to avoid stimuli that symbolize the event (e.g., refusal to fly after surviving a plane crash), emotional numbness, social withdrawal, and
3. hyperarousal, easy startle, irritability.[34]

However, symptoms alone do not qualify an individual for the diagnosis, the person must also suffer incapacitation or overpowering emotional pain.

One plausible theory about the essence of PTSD is that it represents a biologically programmed fear reaction that does not subside, for reasons not fully understood, once the fear-producing situation is removed. Pervasive anxiety and conditioned phobias accompanied by the incessant replay of memories are symptoms of the unabated fear reaction.[35]

The nature of the trauma endured likely plays a role in its development.[36] Among the survivors of the Oklahoma City bombing, for example, 34 percent developed PTSD. All were in the direct path of the blast and most were injured.[37] After a car accident or natural disaster, however, lower rates have been noted, while among rape victims well over half are affected.[38] Fortunately, PTSD usually fades. Conservatively, about two-thirds of cases are resolved within the year, though periodic nightmares or easy startling may linger for additional months or even years.[39]

A number of controversies surround the diagnosis of traumatic stress.[40] First, what is trauma? The answer seem obvious enough, but it actually needs to be spelled out because many experts are now insisting that trauma should be defined as whatever traumatizes a person. In his sweeping 2003 book *Remembering Trauma*, McNally rejects this circularity and defines a traumatic event as one that is unexpectedly life-threatening or horrifying or both.[41] True, someone might feel "traumatized" by a minor car accident, McNally acknowledges, but to say that a fender-bender counts as a traumatic event alongside such horrors as rape, torture, or escape from a burning building dilutes the concept beyond recognition.

Post-traumatic stress disorder did not begin its taxonomic life with a subjective dimension. In 1980, when it was entered into the diagnostic manual, it applied only to the patient who had confronted a severe event outside the range of routine human experience "that would evoke significant symptoms of distress in almost everyone."[42] Gradually, as we will later show, the list of qualifying traumatic events expanded to include events that were witnessed remotely—even witnessed via television— or that happened to someone else. This was a boon to therapism, expanding the franchise of trauma experts and undercutting faith in natural human resilience.

Another point of confusion is whether the word "trauma" itself refers to an event or to an individual's response to that event. Again, this begs clarification because many mental health professionals use the word interchangeably, blurring the distinction. As a consequence, says New York University psychoanalyst Steven Reisner, practitioners and the public alike are "primed" to believe that traumatic circumstances invariably lead to a clinical syndrome.[43]

Then there is the problem of overzealous diagnosing. The *Diagnostic and Statistical Manual* sets out guidelines, but there is only so much a manual can do to ensure that clinicians regard a patient as more than the sum of his symptoms. Mental health workers who adhere too rigidly to the PTSD model, Marilyn Bowman laments, tend to "assume that the reported distress reflects profound inner experience in a way that is more true and more important than other ways of presenting the self."[44]

How Much Pathology Did Vietnam Produce?

Those who campaigned for the inclusion of PTSD did so, at least in part, to validate the suffering of veterans, but the irony is that nobody knows how many Vietnam veterans were actually afflicted with PTSD. In 1972, the *New York Times* quoted a psychiatrist at a veterans' hospital in Minnesota who estimated that "fifty percent of the soldiers returning from Vietnam need professional help to readjust."[45]

A 1982 article in the *Journal of Nervous and Mental Diseases* estimated that 500,000 to 700,000 veterans out of the roughly 3 million who served in the Vietnam theater were "in need of emotional help at the present time."[46] Lifton estimated that at least 900,000 veterans had PTSD despite the fact that only about half a million, or 15 percent of soldiers, were assigned to combat units.[47]

One of the few to challenge the assertion of widespread maladjustment among returning veterans was Jonathan Borus, now at the Harvard School of Medicine. In the early 1970s, when Borus was a research psychiatrist at the Walter Reed Army Research Institute, he published data comparing the emotional and behavioral readjustment of almost 600 Vietnam veterans, most of them assigned to combat units, and about 200 noncombat counterparts who served elsewhere overseas or in the United States. Borus found no difference between the two cohorts of veterans. "From a review of public and professional reports," he wrote, "it seems to me that some mental health professionals have . . . overstepped their data to support their politics."[48]

In the early 1980s the federal government mandated a study of PTSD in Vietnam veterans. The National Vietnam Veterans' Readjustment Study (NVVRS) was released in 1990 by an independent research team.[49] During the mid-1980s—when the men were interviewed for the study—about one quarter still met diagnostic criteria for either full (15 percent) or the less severe form called "partial" PTSD (11 percent) at the time of the interview.[50] Thus, at some time since returning from war—the last soldier was evacuated in 1975—half of the approximately three million Vietnam theatre veterans had suffered either PTSD (31 percent) or the less severe partial PTSD (22 percent).

But this seems implausible. Only 15 percent of men were assigned to combat units, yet *half* of all veterans suffered "clinically significant stress-reaction symptoms," as the NVVRS put it.[51] True, noncombat jobs, such as truck driver, put men at risk for deadly ambush, but studies on psychiatric casualties during the war found the vast majority of cases referred to field hospitals were from support units.[52] Furthermore, they did not experience much combat-related stress; instead, they were sent because of "character problems" and substance abuse.[53]

During the years of most intense fighting, 1968–1969, psychiatric casualties reportedly numbered twelve to fifteen troops per thousand, or a little more than 1 percent.[54] If the readjustment study were correct, the number afflicted with diagnosable war stress vastly multiplied somehow in the years after returning. Again, it does not add up. Finally, as fighting wound down after 1968, psychiatric casualties actually went up. The best explanation seems to be that military discipline and unit cohesion—factors known to buffer soldiers from psychological problems—eroded considerably during that period.

The NVVRS enjoys status as conventional wisdom about the psychological impact of Vietnam. Yet another, less publicized study, was conducted by the Centers for Disease Control and published in 1988 in the *Journal of the American Medical Association*. It was called the Vietnam Experience Study and using different interview methods it found that only 15 percent of veterans ever suffered PTSD and that 2 percent met criteria at the time of the interview.[55] By 1990 a critical mass of scholarship had accumulated showing that Vietnam veterans, as a group, were roughly similar to both Vietnam era veterans (soldiers who did not serve in Vietnam) and nonveterans in terms of income, level of education, divorce rate, suicide, employment, and homelessness.[56]

Controversy Remains

How to explain the apparent explosion in mental illness among Vietnam Veterans within the two decades of fighting in the Vietnam War? One answer is that PTSD takes years to develop. But the problem with this possibility is that delayed onset is actually quite rare—despite its being considered a classic characteristic of combat PTSD as Lifton and Shatan construed the condition. In fact, studies of trauma victims find that symptoms tend to develop within days of the traumatic event, peak within one to a few weeks, and usually fade in intensity within months.[57]

Researchers who have followed victims of mass shootings, industrial accidents, and the Oklahoma City bombing have documented no cases of delayed-onset PTSD (defined as PTSD that does not appear until six months after an event) up to three and four years after the event.[58] Several studies of motor vehicle accident victims found that between 3 and 5 percent developed delayed-onset PTSD and a large study of volunteer firefighters in Australia found that 20 percent were afflicted.[59] But it is exceedingly rare for PTSD to appear out of nowhere after six months. Studies that take into account the presence of subthreshold PTSD symptoms prior to the subsequent development of full-blown PTSD find that, indeed, they already existed in muted form.[60]

Studies of combat and civilian subjects that rely on their

recall of symptoms—a method subject to memory distortion—give a mixed picture. Several found negligible evidence of delayed PTSD or none at all.[61] In two studies, 22 percent and 40 percent of combat veterans said that symptoms of PTSD did not occur until at least six months after their tour of duty.[62] Finally, compelling case reports of veterans of World War II and Korean and Holocaust survivors developing PTSD for the first time decades after their ordeals have appeared in medical journals.[63] Yet it is more likely that these cases represent reactivation of earlier traumatic symptoms due to subsequent crises or personal disruptions, such as retirement or illness in old age.[64]

Another explanation for the high rates of PTSD in the NVVRS could be that researchers used a diagnostic threshold for PTSD that was too low and thus tallied up cases where none actually existed. In particular, researchers did not measure the degree of impairment caused by symptoms; nor were subjects asked about the severity of symptoms.[65] These omissions were significant because many individuals who have occasional, even frequent, symptoms (e.g., nightmares, painful memories) can still function well. It is not uncommon for clinicians to overlook functional measures and concentrate chiefly on symptoms, a circumstance that has spurred active debate about overdiagnosis within the field of psychiatry.[66]

And, finally, veterans, like the rest of us, are suggestible. In World War I the British Army adapted to this fact by discouraging soldiers from thinking of themselves as casualties, lest it induce them to overstate the severity of their distress.[67] In 1917 the British army went so far as to ban the very term "shell shock." The term was replaced with the nonlabel "not yet diagnosed [nervous] or N.Y.D.N."[68] French and British psychiatrists had found that when soldiers with war stress were cared for at the front—with rest, hot food, encouragement, and reassurance—they were far more likely to recover than those receiving longer-term, Freudian-type therapy at hospitals hundreds of miles away.[69]

In the wake of the Vietnam War the PTSD narrative circulated widely in the cultural atmosphere. It could provide a medical-ized story line for many unhappy but not necessarily trauma-tized veterans who invoked PTSD in their "effort at meaning"—a poignant term used by the British psychologist Frederic C. Bartlett to signify the human longing to make sense of one's feelings and circumstances.

Such effort is as strenuous as it is unwitting. Researchers have documented, for example, that people tend naturally to reconstruct the past in terms of their present circumstances, exaggerating the degree of earlier misfortune and trauma if they are currently feeling bad, minimizing it if they are feeling good. Findings from various studies—of Gulf War veterans, car accident victims, witnesses to school shootings, international peacekeepers—are remarkably consistent in this regard. They show that individuals with more severe symptoms of anxiety and depression remember a traumatic event as being worse when they are asked about it a second time many months, or even years, after the first. Those with fewer symptoms, however, tended to recall the event as *less* harrowing than they had previously described it.[70]

Verifying combat histories would have clarified the picture to some extent, but researchers felt that military personnel files were too unreliable for this.[71] True, no data source is perfect, but taking into account the information on personnel files is surely better than relying solely on memories that are over ten years, even two decades, old. A best estimate could be derived from triangulating various sources of information, memory in-cluded. It is simply hard to believe that there were no other in-dependent sources that could verify, at minimum, whether a soldier was within one hundred miles of a combat zone.

These powerful phenomena—effort at meaning and memory distortion—do not deny that some veterans did indeed suffer the crippling anxiety of post-traumatic stress disorder. But we simply do not know how many of them did. This unknown reflects a larger set of uncertainties about how to interpret much of the re-search evidence on PTSD. It has also created an exaggerated sense that otherwise healthy people are brittle in the face of catastrophe.[72]

The VA Treatment Experience

Starting in the midseventies and throughout most of the eighties, veterans received therapy that reflected the dominant technique of the day: an in-depth excavation of wartime memories accompanied by emotional catharsis and reenactment of harrowing experiences.[73] "The primary task of the therapist is listening to their [war] story," wrote a psychologist who directed a PTSD unit during the mideighties at the West Haven Veterans hospital, "If you can 'get it out,' your load will be lightened and your recovery can begin."[74] Like a hot poultice on an abscess, therapy was meant to draw disturbing images and feelings to the surface where they would burst forth in a healing torrent of anger, self-recrimination, and tears.[75] This was not a good way to help the sufferer put his traumatic experience in perspective.

This effort at reviving memory was inspired by Freud. Hypnosis was practiced in shell shock hospitals in Britain during World War I and so-called barbiturate-induced abreaction, or catharsis, conducted by American psychiatrists in World War II who were stationed in psychiatric facilities many miles behind the front lines.[76] In those earlier wars, however, uncertainty among military psychiatrists about the value of such treatment foreshadowed contemporary debates about whether clinicians should extract recollections of trauma or encourage victims to distract themselves from dwelling upon them.[77]

In VA hospitals in the eighties and early nineties, veterans could be hospitalized for up to four months on so-called PTSD units. In group therapy and individual sessions, they told war stories, confessed survivor guilt, and relived nightmarish episodes of combat. On some hospital units, staff strongly discouraged the use of calming medication for anxiety or depression, lest it dull the patient's capacity to engage in exploratory psychotherapy.

From 1986 to 1988, Allan Young of McGill University served as an embedded anthropologist on a trauma treatment ward at a Midwestern VA hospital. Young noted that therapists were enthusiastic about eliciting the "memory narrative," the master war story that would reveal the deep source of the patient's turmoil. Young called it the "Rosetta stone" of the patient's treatment.[78]

No matter what other problems the veteran had—and there were often many: alcoholism, erratic employment, and domestic violence—the staff attributed them to the war. A distinct therapeutic culture coalesced around the idea that combat was the root of all anguish. In such a milieu, a troubled, middle-aged veteran who had only minor complaints of nightmares or occasional disturbing thoughts of Vietnam could find himself misdiagnosed with PTSD.[79]

Years before, in the early seventies, Sarah Haley, a social worker at the Boston VA and leading advocate for Vietnam veterans, had written in a much-cited article in *The Archives of General Psychiatry*, "The only report that should not be accepted at face value . . . is the patient's report that combat in Vietnam had no effect on him."[80] It was in this spirit that one of the therapists observed by Allan Young told a patient: "All I am saying is that the combat experience—even just being in the combat zone—is a traumatic experience. You've got to be changed after this: your priorities are changed, your brain is reordered."[81]

These dynamics helped contribute to a well-known phenomenon in medicine called the "clinician's illusion." It occurs when practitioners generalize too readily from a clinical subgroup to a wider population.[82] The illusion tricks doctors, for example, into overestimating how difficult it is to quit cigarettes or alcohol or lose weight: the patients who are successful don't keep coming back to the doctor with shortness of breath, liver disease, or diabetes. Similarly, trauma clinicians tend not to see individuals who cope successfully. They are prone to repeat the mistake made by psychiatrists who ran "rap" groups for veterans in the seventies and claimed that the bitter, dysfunctional young men who populated those groups were representative of vast numbers of Vietnam veterans.

PTSD Echo Chamber

During the late 1980s, one of us (Sally Satel) observed first hand the unintended consequences of intensive exploration in a specialized inpatient ward. At the West Haven Veterans Affairs Medical Center in West Haven, Connecticut, about twenty patients at a time were admitted to the PTSD ward for a four-month stay. From dawn to dusk patients were steeped in the stories, symbols, and paraphernalia of Vietnam. During group therapy they were encouraged to tell and retell accounts of the war. They wore camouflage fatigues and their old dog tags and decorated their rooms with POW-MIA flags. Under the direction of a drama therapist, the patients staged elaborate reenactments of their traumatic memories. In mere weeks, they had re-created a platoon.

War stories metamorphosed during the patients' tenure on the ward. One patient complained about searing headaches after he met a fellow patient who suffered recurrent pain as a result of being hit by shrapnel above his left eye. Another patient had never mentioned any involvement in an attack on a village but started to talk about it after sharing a hospital room with a veteran who talked frequently about participating in such a raid. The details of the first patient's account were startlingly similar to the recollections his roommate had disclosed.

The PTSD ward seemed to serve more as an echo chamber for pathology than a readjustment facility. The psychologist in charge of the unit was fully aware of these problems. Writing in the *American Journal of Psychiatry* in 1996, he noted soberly that "long-term, intensive inpatient treatment is not effective, and other forms of treatment should be considered after rigorous study."[83] In response, he developed a "second generation" program that focused on repair of family relations, rehabilitation, and adjustment to the community by performing volunteer work or taking a vocational course, for example. Another "helpful strategy" for social adaptation was "not allowing everything [negative] to be attributed to PTSD."[84]

Many veterans themselves found such intensive exploration unhelpful—hardly surprising, given what recent research into "rumination," discussed in the previous chapter, has revealed. According to reports from West Haven researchers, stays on the PTSD wards intensified patients' anger at the government; they began wearing war-related insignia and paraphernalia.[85] Years later, when the same patients were surveyed about their stay, they were more upbeat about the experience, but nearly three-quarters still complained of disabling stress symptoms and remained unemployed; as an entire group, the average amount of time worked at a job one month before the survey was one day.[86] Considerable pathology remained after treatment in other veterans programs in the United States, Israel, and Australia.[87] The most extensive report from West Haven, published in 1997 in the *American Journal of Psychiatry*, found that specialty wards so tightly organized around the war experience were not much benefit to the veteran.[88]

These evaluations proved "controversial, disappointing, and enlightening," according to the West Haven research team.[89] And they had an impact. Today, much of the treatment for Vietnam veterans takes place in outpatient clinics or halfway houses, not hospital wards, and has a practical, work-oriented, rehabilitative emphasis. Therapists focus on patients' problems in daily living; they do not encourage emotional retellings of decades-old war experiences.

Gratifications of the Sick Role

It is easy to see why some veterans coveted the PTSD diagnosis. It bolstered their image as wounded warriors, helped them make sense of failures, and allowed them to attach meaning to pervasive feelings of demoralization, apathy, or irritability.[90] As Paul McHugh, former chairman of psychiatry at Johns Hopkins University, observed, PTSD "conferred a status preferable to such alternatives as personality disorder, alcoholism, or adjustment disorder."[91] The hospital itself became an indispensable social venue to gather with fellow veterans and reexperience the camaraderie and sense of purpose they felt as young warriors. Their time in Vietnam may well have been the most exciting and meaningful period of their lives.[92] Access to this milieu, however, often depended upon procuring a diagnosis of PTSD from VA psychiatrists.

Conditions were ripe, then, for unwitting collusion between the patient and therapist in elaborating the PTSD narrative to explain his distress. As McHugh notes:

[A]nyone expressing skepticism about the validity of PTSD as a psychiatric condition—on the grounds, say, that it became a catchall category for people with long-standing disorders of temperament and behavior who were sometimes seeking to shelter themselves from responsibility—was dismissed as hostile to veterans or ignorant of the mental effects of fearful experiences.[93]

Veterans would have been better served by a skeptical stance on the part of their therapists. Loren Pankratz, a psychologist retired from a veterans medical center in Oregon, has written extensively about patients who distort or manufacture their history and make erroneous assumptions about the cause of their symptoms.[94] His curiosity about both unconscious deception and the feigning or exaggerating of symptoms to achieve a tangible goal (e.g., disability benefits) grew out of his observation that veterans who claimed to suffer chronic war-related stress were especially difficult to treat.[95] Gradually, Pankratz realized that many failed to improve because their treating clinicians were often distracted by dramatic symptoms, such as flashbacks, nightmares, and war stories, and did not focus on practical care.

During his years as a VA psychologist, Pankratz regularly dug into the military records of World War II and Vietnam veterans who told him about especially daring or improbable exploits. Pankratz was not interested in exposing or embarrassing these men, and because he was usually able to redirect them into proper treatment, he had no need to tell them that he knew their stories were false.[96]

Pankratz worked as a VA psychologist for twenty-five years; the embedded anthropologist Allan Young was there for less than one year before he observed a man named Flip. He had "mastered the language of the treatment program. . . . [Flip] disclosed a confusing story about shooting Vietnamese civilians during an evacuation. Soon afterward, he claimed that the [treatment] program was putting everything together for him." About a month after his discharge, Young recounts, new evidence suggested that Flip's military exploits were a fabrication.[97]

Perverse Incentives

In the VA environment, the problem of misrepresentation is also fueled by the disability benefit system. Well over half of veterans who seek treatment for PTSD in the VA system apply for disability—up to 94 percent in one study.[98] A veteran fully disabled by PTSD collects about $2,100 per month tax-free, not an insubstantial sum.[99] Veterans can consult a variety of sources to learn about eligibility for financial awards. No doubt many have used these to obtain deserved care and compensation for their disabilities. But as B. G. Burkett, a former noncombat Vietnam veteran, documents in his explosive book *Stolen Valor: How the Vietnam Generation Was Robbed of Its Heroes and History*, opportunities to commit fraud are spelled out for those who want to take advantage.[100]

In a chapter called "The Vietnam Veteran's Guide to Tax-Free Living," Burkett describes how magazines like *Vietnam* and *Survivalist*, newsletters like the *S-2 Report*, and a booklet from the Vietnam Doorgunners Association called *Post-Traumatic Stress Disorder: How to Apply for 100-Percent-Total Disability Rating*, provide detailed instructions. Some advice: "Tell [the VA] all the symptoms you have just read about [in the booklet]," "let the tears start to come if you are able," "if you enjoyed killing, tell them for sure." Patients are told that getting admitted to a PTSD treatment ward will improve their chances of being declared disabled, "but you will not have to remain in treatment once you receive your award."[101]

It is an open secret that some veterans seeking "total and permanent" disability payment (the highest level of compensation) for PTSD are not as sick as they claim to be. Talk to most VA workers and you will hear about patients who claim severe depression and social withdrawal, yet are seen on the grounds of the hospital joking uproariously with friends day after day. In treatment sessions they prefer to talk about the war or getting disability payments, rejecting practical help with current life circumstances. These patients complain bitterly when not diagnosed with PTSD. And when they do get the diagnosis, they become upset if a clinician notes for the record that they are improving. At some VA centers, compensation-seeking has become such an interference with treatment that patients are told not to expect that "participation in the program will automatically guarantee that you will get a VA disability award for PTSD. . . . We are a treatment program only."[102]

Of course, many patients are sincere about getting care and are helped tremendously. But they must compete for clinicians' attention with patients who have other, more mercenary agendas. Psychiatrists rate veterans who are compensation-seeking as less motivated to participate in treatment.[103] Psychologist Chris Frueh and colleagues at the Charleston Veterans Affairs Medical Center tried to clarify the inconsistency between the veterans' behavior and their reports of duress. They conducted analyses of military records (obtained via the Freedom of Information Act) in a random sample of 100 veterans in a South Carolina VA medical center. Each man claimed to have seen combat, though records confirmed this in only 40 percent of cases.[104]

Misrepresentation among those claiming PTSD for all kinds of traumatic experiences is common enough to warrant a warning in the *Diagnostic and Statistical Manual*: "Malingering [faking] should be ruled out in those situations in which financial remuneration, benefit eligibility, and forensic [or legal] determinations play a role" before making a diagnosis of PTSD.[105] Chris Frueh and colleagues examined several hundred veterans seeking treatment for PTSD. When they compared men with PTSD applying for disability payments to those with PTSD but not applying, they found that the applicants scored much higher on a standard psychological test for malingering.[106]

Misrepresentation of combat experience and symptoms is by no means a new problem. In the 1920s, a British Ministry of Pensions survey found that 57 percent of about six hundred enlisted men drawing pensions for war neurosis had never even left England between 1914 and 1918.[107] As a corrective to the outpouring of pensions in World War I and the subsequent unwillingness of soldiers to return to duty, Britain refused to grant pensions to soldiers while the hostilities were ongoing. This addressed a central dilemma in the management of war neurosis. As British war historian Ben Shephard put it, "how to discourage [soldiers] from developing psychiatric problems while simultaneously behaving fairly and humanely to those who break down; reconciling the needs of the genuinely traumatized veterans with the overriding necessity to deny secondary gain."[108]

One can feel sympathy for veterans who embellish compulsively. And one can also fault the VA for operating a disability benefit system known to reward, and thus sustain, dysfunction. Not only does compensation create an incentive to malinger, distort, exaggerate, but it also sends a damaging message to veterans who have PTSD—namely that PTSD is expected to be chronic, without cure, and incapacitating. After all, the government has given them the clear message: "total and permanent" disability. As Paul McHugh says, "America's war veterans, who are entitled to our respect and support, certainly deserve better than to be maintained in a state of chronic invalidism."[109] Granted, devising a disability system that can balance helping the needy, encouraging their rehabilitation, and weeding out fraud is a daunting social service challenge. As things stand now, a veteran with limited economic opportunities has a strong incentive to take advantage of the system. And, like the memory-distortion problem mentioned earlier, the ease with which symptoms can be deliberately faked or unwittingly exaggerated, and the incentives for doing so, should worry PTSD researchers. Finally, regardless of patients' myriad motives for misreporting symptoms, the fact that so many do so makes the possibility that veterans still suffer war-induced pathology appear more commonplace than it truly is.

Exporting PTSD

Several years ago a U.S. government resettlement project for Albanian Kosovars in Fort Dix, New Jersey, was staffed with mental health specialists prepared to treat high rates of PTSD among the refugees as a result of the traumas of war and resettlement in a foreign country.[110] Yet only three of the three thousand refugees were found to need psychiatric care, and those three had suffered from mental illness prior to resettlement. Their medicine had been lost in the migration, but once back on their medication the refugees improved considerably.[111]

Similarly, the Overseas Development Institute, a London-based think tank, found that referral for specialized psychological help in Kosovar communities was "extremely low."[112] And when researchers who evaluated a program of assistance to victims of war in Bosnia-Herzogovina and Croatia for the European Community Humanitarian Office discovered heavy use of its mental health clinics by internally displaced Bosnians and Croats, they soon realized that the refugees were using the facilities mostly "to create new social networks and make contacts. . . . The staff seemed [*sic*] to attach more importance to organized activities—especially individual therapy—than do the beneficiaries," said the Humanitarian Office report.[113]

These observations challenge the assumptions of therapism. According to the British psychiatrist Derek Summerfield, trauma experts expect "that without trauma programmes there will be a postwar crop of psychiatric disorders."[114] This is what psychiatrist Soren Buus Jensen predicted when he told the *New York Times*:

Based on what we know about Vietnam veterans and Holocaust survivors, there is no doubt in my mind that post-traumatic stress is going to be the most important public health problem in the former Yugoslavia for a generation and beyond.[115]

Jensen's prophecy reflects the prevailing wisdom in international aid agencies since the early- to midnineties.

The nonprofit U.S. Committee for Refugees claims: [R]efugees mental health providers and resettlement workers are increasingly aware that refugees and survivors of torture need greater, earlier access to . . . mental health care services to help them deal with both the trauma from which they fled and the challenge of adjusting to life in the United States.[116]

In its manual *Psychosocial Training and Support Program*, CARE International, an independent relief and development agency, claims that "almost everyone in Kosovo will consider her- or himself traumatized."[117] As a result of such convictions, clinics are now dispensing Western-style psychotherapy in the farthest reaches of the globe.

According to one critic, influential relief agencies like UNICEF, the UN High Commission on Refugees, CARE, US-AID, and the U.S. Office of Refugee Resettlement have contributed to a burgeoning "PTSD movement."[118] Patrick J. Bracken, psychiatrist with the University of Bradford, England, and Celia Petty of Save the Children Fund express concern about an "explosion" of interest in trauma and program initiation that "happened so quickly and with so much urgency that there has been little reflection upon its relevance to non-Western societies."[119]

Nowhere is the therapistic fallacy that crisis leads inexorably to widespread mental illness better exposed than in the experience of subjects who do not share our therapeutic culture.[120] Just because we can identify mental symptoms or syndromes in people from different cultures does not necessarily indicate—as cultural anthropologists have long recognized—that individuals find these symptoms intolerable or are rendered dysfunctional by them.[121]

A study of Rwandan adults conducted by the African Medical and Research Foundation illustrates this point. As eyewitnesses to massacre, these men and women had seen relatives and friends hacked to death. Up to 90 percent of them said they had trouble sleeping, poor concentration, bad memories, and thoughts of killing themselves. Yet when asked about their attitudes and capacities, they gave positive answers. Asked, "Are you interested in activities like work and play?," 77 percent said yes; asked, "Does your future seem good?," 57 percent said yes; asked, "Can you protect yourself and your family?," 75 percent said yes.[122]

When Summerfield and his colleague, Leslie Toser, looked for the symptoms of PTSD among Ugandans who had suffered atrocities, they found that the symptoms "were often present,

[but] they seldom dominated the person's account of his or her suffering." These people were "clearly not psychiatric casualties."[123] Over a six-year period, William Sack followed about fifty Cambodian refugee teenagers and found that they functioned well, despite most reporting symptoms of PTSD.[124] Joan Giller, a physician working with the London-based Medical Foundation for Caring for Victims of Torture, administered diagnostic questionnaires to Ugandan women who had been repeatedly raped. "The results did show quite clearly," she reports, "that there was no correlation at all between how well a person appeared to be functioning socially and the degree of symptomatology on the psychological scores."[125]

Drawing on his work with Bosnian refugees resettled in California, Harvey Weinstein, psychiatrist and director of the Human Rights Center at Berkeley, cautions his colleagues not to restrict themselves to looking at symptoms: "At the extreme, if we think about these symptoms as a manifestation of psychiatric disturbance, then we are left with diagnosing the people of an entire nation with a psychiatric disorder."[126] Weinstein warns that diagnosis and treatment can backfire, "the American focus on uncovering and catharsis may not be the most effective strategy for many Bosnians as they seek security and safety."[127] He quotes a twenty-five-year-old Bosnian mother:

> That is normal. The pictures are in my head. I saw many killed.
> I see pictures of people I knew killed. I see them at night and I
> think about it. That is hard. If I talk to someone about it, I see
> more, I remember more, and it is more difficult at night. If I
> keep myself busy, I don't think that much.[128]

Perhaps the clash of idioms is best expressed by a Russian woman who was a survivor of World War II. "I did have nightmares," she told an interviewer, "But what is this post-dramatic [sic] stress?"[129]

"Dwelling on the Past Is Discouraged"

Even when refugees themselves claim to be overwhelmed and are receptive to help, there is no guarantee that they will welcome Western models of care or benefit from them. Carola Eyber and Alastair Ager of Queen Margaret University College in Edinburgh interviewed Angolans who had lost their homes and families in the decades-long civil war and were displaced within their own country.[130] Those having particular trouble coping were given *conselho* (advice or consolation) by elders, church groups, and family members. Distraught individuals were advised to appreciate that death is inevitable and instructed not to "think too much" about the tragedy. Eyber and Ager reported that "dwelling on the past is discouraged and seen as destructive because survivors need to take responsibility for themselves and their family." They concluded that "psychosocial programmes that attempt to use counseling are unlikely to be popular," with displaced Angolans.

Social workers helping Zimbabwean victims of civil war experienced a similar revelation. According to a report in *The Lancet*, the workers, who were part of a nongovernmental aid group called Amani, went to communities in the western part of Zimbabwe "expecting to offer counseling services in keeping with the Western expectation that post-traumatic stress disorder or mixed anxiety or depression would be the most prevalent disorders." But these were not the problems that the Zimbabweans claimed to have. Instead, they spoke of bad behavior in children, failure to marry, illness, floods, and crop failure— crises they attributed to the fact that their murdered ancestors had not received a proper burial. Amani's response to the villagers' situation was to abandon one-on-one therapy in favor of traditional community conflict resolution and public truth-telling. One "therapeutic" activity was to help exhume bodies so the villagers could rebury them according to their customs.[131]

Finally, refugees who are distressed and in despair may not consider violence or loss to be the primary causes of their anguish. In fact, the distress reported by refugees often proves to be more closely linked to the effects of forced migration and resettlement.[132] Although psychologist Kenneth Miller of the Bosnian Mental Health Program in Chicago saw much suffering among his clients—they had been interned in concentration camps before migrating to the United States—the most successful feature of his program was not therapy, which most clients rejected, but efforts aimed at relieving their loneliness, worry over economic survival, and loss of occupation. The remedies took the form of creating social networks, education, and job training.

Similarly, when Joan Giller offered counseling to Ugandan rape victims, none of the women accepted it. "They wanted advice, medication, practical and financial assistance, and reassurance."[133] Patrick Bracken finds that it is often the "demoralization" of being in exile, not discrete horrors in their homeland, that torments asylum seekers. The best solution, he found, is to help refugees deal with practical concerns such as jobs, housing, schools, legal support, and access to immigration authorities.[134] How unfortunate if crisis counselors unwittingly undermined the refugees' resolve by insisting they were traumatized and helpless.

Marita Eastmond, a Swedish anthropologist who studied Bosnians living in Sweden, is another scholar who has questioned the wisdom of a psychologized approach to resettlement. She found that male heads of families who were offered employment reported a far greater sense of well-being and optimism than those who were provided psychological attention, but not employment, when they arrived in Sweden. One year later, the majority of adults offered therapy instead of employment were on indefinite sick leave. Her observations prompted Eastmond to wonder "whether extensive psychological assistance may in fact facilitate and maintain a sick role as traumatized victims and promote helplessness, in the absence of other structures to constitute a meaningful life."[135]

Similarly, the Albanian Kosovars at Fort Dix surprised mental health workers when they framed their suffering in historical and political contexts rather than in clinical terms. Refugees politely declined to tell their "trauma stories" to the mental health workers. Instead they wanted to recount their ghastly experiences and harrowing escapes to Amnesty International and war crime interviewers from the State Department. They regarded their stories as political, not personal, testimony and, according to Gozdziak and Tuskan, "took pride in their ability to contribute to the international investigation of war."[136] The mental health workers—who routinely encourage the sharing of war stories to help refugees "work through" their traumatic experiences—felt they had missed an opportunity to help.[137]

It also deprived them of an opportunity to diagnose PTSD. Such pressure is often felt by well-meaning workers who use the diagnosis chiefly as a way to signify the seriousness of the abuse inflicted on their clients. In other words, if one did not get PTSD from his ordeal, how bad could it have been? Perhaps authorities will not believe a victim if he does not carry a diagnosis. Summerfield speculates that such utilitarian thinking is behind a good proportion of the PTSD diagnoses assigned.[138]

The upheaval of one's physical and social world is a devastating ordeal. It will cause some refugees to slip into a pathological state requiring psychiatric care. This is why it would be reckless to interpret refugee suffering solely in political or social terms. Nevertheless, a reflexive invocation of Western practices may do more harm than good by spreading the gospel of therapism.[139] At worst, it erodes confidence in local wisdom, siphons off money that could be used to repair communities, and distracts attention from practical engagement with everyday life—the activity that refugees and other survivors of political brutality find most beneficial.

Defining Trauma Down

Let us now turn from the refugee experience, in which people tend not to perceive themselves as psychologically damaged by adversity, to a cultural phenomenon—American personal injury litigation—wherein mental states are all too readily framed as pathological.[140]

In 1994, the definition of post-traumatic stress disorder in the *Diagnostic and Statistical Manual* was modified once again. First, the range of events that could count as "traumatic" was expanded to include hearing about the unexpected death of a loved one or receiving a fatal diagnosis such as terminal cancer. No longer did one need to experience a life-threatening situation directly or be a close witness to a ghastly accident or atrocity.[141] In other words, experiencing "intense fear, helplessness, or horror," after watching the September 11 terrorist attacks on television, for example, could qualify an individual for PTSD.

This diagnostic mission creep gave personal injury lawyers and their expert witnesses wide latitude to allege mental injury.[142] According to Alan Stone, psychiatrist and professor of law at Harvard University, "no diagnosis in the history of psychiatry has had a more dramatic and pervasive impact on law and social justice than PTSD."[143] As Ralph Slovenko, professor of law at Wayne State University, observes:

> PTSD is a favored diagnosis in cases of emotional distress because it is incident specific. . . . Thus plaintiffs can argue that all of their psychological problems issue from the alleged traumatic event and not from myriad other sources encountered in life.[144]

Many lawyers warmly welcomed the fourth edition of the manual, released in 1994. A newsletter from the California Trial Lawyer Association featured the question: "The New DSM

IV—Is It Easier to Prove Damages?" The answer: "Yes, of course."[145] Proving the association right, victims of minor auto accidents now regularly claim to suffer from PSTD.[146] Plaintiffs alleging wrongful job termination, false arrest, and medication side effects have also invoked PTSD.[147] An Arkansas man claimed PTSD after he was given the wrong prescription medication by Wal-Mart; he won a settlement after he unknowingly took the wrong pills for two days without ill effect.[148] In the realm of employment litigation, workers have successfully sued or settled for large awards, claiming that sexual harassment or exposure to foul language gave them PTSD.[149] In her harassment suit against President Clinton, Paula Jones claimed their encounter caused her PTSD.[150]

"The PTSD diagnosis is eagerly sought by many plaintiffs looking to cash in on their workplace misfortune," writes attorney James McDonald Jr. "An expert witness's attaching a PTSD label to a plaintiff (whether or not any valid scientific basis exists for doing so) suggests to a jury that the plaintiff has suffered horrible torment akin to that suffered by torture victims and prisoners of war."[151] By enlarging the repertoire of abuse excuses, lawyers and their mental health experts-for-hire trivialize both truly horrific events and the legitimate psychiatric disturbances they can engender.

A number of theorists and clinicians have claimed that sexual harassment can produce PTSD. Claudia Avina and William O'Donohue, psychologists at the University of Nevada, argue in the *Journal of Traumatic Stress* that sexual harassment, such as telling off-color jokes, constitutes a legitimate trauma.[152] The "threat to physical integrity"—a diagnostic requirement—is met, the authors contend, because harassment can pose a financial threat, a "violation of personal values," and helplessness. This creative logic permits them to argue that "victims can be seen as legitimately suffering form a serious mental disorder and [should] be compensated for this."[153]

Journalist Ted Conover spent several months as a guard in

Sing Sing, New York's notoriously menacing state prison, in preparation for writing an exposé on prison culture. After his acclaimed book, *Newjack: Guarding Sing Sing*, was published in 2000, Conover had nightmares about being attacked by knife-wielding inmates—though this never happened to him during his tour at Sing Sing. When Conover mentioned the nightmares in passing to a group of medical professionals at a convention of the American Public Health Association, a psychiatrist in the audience "suggested it was probably post-traumatic stress disorder."[154] Conover acknowledges that he expects to be haunted by aspects of his experience, but adds, "I don't want to suggest that I went through anything like what soldiers who saw combat in Vietnam did."

Yet, comparisons to Vietnam veterans are made too promiscuously. Some professional football players are said to have "developed post-traumatic stress disorders comparable to those experienced by some Vietnam veterans" from playing football; during the agricultural depression of the 1980s mental-health workers said that "psychologically, rural Iowa resembles a Vietnam veteran with post-traumatic stress disorder"; teenagers pressed to overachieve by their "hothouse style of upbringing are now suffering post-traumatic stress syndrome like Vietnam veterans."[155]

In the fall of 2002, the *Boston Globe* ran a story about three local therapists who were campaigning for recognition of a new diagnosis: Post Traumatic Slavery Disorder.[156] In their view, drug abuse, broken families, crime, and low educational attainment in segments of the black community could be directly linked to the trauma of slavery, and "black people as a whole are suffering from PTSD." Satirists could barely contain themselves. One suggested "post-traumatic déjà vu disorder—the feeling one gets after one has experienced trauma before it happens." Another offered "post-traumatic birth disorder," which is "brought on by the pain, insensitivity, embarrassment, and forced relocation that the victims had to endure as a result of the birth process, not to mention the indignity and violence associated with that first spanking."[157]

Even the idea of being "traumatized" is cropping up in unlikely contexts. When the actress Gwyneth Paltrow received an Oscar for her role in *Shakespeare in Love*, she recalled, "I felt exposed and embarrassed [at the awards ceremony]. The next day I got really ill. It was post-traumatic stress from the adrenaline shock my system suffered."[158]

The comic writer Andy Borowitz captured the phenomenon with his bulletin: "Small Children May be Traumatized by Ann Coulter, Psychologist Says: 'Few Coping Strategies for Exposure to Banshee-like Pundit'":

> "Mommy, make the scary lady go away." Those are the tearful words of Kaylee Brodkin, 7, of Gary, Indiana, who for the last five days has been awoken in the middle of the night by terrifying nightmares—nightmares featuring television pundit/author Ann Coulter. With the ubiquitous Ms. Coulter currently on a national book tour [in summer 2003], little Kaylee's story is far from an isolated occurrence.[159]

Borowitz cites the advice of a fictional psychologist, Harmon Densmore: "More and more these days, we are seeing small children who have been traumatized by Ann Coulter."[160] Densmore urged parents to limit children's television exposure to her. His advice could well have been used a year later by viewers who were shocked by the scraggly looks and blustery demeanor of filmmaker Michael Moore, ubiquitous on television as he touted his film *Fahrenheit 9/11*.

Unrealistic Legacy

With the first major troop rotation out of Iraq in the winter of 2004 there was worry about large numbers of PTSD casualties. Parallels were explicitly drawn between Iraq and Vietnam soldiers.[161] One well-publicized study of psychiatric casualties conducted by military psychiatrists at Walter Reed found that 8 percent of Iraq veterans with combat exposure, not one-third, had developed PTSD within three to four months of their return.[162] In the spring of 2004, the Veterans Affairs Department reported that 0.4 percent of soldiers separated from active duty in Iraq had thus far been treated for PTSD.[163]

Psychiatrist Matthew Friedman of the National Center for PTSD was quick to remind readers of the Walter Reed study that the NVVRS findings were much higher. He warned that the relatively modest 8 percent figure of PTSD among Iraq veterans could "underestimate the eventual magnitude of this clinical problem."[164] Historian Eric Dean foresaw such an interpretation when he wrote in 1997, "the Vietnam veteran has come to dominate and condition our thinking on the matter of the psychological repercussions of warfare."[165]

And along with other related developments—a diagnosis, PTSD, that was initially believed to represent a typical reaction to trauma; a national survey of PTSD among veterans that yielded improbably high rates of mental illness; a veteran's treatment and disability system that often entrenched rather than dissipated symptoms; reframing of normal reactions to loss and tragedy as pathological—the notion that we are too often unfit to cope with adversity became accepted wisdom.

But the conditioning goes beyond warfare. PTSD and Vietnam are so intertwined they have formed an archetype for the experience of adversity in our culture. Today, PTSD is an important cultural narrative for suffering. The legacy that began in the early 1970s with Dr. Lifton's Vietnam veteran rap groups remains influential today. It is a tendency to confuse pathos with pathology, to presume fragility in the face of adversity. Whether operating in the third world or in their own backyard, mental health workers forget how frequently survivors find sustaining meaning in heartbreak and how often they persevere nobly.

In the next chapter we examine the country's responses—
and those of the mental health profession—to the September 11
attacks. Although many psychiatrists, psychologists, and counselors predicted a national mental health crisis featuring an epidemic of PTSD, no crisis materialized. The mental health
profession had an opportunity to affirm that most of us would
meet the challenge without psychological damage. Instead, in
the best tradition of therapism, it accentuated the themes of
threat and loss.

6

———

September 11, 2001:
The Mental Health Crisis
That Wasn't

On September 14, 2001, three days after the terrorist attacks on
the World Trade Center and the Pentagon, a group of psychologists sent an open letter to the American Psychological Association.[1] The nineteen signatories, all established experts in trauma
research and treatment, were concerned that thousands of people in New York City and elsewhere would receive dubious,
even damaging, counseling. "In times like these," the letter said,

> it is imperative that we refrain from the urge to intervene in
> ways that—however well-intentioned—have the potential to
> make matters worse. . . . Unfortunately, this has not prevented
> certain therapists from descending on disaster scenes with well-
> intentioned but misguided efforts. Psychologists can be of most
> help by supporting the community structures that people natu-
> rally call upon in times of grief and suffering. Let us do what-
> ever we can, while being careful not to get in the way.[2]

The letter voiced a second powerful warning: not to mistake
normal reactions—intense sadness or sleeplessness, jumpiness
and so on—for mental abnormality. The letter was posted on-
line and picked up by a *New York Times* science reporter who fast-

tracked the controversy into Sunday's paper, five days after the attacks.[3] As Gerald Rosen, a Seattle psychologist and one of the letter's authors told the reporter, "The public should be very concerned about medicalizing what are human reactions."

By then, however, the trauma industry—dubbed the "National Guard of Therapists" by one magazine—had shifted into high gear.[4] Roughly nine thousand counselors raced to lower Manhattan, advocating, in the words of one observer, "intervention for any person even remotely connected to the tragedy."[5] As psychologist Charles Figley, founder of the Journal of Traumatic Stress, told the *Los Angeles Times*, "there are not enough traumatologists to help everybody."[6]

Spencer Eth, a psychiatrist at St. Vincents Catholic Medical Centers in New York City, foretold "huge increases in the prevalence of traumatic grief, depression, post-traumatic stress disorder, and substance abuse in the New York City metropolitan area at the least . . . [the] psychiatric toll will be enormous."[7] Neal L. Cohen, a psychiatrist and New York City commissioner of Health and Mental Health, told Congress, "We face the possibility of a sharp increase in chronic and disabling mental health problems."[8] Richard Mollica, a Harvard psychiatrist, forecast that "starting around the Thanksgiving holiday and through the New Year, a major mental health crisis will emerge in the city and surrounding area."[9] The president of the New York State Psychiatric Association predicted that psychiatric problems would continue to emerge over several years, including among those who were watching television coverage of the attack.[10]

Granted, these urgent statements were made soon after the attacks, while our collective nervous system was still reverberating from the shock. Yet weeks and months later, when cooler heads might have prevailed, the warnings remained frantic and grim. In June 2002, for example, the Office of Mental Health projected that two million New Yorkers, or one in four, would need counseling.[11] And one year after the attack, the president of the Washington, D.C., Psychiatric Society was still worried

about mental health manpower: "There are not enough psychiatrists, psychologists, social workers, or other crisis counselors
to treat the fallout from a massive, unimaginable horror."[12]

The dire predictions of psychological injury prompted a
Washington Post reporter to correct the misimpression: "Even
though it is commonly believed that post-traumatic stress disorder is universal among trauma victims—a fallacy that some
mental health counselors are perpetuating in the aftermath of
this tragedy—epidemiological studies show otherwise."[13] In response to the apprehension about whether people could cope, a
skeptical reporter with *USA Today* was finally forced to ask,
"Does everyone who goes through trauma need a therapist?"[14]

The answer, of course, is no.

Life Before Counseling

In this era of grief and trauma counseling, one is tempted to ask
how humanity managed to survive for thousands of years before
its advent. The secular assumptions of our age are largely responsible for the flourishing of the trauma industry. In previous
eras we were more likely to seek solace from a priest or minister
or to accept a transcendent explanation for catastrophe. A sense
of fate and mystery, so necessary to people with little or no control over their natural environment, kept feelings of cosmic betrayal at bay. We were once fairly reconciled to what could not
be changed. Now we want answers.

Modernity brought estrangement from death and dying.
Urbanization severed intimate connections with nature's cycles
of life and death. Advances in medicine meant fewer encounters
with morbidity and loss; meanwhile, dying itself was se-
questered in hospitals. With migration to the big cities, families
and communities dispersed, making mourning a more private
affair. As society became more technologically proficient, it also
grew less tolerant of discomfort and more reliant on quick fixes.

Our inexperience with communal coping helped set the stage

for the trauma industry. So did the ascendance of psychological man, a product of the late-nineteenth-century idea that many of our problems are mental in origin. Our greater affluence soon allowed us to purchase that fix in the form of experts, both credentialed and self-anointed. Other enabling trends came somewhat later; most prominently a common faith in the power of catharsis, the confessional culture of popular media, and the normalization of discussing personal problems in public.

The media played their role, depicting trauma counselors as a staple of the disaster scene. Media exposure in turn allowed the industry to market itself as a remedy for suffering. This appealed to concerned managers and officials trying to deal with crises—and alerted lawyers to potential negligence should institutions fail to provide counseling. Thus, an industry was born, and therapism made inroads into the domain of communal tragedy.

The Trauma Industry

Trauma counseling flowered in the midnineties with the Oklahoma City bombing in 1995—where counselors reportedly fought over patients "because there were simply not enough to go around"—and the TWA Flight 800 air disaster in 1996.[15] After the Columbine High School massacre in 1999 counselors logged fifteen hundred hours talking to students in the first week alone, according to *Time* magazine.[16] When school resumed, every classroom was equipped with a counselor whose job was to urge the teens to recite their most painful thoughts, feelings, and bodily sensations in a process called "psychological debriefing." Typical questions included "What were the first thoughts that raced through your mind at the time of the crisis?" and "What was the worst moment for you?" Students who found this activity too overwhelming—and, as we will see, the procedure has been faulted for tampering with the mind's natural protective defenses—were excused from class so they could sit in the "safe room" with a psychologist.[17]

Today's version of psychological debriefing bears little resemblance to its precursor: military operational debriefing. After a significant battle in World War II, soldiers were "debriefed" by their superiors. The aim was to establish what happened for historical purposes, identify plans that had gone awry or well, share experiences, boost morale, and facilitate troops' rapid return to duty. The mitigation of distress was a welcome byproduct, but operational debriefing was not designed as a psychological aid, and, according to a standard military textbook, "emotional reactions are recognized and validated but not emphasized."[18]

In the 1960s and 1970s these frontline principles were translated into peer-to-peer support activities for rescue workers. Firefighters, paramedics, and other emergency workers who routinely witnessed horrible scenes of carnage and risked their lives in the line of duty would gather to review the logistics of an operation and talk about their experience.[19]

Over time, the debriefing process was extended to civilians. As a form of psychological first aid, it joined—and sometimes displaced—traditional crisis work, which had grown out of crisis theory elaborated in the 1960s. The basic tenets of crisis theory are that people who have endured a life-threatening event are not sick and that crisis intervention is not necessarily a mental health service. The main job of a crisis worker or counselor is to help the client find concrete, realistic solutions to the problems created by the event.[20] The crisis model views victims as fundamentally durable; with respite, reassurance, and resources, they can recoup.

This perspective differs fundamentally from the more recent trauma debriefing model, created by Jeffrey T. Mitchell, a former paramedic and firefighter. In the late 1980s Mitchell began to market his crisis philosophy that virtually all victims are at risk for trauma-induced mental illness. If crisis workers shore up people who are basically sound though temporarily in disarray, psychological debriefers give a mixed message. On one hand, they tell victims that stress reactions are normal, and yet warn that without their intervention such reactions can easily blossom into post-traumatic stress disorder.[21]

All manner of setbacks qualify a worker for psychological help. According to *Psychotherapy Finances*, a newsletter for entrepreneurial therapists, "workplace trauma isn't just about bank robberies or shooting sprees . . . for every high-profile incident there are thousands you never hear about."[22] When a tasteless cartoon about firemen appeared in the *New York Post* two years after the September 11 tragedy, the Fire Department of New York City sent counselors to a company that had lost men on September 11. "We wanted to make sure the guys were alright," a FDNY official told the New York *Daily News*.[23]

Business and corporate managers have jumped on the psychological debriefing bandwagon, persuaded by its purveyors that without their help worker productivity will suffer and mental health costs will soar. Organizations that do not offer debriefing for workers exposed to on-the-job trauma "may put themselves in medical-legal jeopardy," warns Landy Sparr, a psychiatrist at Oregon Health and Sciences University.[24] Some psychologists even tell employers that they have 48 hours to act after a disaster, otherwise employees may "jump ship" or "come down against the company."[25]

In 1997 an Australian railway worker successfully sued the State Rail Authority of New South Wales over the employer's obligation to provide debriefing after accidents.[26] Three years later a policewoman who investigated child abuse won an award against the New South Wales Police Service because it did not protect her from developing job-related PTSD.[27] In the United Kingdom, more than two thousand veterans of the Falklands War, Northern Ireland, the Gulf War, and Bosnia sued the Ministry of Defense for over $200 million because they had received no trauma counseling at the time of their service; they claimed they are now suffering from preventable PTSD.[28] That suit was unsuccessful, but in the spring of 2003, a group of Canadian peacekeepers suffering from PTSD announced they were filing a $60 million lawsuit against the Canadian Armed Forces, alleging their psychological problems had been ignored.[29]

It is easy to see why trauma counselors are popular. Litigation fears aside, managers do care about their employees. Individual Manhattan businesses spent tens of thousands of dollars on trauma counseling for one to three weeks; in total, Crisis Management International, one of the largest counseling firms, billed $4 million for services to about two hundred companies.[30] To them, psychological debriefing—which generally takes place in a group of ten to twenty victims and is led by a counselor—may appear to be a humane response to psychological distress. "There is even an influential view that psychological debriefing ought to be routinely prescribed after all traumatic events," note psychologists Justin Kenardy and Vaughan Carr. "If there were compelling evidence that debriefing contributes to the recovery of an individual this position might be defensible. But this is not the case."[31]

Recently, psychological debriefing has lost some ground. The British military, which employed it for many years, is now reconsidering the practice. The British psychiatrist Simon Wessely describes the Royal Marines' current approach as providing a brief training course to all ranks:

> The rationale is that when a traumatic event happens to a unit, those members of the unit will be able to offer each other commonsense, low-key, supportive intervention that is firmly rooted in organizational culture and involves no outsiders, and no risk of "professionalizing" normal distress.[32]

A progressive trend in corporate crisis management parallels the British military's effort to avoid "professionalizing" the process. Importing packaged workshops and group therapy run by outsiders who are unfamiliar with a particular workplace, organization, or community may be slowly falling out of fashion. Some psychologists are now even warning that compulsory debriefing might itself be grounds for litigation.[33]

Thus, Bruce Blythe, CEO of Crisis Management International, concerned about the poor track record of debriefing, had changed his approach by the time the second anniversary of September 11 came around.[34] He calls himself a "recovering debriefer."[35] Two years earlier, the Atlanta-based company had sent hundreds of trauma counselors to debrief the employees of its corporate clients. Now its Web site informs prospective clients that the company no longer engages in "rehashing of graphic details and pathologizing."[36] Ironically, Blythe warns, the provision of debriefing may itself soon be cause for lawsuits alleging negligence or malpractice in an organization's crisis response.

The enlightened manager, Blythe suggests, should deal with crisis by promoting a sense of safety and group cohesion. He should disseminate information—how rescue efforts are progressing, how coworkers are faring—and clarify practical matters such as access to housing, food, transportation, and so on. Mental health care referrals are to be made as needed on a case-by-case basis. This strategy, which has been adopted by Crisis Management International, fosters good communication, bolsters existing programs and relationships, and emphasizes natural avenues of support.

New York City Mayor Rudolph Giuliani grasped this intuitively. On September 11 he spoke to New Yorkers as mature adults, giving practical advice, telling them what he knew and did not know. He asked people to help each other out. The mayor was deeply human—when asked how many casualties there were, he replied, unforgettably, "more than any of us can bear"—yet he never urged New Yorkers, en masse, to seek psychological help or invited trauma experts to lead the city in a group cry.

Trauma Tourism?

The International Critical Incident Stress Foundation (ICISF) near Baltimore is the largest psychological debriefing training outfit in the world. A few months after September 11, Anne Kadet, a reporter for *Smart Money* magazine, attended a debriefing seminar given by the foundation as part of her research for an article on crisis counseling. "The instructor told us that in light of September 11, learning [debriefing] was 'practically an act of patriotism,' " Kadet said.[37] Appealing to patriotism was a shrewd promotional tactic, for debriefing is a technique, as we will show, of dubious clinical value.

With a virtual monopoly on debriefing training, ICISF appears to be prospering both at home and abroad. Its clients include the FBI, the Coast Guard, the American Red Cross, and U.S. Air Force bases worldwide.[38] It has training programs in Canada, Europe, the Caribbean, Central and South America, and Australia.[39] In Canada and the United Kingdom, counselors are routinely deployed after mass disasters, and in Australia an estimated $35 million a year is spent on intervention.[40] In 1997, the United Nations granted the foundation "special consultative status."[41] Thousands of workers in state rescue and firefighting agencies are among the thirty thousand people trained annually by the ICISF.[42]

Anyone with a high school diploma is eligible for the foundation's course. In some circumstances, an ICISF certificate grants the bearer access to disaster sites that an advanced clinical degree does not. For example, in 1995 a group of psychiatrists from Yale that included respected experts in traumatic stress offered to help with victims of the Oklahoma City bombing. Emergency officials turned them away because they lacked certification from the International Critical Incident Stress Foundation.[43]

The certificate, then, doubles as a coveted passport to disaster sites—even though it is awarded to anyone who paid the $190 course fee and shows up for the lectures. Is it any coincidence that critics of the crisis management business have taken, tongue-in-cheek, to calling volunteer crisis counselors "trauma tourists"?[44] There is no doubt that the volunteers are well meaning, but neither is it any secret that some of them have a voyeuristic urge to be part of a historic moment or a media event.

This urge "can cloud their judgment about whether they are providing services for themselves or others," observed Anand Pandya, a psychiatrist with Disaster Outreach Psychiatry, a volunteer organization in New York City.[45] Yvonne McEwen, former head of the department of trauma management and victim assistance at the Abertay Fife University Centre in Scotland, portrays trauma counseling with dismay as "the glamourous, high-profile end of the [caring professions] with everybody wanting to get in on the act."[46] "Disaster vultures" was the name given to overly enthusiastic mental health professionals who rushed into the scene at the Oklahoma City bombing in 1995. "Their credibility in the future would be their claim to have worked in Oklahoma City," observed a dismayed local psychologist.[47]

Psychological debriefing is an enterprise that has operated outside of conventional clinical boundaries and oversight. Richard Gist, a psychologist with the Kansas City, Missouri, fire department and an outspoken critic of the trauma industry, describes it as

a prolific and parochial subculture of providers whose understanding of these highly complex issues is often limited with near exclusivity to proprietary instruction in the form of traveling seminars, trade magazines, and paperback books, rather than the refereed venues of empirically guided professional practice.[48]

Trauma School

In the summer of 2002, one of us (Satel) spent two days in a hotel ballroom outside Baltimore with about two hundred men and women—nurses, social workers, rescue volunteers—seeking ICISF certification in the basics of crisis counseling.[49] She listened to lectures about traumatic stress. Much of what the instructor said was obvious: that routines should be preserved after a crisis, that too much alcohol is bad, that depriving oneself of sleep is unhealthy, and so on. The "experts" had appropriated common sense as if it were their own special province.

Then came a session on psychological debriefing (also known as critical-incident stress debriefing), the centerpiece of trauma counseling. Our instructor acknowledged that debriefing had come under attack, but promptly dismissed the critics, maintaining that psychological debriefing was proven to thwart the development of PTSD.

The instructor peppered us with a series of half-truths and outright misstatements. We were told, for example, that PTSD "rarely goes away by itself," that there are no factors that predispose a person to develop PTSD, and that people who "hold it in do worse"—all untrue statements. The course manual stated that debriefing compensates for "the failure of the [victim's] usual coping strategies." Moreover, unless psychological debriefing took place soon after the crisis, a so-called trauma membrane would form around the victim and "thicken" so that he would no longer be receptive to help.[50]

We learned how to conduct a psychological debriefing by breaking up into groups of eight. Each group was provided its own tragic scenario. In ours, we were supposed to be telemarketers busy on the phones one morning when a coworker's drunk and jealous ex-husband burst into the work area with a gun and shot one of us in the shoulder. After the injured coworker was taken away in an ambulance, the rest of us gathered to be debriefed by our eighth colleague, who was assigned the role of an outside debriefer. Following the directions in our course manual, the role-playing debriefer encouraged us to talk about how scared we were, rehashing in the most graphic language how the blood had spurted from our colleague's wound, how we had panicked and had thought we would all be killed. This was our "opportunity for catharsis, an opportunity to verbalize trauma," said the manual.[51]

Such opportunities are precisely what the nineteen psychologists warned against in their open letter to the American Psychological Association when they spoke of therapists "descending on disaster scenes with well-intentioned but misguided efforts." And with good reason. Research shows these efforts at debriefing to be ineffective in preventing the development of PTSD or related symptoms, and, at times, to actually be harmful.[52]

Most random-assignment studies of individuals who have suffered accidents, assaults, or burns show the same degree of improvement, whether patients were debriefed in a one-on-one session by a therapist or instead received general support or no intervention at all.[53] Two such studies, however, found that debriefing actually impeded recovery. In one, debriefed burn victims were three times as likely as the control group to develop PTSD after one year.[54] In the other study, a three-year follow-up of car accident victims, anxiety, level of functioning, physical pain, and degree of preoccupation with the accident improved more slowly in the debriefed patients than in the control group.[55]

Britain's National Health Service, the North Atlantic Treaty Organization, and the World Health Organization all cautioned against the use of debriefing as possibly harmful.[56] In the fall of 2002, the National Institute of Mental Health (NIMH), in collaboration with the U.S. Departments of Defense, Justice, the Department of Veterans Affairs, and the Red Cross, released a report on psychological interventions in the wake of disaster.[57] "A sensible working principle in the immediate [aftermath] is to expect normal recovery," said the report.[58]

How can debriefings make things worse? First, venting emotions and reviewing experience repeatedly in the immediate aftermath of a crisis can interfere with victims' natural adaptive instinct to distance themselves emotionally.[59] They may start ruminating about the event—fixating on why it happened, how life is now ruined, whether revenge is possible—thus intensifying intrusive memories and overall distress.[60]

Second, debriefing might lead people to believe that they have now received "treatment" for distress and no longer need to, or should, disclose their anxieties to family and friends. This deprives victims of the comfort and reassurance that are usually best supplied through established, intimate relationships. Paradoxically, knowing that professional debriefers are involved may even cause family and friends to hang back. Third, by warning participants of the kinds of reactions that could develop over the coming weeks, debriefers might inadvertently prime victims to interpret otherwise normal reactions as pathological or as the beginning stages of PTSD.[61] (In doing so, debriefers violate a lesson first learned in World War I, wherein frontline doctors took great pains to avoid suggesting pathological symptoms to shell-shocked soldiers.)

As Simon Wessely has remarked, "The toxic effect of counseling is that some people begin to see themselves as having a mental health problem when they do not."[62] The Stanford psychiatrist David Spiegel concurs: "[I]n the immediate aftermath of trauma . . . such predictions may induce rather than prevent certain emotional reactions."[63] As Richard Gist puts it, psychological debriefing can be a self-fulfilling prophecy: "I did not think of myself as sick until you sent for a remedy."[64]

One Size Fits All

The doctrine of the trauma industry holds that all of us are at equal psychological risk and all should receive the same kind of professional attention. Victims are interchangeable. How else can the application of assembly-line techniques, with little regard for the victim's privacy, be justified? With so little faith in an individual's natural ability to tolerate emotional pain, the trauma industry is bound to undermine his confidence in his capacity to cope. Since the victim's perception of his competence is so vital to successful coping, this assumption of the trauma professionals is particularly lamentable.

Furthermore, urging individuals to undergo debriefing before the "trauma membrane thickens," as our trauma instructor warned, is ironic considering the origin of the term. The psychiatrist Jacob Lindy, who treated survivors of the devastating Beverly Hills Supper Club fire outside Cincinnati in 1977, coined the term to describe not a debriefing-resistant cocoon, but a small network of trusted friends who buffer the victim from additional stress.[65] A properly functioning trauma membrane, in Jacob Lindy's sense, might well act to keep debriefers away!

Proponents of psychological debriefing rebut their critics on several counts.[66] First, they charge, the studies cited above employed hour-long debriefing sessions one-on-one with individual subjects, even though debriefing in the field after disaster is most often conducted with groups of victims over a period of three to four hours. Second, the study subjects were all physically injured, while debriefing as it is practiced in the field also targets noninjured and indirect victims such as civilian rescuers, frightened bystanders, and remote witnesses. Third, none of the studies had been done on professional rescue personnel, popular subjects of debriefing services.

Ultimately, the burden of proving that debriefing works for any of these populations falls on its proponents. Until they have scientifically demonstrated that debriefing ever benefits victims, it makes little sense for them to criticize departures from their methods.[67] What is already clear, however, is that three of the assumptions that underlie debriefing have been discredited: first, rehashing the traumatic event is helpful; second, most people require early intervention; and third, all trauma victims should receive the same intervention.

It bears repeating that mental health professionals have a potentially important role in caring for people still suffering from intense anxiety and phobias several weeks after a traumatic experience. In such cases, a tested cognitive behavioral treatment can be very helpful.[68] Over several sessions a patient is guided though increasingly vivid recollections of the event until his emotional reactions to them fade and he can confront places and activities he has been avoiding out of fear. Irrational thoughts and false assumptions about risk are examined in the process. As for medication, a number of drugs have been approved for PTSD and can be used successfully in combination with exposure therapy.[69]

Imaginal exposure is combined with cognitive exercises (called restructuring) to alter unrealistic beliefs, questions and distortions upon which the patient dwells, often obsessively (such as, "How could I have prevented this?" "If I had only done X . . . ," or "I'll never be safe again.") There is some evidence that people cope more successfully when they see a difficult situation as a trial they can overcome rather than an ordeal that has defeated them. Thus transforming "threat appraisals" into "challenge appraisals" is a strategy some therapists have fruitfully combined with exposure work.[70]

This kind of formal treatment differs from debriefing in many important ways. First and foremost, it is completely voluntary. Second, it takes place weeks after trauma-induced stress sets in, when it is fairly clear that the person's own coping ability has failed. Debriefing, on the other hand, takes place before this becomes obvious, and in the process it may disrupt the natural coping process of victims who would otherwise cope well. Third, therapy takes place over several sessions; debriefing is typically a one-time encounter. Fourth, responsible therapy weaves cognition and desensitization together—debriefing is too often about releasing raw emotion.

Where Are All the Patients?

In October 2001, Sharon Kahn, a senior psychologist at Coney Island Hospital, manned the phones at a televised call-in show sponsored by PBS called *Reach Out to Heal*. Experts described the symptoms of traumatic stress and viewers were urged to call in with questions and to get referrals for help. Ms. Kahn took calls all evening. She referred two people for therapy. The vast bulk of calls were queries about the resumption of regularly scheduled programming.[71]

"There were a lot of therapy experts here in New York who were quite happy to tell everyone that firefighters would have PTSD," Malachy Corrigan told the *New Yorker*.[72] Corrigan is the director of the Counseling Service Unit of the New York City fire department. By the late fall of 2003, Corrigan estimated that fewer than one hundred of the thousands of firefighters and emergency service personnel involved with rescue operations after September 11 had developed PTSD.

Other clinicians remarked on the dearth of new patients. "Most of the patients I have seen, ranging from those who ducked falling bodies and debris to those who were miles from Ground Zero, presented with exacerbations of preexisting mood, anxiety, psychotic, and substance abuse disorders," wrote John Markowitz, a psychiatrist at Weill Medical Center, in *Psychiatric Services*. Rachel Yehuda, director of the Traumatic Stress Studies Division at Mount Sinai, said that despite widespread media and education on treatment, the volume of new patients in the fall of 2001 was low.[73] "Many people were coming to treatment," she said, "but those were people that had already been in treatment, particularly for past PTSD and anxiety disorders."

Across the country, mental health professionals braced for epic caseloads after September 11. Yet in the end, the demand for their services was modest. According to the New York Academy of Medicine, which conducted numerous surveys after the terrorist attacks, roughly 19 percent of New Yorkers said they saw a mental health professional within the eight weeks after the event, but this was little more than the 17 percent who did so eight weeks before the attack.[74] "Existing therapeutic relationships and informal sources of support were the primary mental health resources for most people within the first few months," according to Doctor Sandro Galea of the Academy.[75]

According to an Academy study published in 2004, there was no evidence that the predicted waves of delayed PSTD were surfacing, at least within the first five months after the attacks. Mental health service use declined steadily within the first five months after attacks to virtually pre–September 11 levels.[76] "The increase was not clinically significant," Dr. Joseph A. Boscarino, the study's lead author, told the *New York Times*, "We expected higher use rates."[77]

Concerned that September 11 would destabilize Vietnam veterans with PTSD, VA administrators in New York geared up to provide supplemental clinical resources.[78] They never had to deploy them, however.[79] Usage patterns in forty VA medical centers, including those in New York City, Washington D.C., and Oklahoma City showed modest change as well, according to Robert Rosenheck and Alan Fontana of the Veterans Affairs Northeast Program Evaluation Center.[80] They compared visits for any mental disorder, medical clinic visits, and admissions to inpatient psychiatric wards at six months before and after September 11 for three years—1999, 2000, and 2001—and found no significant increase in new patients or in the use of VA services for the treatment of PTSD or other mental or physical disorders. "Veterans were able to cope with their emotional experiences successfully enough that they did not seek increased professional assistance," the researchers wrote in the *American Journal of Psychiatry*.[81]

Using projections based on utilization in the previous year, Ellen Weissman and colleagues at the Bronx Veterans Affairs Medical Center examined clinics in New York and New Jersey veterans facilities. They found increases in the number of total outpatients treated for PTSD of less than 2 percent within the six months after September 11. Greater increases, however, tended to occur in peripheral areas rather than in the immediate New York area.[82] Also, no "new" cases of PTSD appeared until March 2002 (a new patient was defined as one not having received VA care within the previous thirty months). These small increases occurred in the context of extensive outreach to area veterans already established as patients at those facilities; what's more, there was no relationship between increases at various VA facilities and their proximity to Ground Zero. Such geographic and temporal aberrations make it difficult to conclude that September 11 was the cause of the increase, as the authors themselves acknowledge.

The Walter Reed Army Institute of Research examined a military health systems database that recorded all outpatient visits logged at military treatment facilities from September 11, 2001, to February 9, 2002. Comparing this twenty-two-week window to the same time period in the previous two years revealed no increase in visits to mental health clinics.[83] In late 2002 the federal Substance Abuse and Mental Health Services Administration released data on patterns of treatment use in New York City and surrounding areas.[84] Seasonal effects were ruled out by comparing similar time frames from 2000. Comparing the first three quarters of 2001 to the fourth, researchers noted "relatively few significant changes," including some small declines, in use of mental health and drug treatment services. Researchers also noted no increase in rates of mental health disorders or of distress in either the general population or those with a history of problems.

Similarly, prescriptions for antianxiety medications, sedatives, and antidepressants showed little new use. A survey of New York City residents taken about one month after September 11 found that 9 percent used psychiatric medications in the month before the event compared with almost 12 percent within the month after.[85] Ninety-seven percent of those using medications postdisaster were already taking them in August 2001.

A more definitive assessment by pharmaceutical industry analysts found that September 11 had a minimal effect on the dispensing of these medications in New York City.[86] Although prescribing was elevated in the late fall of 2001 leading up to the Thanksgiving and Christmas holidays, this pattern closely followed the trends observed in the previous two years (May 1999 thru April 30, 2000, and May 2000 thru April 2001), during which prescribing bumped up a few weeks before Thanksgiving and then trailed off after the New Year.[87]

Diagnosis: Rational Distress

In November 2001 a national survey of Americans' reactions to September 11 appeared in the *New England Journal of Medicine*.[88] It was conducted within five days of the attacks and found that 90 percent of the 560 respondents claimed to be "upset" or had trouble sleeping and concentrating. "By intervening as soon as symptoms appear," the survey's authors wrote, "physicians, psychologists, and other clinicians may be able to help people identify normal stress reactions and take steps to cope effectively."[89]

Putting a pathological spin on otherwise normal human reactions—in the fine tradition of therapism—was a widespread phenomenon.[90] In any event, the vast majority of people managed well without experts. Surely, a small fraction of New Yorkers developed clinically significant problems requiring care, but this relatively crude survey and even the more detailed ones that followed were not sensitive enough to tell us how many.

In March 2002, the New York Academy of Medicine published results of a phone survey of about one thousand Manhattan residents conducted within two months of the attack.[91] Subjects were asked whether they had intrusive memories or distressing dreams, made efforts to avoid thoughts associated with the trauma, or had difficulty falling asleep or concentrating. Among the sample of Manhattan residents living uptown, 7.5 percent were found to have developed PTSD. Those living closer to the World Trade Center had PTSD at almost three times that rate. The survey was much-touted as showing the prevalence of PTSD, but erroneously so, because researchers neglected to assess the severity of the symptoms and degree of impairment. Without this information, it is impossible to determine how many people actually developed PTSD.[92]

At a symposium held by the New York Academy of Medicine in September 2002, Howard Telson, a New York City psychiatrist, was one of many to express dismay at the imprecision of the study: "You have government officials announcing that they are changing policy and planning based on the conclusions of the [New York Academy of Medicine] work, yet the conclusions in many of these studies are based on assumptions and ill-defined terminology."[93] Despite the academy's questionable estimates of PTSD cases, its subsequent studies were consistent with the universal tendency for distress to abate with time. When the group did another survey four months later, it estimated 1.7 percent of the respondents had PTSD, and at six months this had dropped to 0.6 percent.[94]

In August 2002 the *Journal of the American Medical Association* published a report by the Research Triangle Institute in North Carolina.[95] About 2,300 people across the country and in New York City who had already been responding to periodic Internet-based health questionnaires (as part of another ongoing institute study) showed little increase in overall "psychological distress" within the two months after September 11.

When the institute researchers asked specifically about PTSD-like symptoms, however, 11 percent of New Yorkers were judged to have "probable PTSD," compared to a rate of 4 percent in the rest of the country and less than 3 percent in Washington, D.C., site of the other attack. As in the New York Academy study, however, this survey's design allowed only for assessment of stress, not ascertainment of PTSD. The research team used the qualifier "probable" because it employed a screening instrument; a more detailed interview assessing degree of impairment and duration of symptoms would be required to make a formal diagnosis of PTSD.

In an accompanying editorial, Carol North and Betty Pfefferbaum, psychiatrists at the Washington University in St. Louis, who conducted studies of PTSD after the Oklahoma City bombing, wrote:

> Most individuals directly involved in catastrophic events did not develop diagnosable psychiatric illness, but the majority report experiences such as sleep disturbance, loss of concentration, or feeling emotionally upset afterward. Rather than labeling such psychological effects as "symptoms," which unnecessarily implies pathology . . . language such as "reactions" or "responses" might better describe the normative, expected response to extraordinarily upsetting events.[96]

On the first anniversary of the attacks, the *Journal of the American Medical Association* published another survey, this one from the University of California, Irvine—the first survey to canvas the same individuals at several points in time.[97] Interviews with almost 3,500 subjects residing outside New York City were conducted in three waves—between two and four weeks after September 11; again at two to three months; and then at about seven months. Again, data were insufficient to make diagnoses, but PTSD-like symptoms related to the attacks declined over time. "Rather than considering these symptoms as evidence of psychiatric disorders per se, their presence in a substantial proportion of individuals may in fact represent a normal response to an abnormal event," the Irvine researchers concluded.[98]

Project Liberty

"Whatever you are struggling with, you are not alone," said the actor Alan Alda on radio stations serving New York City. "Now is the time to feel free to feel better," he intoned.[99] For about a year after the attack on the World Trade Center, star-studded public service announcements were ubiquitous in subways, buses, and newspapers around New York City. They were sponsored by Project Liberty, the name given to the crisis counseling program in New York City funded by the Federal Emergency Management Agency and run by the New York State Office of Mental Health.

Project Liberty's four thousand counselors offered reassurance and advice. They met with groups of people and with individual clients. They made house calls, arranged to meet clients on park benches or at their workplaces. Between one third to one half of all clients were employees whose supervisors encouraged them to participate in group sessions run by Project Liberty counselors.[100] Counselors typically made one to two visits and occasionally referred clients to a licensed professional if they seemed in need of further help. In all, 10 percent of all clients seen received referrals. One-third of those went to people who lost family members or were themselves in palpable danger at Ground Zero. Presumably, the rest comprised mainly rescue workers, school children, and unemployed or disabled people.[101]

When the New York State Office of Mental Health applied for its first FEMA counseling grant right after September 11, it estimated that 1.5 million New Yorkers would need counseling. A grant of $23 million came through promptly in October. As of June 2002, about 120,000 had sought assistance, not even one-tenth the projected number.[102] Yet around that time, FEMA announced another grant, of $132 million—nearly six times as large—in response to a second request for counseling funding. This time, the Office of Mental Health projected that two million New Yorkers, or one in four, would need counseling ("to allow necessary healing to continue").[103]

More ads were run, asking, for example, "Do you still feel the impact of the World Trade Center disaster?"[104] As of the spring of 2003, Project Liberty was still offering training courses such as "Grief and Survivor-Guilt Intervention Training." It would continue to do so until the end of the year. By summer, about twenty million brochures advertising Project Liberty had been distributed and hundreds of posters placed in bars, bathroom stalls, community centers, and neighborhood fairs.[105]

In the late spring of 2003, about a year after the second FEMA grant was awarded, $90 million remained unspent, according to the New York *Daily News*.[106] Although the value of the help offered through Project Liberty was not in question, its cost and scope attracted criticism. A story in New York *Newsday* headlined "Therapy Overkill?" captured the sentiment of several psychologists who labeled the project a "waste of time and money" aimed at "millions who had no direct connection to the disaster."[107]

Recruiting clients was a priority. "In New York City," said Rachel Yehuda of Mount Sinai, "the strong feeling was that if [the clients] don't come to you, you've got to go to them. The idea was to institute portable Project Liberty units of people to walk the streets looking for people to help."[108] In the winter of 2002, Lynne Rosen, a psychotherapist in Brooklyn, got a part-time job offer in just that spirit. She was contacted by a representative of a Queens-based mental health center to "reach out" to the traumatized residents of Brooklyn and Staten Island. The center would pay her with funds obtained from Project Liberty. Rosen's assignment was to sit in the waiting room of a general practitioner's office and approach patients as they came in for their medical appointments. She was to ask them where they had been on September 11 and whether they were having any psychological problems because of it. If so, she was to refer them to a center therapist.

The center wanted Rosen to talk to the patients about PTSD, she said, "even if they responded to the question about symptoms with a definite no." So she asked the center's representative how he justified such aggressive conduct. " 'We all continue to be deeply affected by September 11,' he told me indignantly," Rosen said, "and he lectured me that future psychiatric symptoms could still develop."[109] Rosen turned down the offer because she could not picture herself "accosting these unsuspecting people and burdening them with unnecessary anxiety about an event that happened over six months ago and that, they said, did not have a lasting effect on their well-being."

The outreach component of Project Liberty was a classic embodiment of the therapistic sensibility. As the late psychologist Bernie Zilbergeld described it in *The Shrinking of America*, this sensibility holds that (1) people really are sick even if they don't appear to be, and especially if they deny it; (2) everyone can benefit from therapy; (3) normal problems are to be made into mental health issues; and (4) those problems are widespread and are unlikely to be solved without professional help.[110]

On the whole, the people who used Project Liberty's services said they were "satisfied," according to the project administrators. Some number had genuinely benefited from the emotional support, coping advice, or referral for more intensive therapy. Yet, many intervention studies have found that perceived helpfulness often bears little relationship to improved measures of distress.[111]

In this particular instance, some of Project Liberty's "satisfied" customers had simply wanted practical assistance with matters such as death certificates or financial aid. Others were simply touched and grateful that a caring person would visit their home and talk with them. Others may simply have wanted care at no cost. And some clients had likely been contemplating psychotherapy even before the terrorist attack, but hanging their distress on the hook of September 11 was a socially acceptable way to get psychological help.

This is not to say such people do not "deserve" psychotherapy, only that their participation in Project Liberty's referral services did not signify a need to resolve trauma-related problems. In all, then, Project Liberty saw a variety of clients, among them the truly needy, the lonely, and the opportunistic.

Since Project Liberty was without precedent, it raised important questions for planners. One was whether all-out marketing of counseling services could inadvertently cause further distress. For example, did Project Liberty's blast advertising unwittingly print as pathological New Yorkers' normal distress? In light of the well-established fact that individuals' efforts to make sense of their reaction to tragedy play a key role in how well or poorly they cope, public messages must be tailored to foster expectations that the average individual will manage.[112]

Social scientists speculate—and the experience of anyone who is a parent tends to confirm—that immediate and highly visible attempts to help people negotiate a task that they could have managed on their own can undercut their sense of personal agency. Psychologists call this overhelping.[113] Does encouraging citizens to use counseling services signal to them that policymakers, health officials, and politicians lack faith in their capacities? Does this, in turn, erode their trust in themselves? Does the overestimation of a population's need for help contribute to collective anxiety?[114] When does consulting an "expert" about distress provide useful support, and when does it deprive the client of the experience of struggling, often in novel ways, to master his trials? These are hard questions to answer—but steeped as we are in therapism, we must be reminded even to ask them.

Pessimism, Pathologizing, and Profiteering

Private charities made mental health services a priority after September 11. They "have taken perhaps the most aggressive stance ever in pushing mental health therapy for families and others affected by the attacks," noted the *Washington Post*.[115] In the summer of 2002, various New York City–based charities along with the Red Cross announced combined grants of almost $250 million over five years to "address the enduring problem of psychic damage—grief, stress, trauma—in the aftermath of September 11."[116] A year later these same charities announced a collaborative effort "to encourage people affected by the 9/11 attacks to take advantage of financial assistance for confidential mental health and substance abuse assistance."[117]

Indeed, money was pouring forth, even as evidence consistently showed that most people were improving with time. Polls taken by the Pew Research Center, the Marist Institute for Public Opinion, ABC/*Washington Post*, and RAND within six months of the attacks all showed declines in problems such as sleeplessness, trouble concentrating, and intense worry about future attacks.[118] Volumes of data on traumatic response confirm that rates of stress and PTSD decline with time.[119]

Why then did the money keep flowing? Partly because mental health planners, lacking data on nonpathological responses to terrorist attacks, relied on models that were inappropriate—chiefly from the Oklahoma City bombing and other mass disasters where death or injury was widespread.[120] The victims of such events bore little resemblance to the vast majority of New Yorkers, who, while deeply shaken, even devastated, were never in mortal peril.

In addition, officials believed more people would use trauma services in the future. "Based on our experience, we know that thousands more need these services but have not come forward," said the administrator of the American Red Cross's September 11 Recovery Program.[121] Once they recognized that they needed help, or got over their fear of being criticized for seeking it, the assumption was, many more New Yorkers would be getting therapy. "It can take months and even years for some people to recognize that they need help coping with the tragedy," said the director of public education of the Mental Health Association of New York City.[122] Indeed, fully three years after the attacks, the association was still advertising counseling services for reactions to 9/11.[123]

Continued funding was also justified by the expectation that symptoms had yet to manifest themselves.[124] Said Joshua Gotbaum, the chief executive of the September 11th Fund, "We know that many people affected by September 11 will need some form of counseling and that many of them will not realize it for months or even for years."[125] Dr. Paul Ofman, chairman of emergency services at the Red Cross in Greater New York, also expected to see delayed reactions: "While for some people, the impact on their mental health is evident right away, for a noteworthy minority of individuals, the impact won't become evident until months or even years after the disaster."[126] According to Trish Marsik, director of Project Liberty for the city, "People are going to continue to have reactions. We can't predict when that is going to happen."[127]

As we saw in the previous chapter, psychiatrists working with Vietnam veterans in the 1970s and 1980s oversold the concept of delayed PTSD—defined as symptoms that develop at least six months after the traumatic event. We now know that symptoms destined to blossom into PTSD generally appear immediately or soon after the event. In the Oklahoma City bombing tragedy, for example, 94 percent of the victims who developed PTSD had the full complement of symptoms within days to a week of the blast.[128]

It is not uncommon for a patient to come to treatment after many months of suffering, but this generally means he delayed seeking treatment rather than that he experienced a delayed onset of symptoms. Individuals may have smoldering symptoms that fall just below the threshold for diagnosis; a subsequent stress or loss of support can tip the equilibrium, making their symptoms more obvious or harder to bear.[129] And, finally, delayed PTSD, to the extent it occurs at all, is limited to direct victims, not to individuals who were not personally threatened.

Still other individuals who appeared to have delayed PTSD were already troubled by various life problems before September 11 but found their worries brought to a boil afterward. Some even unwittingly attributed their anxieties solely to the attack—after all, in deciding what is wrong with us, we are often influenced by so-called illness narratives endorsed by therapists or the media. However, these are not true cases of trauma-induced distress, and successful treatment lies in addressing the root worries and circumstances.

Finally, money flowed because service providers were eager to take it. Daryl Regier of the American Psychiatric Association issued a canny prediction when he told the *New York Times*, "There are going to be people coming out of the woodwork to capitalize on this large amount of money that's available, some of whom will be completely legitimate." And, Regier added, some of whom will not be.[130] As Reuters reported, "A whole new era of mental health services could be opening up for longer-term care [for stress relating to the terrorist attacks] in what could be a boon for individual counselors and the companies who act as industry middlemen."[131]

A Brief Modern History of Response to Calamity

In New York City on September 11 there was a strong, spontaneous show of collective resolve and organization. Near Ground Zero, members of one tenant association helped direct the streams of people running from the World Trade Center; they formed an "urgent needs" team to check on homebound residents; they acted as volunteer cashiers in stores when paid employees could not get to the area.[132] The calm and orderly behavior of workers evacuating the World Trade Center towers themselves surely kept the death and injury tolls from rising. In the largest waterborne evacuation in our history, half a million people left lower Manhattan. Barges, sailboats, and ferries, with no instructions, put into the port as the towers burned. "If you're out in the water in a pleasure craft and you see those buildings on fire," said Lee Clarke, a sociologist at Rutgers University, "in a strictly rational sense, you should head to New Jersey. Instead people went into potential danger and rescued strangers."[133]

According to the sociologist Henry Quarantelli, a pioneer in the field of disaster research, such constructive responses are typical. "Mythical beliefs to the contrary," he writes, "disaster victims do not panic, they are not passive, they do not become caught up in [selfish and] antisocial behavior, and they are not behaviorally traumatized."[134] Monica Schoch-Spana, a medical anthropologist with the Johns Hopkins Center for Civilian Biodefense Strategies, laments the predominance of the "pathological model." So often, she says, officials and mental health planners neglect the positive human elements that crisis elicits, such as "reasoned caution, resourcefulness, adaptability, resiliency, hopefulness, and humanitarianism."[135]

Half a century of research on natural disasters and industrial accidents reveals a relatively benign picture of human response in the face of uncertainty, calamity, and fear.[136] The Center for Disaster Research at the University of Delaware has conducted hundreds of studies of events such as floods, earthquakes and tornadoes, chemical emergencies, and building collapses. Again and again researchers have found that people rarely panic, lose control, or lapse into passivity, though this is not to say they are unafraid.[137] Danger in enclosed and overcrowded places with no obvious exit is more likely to produce panic, though even then it is common for many of the entrapped people to try to help others.

A good example is the collapse of the suspended walkways in the lobby of the Kansas City Hyatt Regency in 1981, which killed 110 people. "An initial impulse to open clinical services for those affected rallied many staff but virtually no clients," wrote the firehouse psychologist on duty. "Attention quickly shifted from clinical intervention toward community-based approaches to information, empowerment, and peer support."[138]

Rutgers's Clarke has observed: "The rules of behavior in extreme situations are not much different from rules of ordinary life. . . . The most consistent pattern in disasters is that people connect in the aftermath and work to rebuild their physical and cultural environments."[139]

Civilian populations under sustained assault have also shown impressive fortitude, despite dire predictions of mental breakdown. On the eve of World War II in England, Philip Vernon, a noted British psychologist, wrote:

> [T]he stimuli presented by a heavy air raid are far more intense and more terrifying than civilized human beings normally experience. . . . In the summer of 1940 when raids on a large scale seemed imminent in Britain, many of us were apprehensive lest they should lead to widespread panic and hysteria.[140]

In 1936 the psychiatrist John Rickman, writing in *The Lancet*, advised, "Since air raids may produce panic in the civilian population it is well to consider the factors that facilitate or diminish panic, and what steps, if any, may be taken against it."[141] Accordingly, British authorities made arrangements to disperse city dwellers and establish special psychological clinics called Neurosis Centers.[142] Psychiatrists advised the government that there would be three psychiatric casualties for every physical one when the bombs began to fall.[143] When they did, in September 1940, some people did experience "air-raid phobia," a reaction described by the Viennese-born neurologist Erwin Stengel as "a persistent and excessive fear of air raids. . . . which increased toward nightfall." The wail of sirens precipitated an acute attack. But instead of occurring on a wide scale as expected, Stengel noted, this condition turned out to be relatively rare.[144]

The British psychologist Irving L. Janis collated the official reports on psychiatric casualties during the Blitz.[145] Among his findings:

[P]sychiatric reports on civilian reactions to bombing indicate that heavy air attacks produce sizeable incidence of emotional shock cases with acute anxiety symptoms. Most of these cases appear to be capable of fully recovering, either spontaneously or in response to simple forms of psychiatric treatment within a period of a few days up to a few weeks.[146]

Similarly, in a report to the British Medical Research Council, the psychiatrist Aubrey Lewis concluded, "air raids have not been responsible for any striking increase in neurotic illness."[147] Years after the war, W. Linford Rees, a former president of the Royal College of Psychiatrists, told an interviewer, "One interesting thing was that although London was being bombarded at that time, I, a young psychiatrist, looked after nearly all the outpatient clinics for the whole of London. What that shows of course is that there wasn't a tremendous demand for outpatient treatment."[148] After fifteen months of terrifying bombing, food shortages, sleeplessness, and family bereavements, there was no increase in hospital admissions in the Bristol area, and in Coventry there was even a decrease in visits to outpatient clinics.[149]

During the Blitz, from the autumn of 1940 to the summer of 1941, more than 43,000 civilians were killed across Britain including almost 5,500 children. More than 190,000 bombs were dropped and over one million homes in the London area alone were destroyed or damaged. Yet over all, as the psychologist Stanley J. Rachman showed in his book *Fear and Courage*, "the resilience that people displayed under air attack was so unexpected and remarkable that the surveys and statistical analyses [compiled by Janis] inevitably fail to convey how people coped."[150]

The British government commissioned several surveys to understand why rates of mental breakdown were so low. According to the British historian Ben Shephard, the explanations ranged from feelings of solidarity and a sense of shared purpose induced by the war to psychiatrists' practice of dealing briskly with patients, encouraging them to "return to their normal work and resist the temptation to exaggerate the experiences through which they passed."[151]

A recent review of British intelligence and clinical reports from World War II by Edgar Jones and colleagues of King's College Medical School in London, questioned whether perhaps many psychiatric casualties had gone unreported, thus creating a false impression of resilience.[152] The "morale of the bombed," as a 1940–1941 public opinion measure put it, largely depended on the quality of the information they got and whether food, health care, and facilities for children were provided. Local doctors reported more complaints of stomach ailment and other psychosomatic symptoms. Morale did falter occasionally, but Jones and colleagues found little evidence that admission to mental health facilities increased. Cities with the best morale tended not to suffer economically and to have citizens who were already acclimated to raids through previous exposure to bombing earlier in the war and who could undertake constructive roles in helping with the war effort.

In the last chapter we mentioned Anna Freud's observation of children. That little children "should thus come into close contact with the horrors of war," she wrote in *War and Children*, "led many people to expect that children would receive traumatic shocks from air raids and would develop abnormal reactions very similar to the traumatic or war neuroses of soldiers of the last war."[153] Children around ages five, six, and seven did become agitated when sent into foster care or relocated into the countryside away from their parents; those remaining with their parents showed anxiety chiefly if their mothers were highly distraught. But as Freud and her coauthor, Dorothy Burlingham, wrote:

> So far as we can notice, there were no signs of traumatic shock to be observed in these children . . . this observation is borne

out by the reports of nurses and social workers in London County Council Rest Centers where children used to arrive . . . straight from their bombed houses.[154]

In fact, children who remained in London with their parents fared better emotionally than those sent to live in the countryside.[155]

Years later in another part of the British Isles, a similar phenomenon was evident. In Northern Ireland, urban terrorism has raged intermittently for about thirty years. When riots broke out in 1969, psychiatrists expected an increase in hospital admissions and clinic attendance. Yet a review of studies from Northern Ireland published in 1988 in the *British Journal of Psychiatry* states, "The campaign of terrorist violence does not seem to have resulted in any obvious increase in psychiatric morbidity."[156]

It might seem that the elderly would be especially prone to fear and panic, since physical limitations put them at the mercy of all sorts of man-made and natural calamities. But evidence from an Israeli nursing home showed otherwise. Renee Garfinkle studied a group of elderly Israeli nursing home residents during the Gulf War, when thirty-nine Iraqi SCUD missiles hit Israel in the space of six weeks.[157]

Garfinkle was expecting especially high rates of distress among Holocaust survivors, not only because they had already been through one horrific experience but also because the poison gas that Iraq had threatened to release over Israel could be a reminder of Nazi gas chambers. But she found that six months after the war, neither mental nor physical complaints had increased. "Under the current paradigms of stress, coping, and adaptation," Garfinkle noted, "we predicted long-term deleterious effects of the prolonged stress of bombing in this group of frail elderly. We found no such effects."[158]

It is possible that rather than being especially vulnerable this population was especially psychologically fit—after all, at an

ONE NATION UNDER THERAPY

average age of eighty-three, those still surviving were among the more robust. It is also possible that older people, by virtue of their life experience, tend to be more psychologically prepared to die, more philosophical about death, or to have perfected ways of coping over the years.

Regardless of the reason, the important fact is that predictions of fragility on a grand scale were not realized. Indeed, another study—of Israeli Holocaust survivors who developed cancer in old age—found that over 80 percent adapted very well.[159] These and other studies contrast with the early research that stressed Holocaust survivors' long-term pathological outcomes.[160] Some of those reports are skewed by their selection of subjects (e.g., clinical populations; compensation-seekers) or are unreliable from a research standpoint because they did not use standardized assessments. Subsequent inquiries reveal that the large majority of Holocaust survivors have been productive in their work and family lives, despite heterogeneity in emotional health among them.[161]

In the summer of 2003, the first study examining the psychological impact of terrorism in Israel appeared in the *Journal of the American Medical Association*.[162] A research team from Tel-Aviv University conducted phone interviews with about five hundred randomly selected Israelis, almost half of whom had either been personally endangered by a terrorist assault or had friends and relatives who were. While two-thirds of those surveyed felt a "low sense of safety," a little over 80 percent expressed optimism about their personal future. Three-quarters felt they would be able to function effectively in a terrorist attack and only 5 percent felt the need for professional help. "Considering the high levels of direct and indirect exposure to trauma in the sample, much more distress might have been expected than was actually found," the authors stated.[163]

Although mass disaster ushers in anguish, it is suffering with a collective aspect. Emile Durkheim famously noted that group cohesion tightens during times of communal threat. Individuals are not isolated in their misery. The close embrace of public mourning cushions shock and sorrow to some degree, partly explaining why psychiatrists have occasionally observed a fall-off in distress during crisis. Also relevant are attitudes toward adversity. One popular theory is the notion of "shattered assumptions."[164] Once people have endured tragedy, they are less inclined to the fundamental belief that they are worthy and their environment is benevolent, meaningful, and controllable. If one's worldview accommodates the likelihood of horror, one is prepared for it and better able to cope when tragedy does at last strike.

If expectations can ameliorate the psychological impact of traumatic events, so can the meaning individuals assign to them. Numerous studies have shown that ideological commitment to a cause plays a protective role. Thus, for example, torture victims and prisoners of war who believed that enduring their abuse was a form of political resistance were less likely to develop PTSD than their unprepared and ideologically uncommitted counterparts.[165] These findings suggest that a feeling of control and a sense of commitment to a cause are buffers against PTSD.[166]

Today we confront not only natural and technological disasters but also terrorism. Comparatively few data exist on effects of the latter, but it seems likely that unprecedented acts of biological and chemical terrorism have the potential to generate greater psychological distress than more familiar kinds of assaults. An invisible, odorless miasma is ideal for generating disruption. By maximizing novelty, undetectability, and uncontrollability, the threat of biological and chemical agents seems more dangerous and thus more likely to produce anxiety.[167]

Nonetheless, Schoch-Spana and Thomas Glass, an epidemiologist at Johns Hopkins School of Public Health, argue that the public can be recruited as active participants in a response to bioterrorism. This would require giving them information and instructions about how to protect themselves, allowing a free and continuous flow of information between officials, the media, and the public, and cultivating trust between biodefense leaders and the media.

Post-Traumatic Growth

The wise counsel of the nineteen psychologists we introduced earlier was drowned out by the urgent doom-saying of many health professionals whose philosophy resonated with the ethos of therapism: pathologizing normal human emotion, promoting the illusion that we are very fragile beings, and urging grand emotional displays as the prescription for coping.

According to the U.S. Surgeon General, "today there is no greater mental health issue facing us as a nation than the effects of terrorism and war."[168] Randall Marshall, psychiatrist at the New York State Psychiatric Institute and head of a citywide treatment consortium for September 11 victims, concurs. "The challenge for psychiatrists," he says, "is how to help people live in a world that is constantly under threat."[169] Ezra Susser, at the school of public health at Columbia University, has pressed for "a determined [public health] effort to help the population withstand such attacks on the psyche."[170]

In our trauma-conscious society, many mental health professionals seem eager to take charge of managing the collective anxiety surrounding terrorism and its aftermath. But perhaps one of the lessons from September 11 is that the clinician's role in a shocked and heartbroken world is actually quite limited. Naturally, professionals should be ready and available to treat people with disabling levels of distress, but in general the people's psychological well-being is best maintained through nonclinical means.

Consider what we know about human response to crisis. Under threat, citizens are ravenous for information and require practical resources. They need a social scaffolding in the form of civic order and some minimal infrastructure to support the bedrock institutions and relationships—families, communities, and houses of worship—that have always served them in times of uncertainty and immense sorrow.[171] Opportunities for citizens to respond actively and constructively to catastrophe—by giving blood, donating money, or volunteering—are important. All of these can enhance social cohesion and channel nervous energy.

The best formula we now seem to have for fortifying psyches amid collective disaster is to minimize disorder, uncertainty, and economic devastation. For the majority, mental health will follow naturally. For those overwhelmed by events, mental health professionals should be ready to help. That is their job.

Research is needed to tell us what more (and what less) the professionals should be doing. It is quite possible, for example, that there is indeed a role for preventive psychiatry. In fact, one of the most pressing questions for the profession is how to predict which individuals will develop mental illness. And, if we can identify this subset, what kinds of psychological interventions, if any, are useful in preventing them from falling ill?[172] For the general population there is currently little beyond psychological first aid—reassurance, resources, and referral to mental health services if needed—that should be offered. And in making themselves available, professionals should guard against suggesting pathological interpretations of distress to people who do not need help.

The psychiatrist Paul Chodoff has studied his colleagues' penchant for "medicalizing the human condition." They do this, he writes, by applying

a diagnostic label to various unpleasant or undesirable feelings or behaviors that are not distinctly abnormal [and] that . . . are not readily distinguishable from the range of experiences that are often inescapable aspects of the fate of being human.[173]

Astute clinicians, psychologists, sociologists, anthropologists, and historians are chipping away at the pathological model of human distress inspired more than thirty years ago by antiwar psychiatrists. According to psychologists Richard Tedeschi and Lawrence Calhoun, the "conventional approach to trauma outcomes focuses on the negative aftereffects, in the worst cases, the development of post-traumatic stress disorder, [but] post-traumatic growth may actually be the more common outcome."[174] In their book, *Posttraumatic Growth: Positive Changes in the Aftermath of Crisis,* Tedeschi and Calhoun bring together scores of studies that complement their own findings that about two-thirds of trauma survivors can point to ways they have benefited from their struggle to cope with the ways a traumatic experience once shattered their lives.[175]

Similarly, Rudolf Moos, a psychologist at Stanford University, has found that more than half of all people who experience crises report some benefit from them: "For many people life crises are the catalysts . . . lead[ing] to greater self-reliance, better relationships with family and friends, new problem-solving skills."[176]

One of the lessons of September 11 is that the mental health profession must find a balance between offering its services and promoting them too eagerly, between letting people know help is available and suggesting to them that they need help when they do not. On September 11 the helpers toiled in good faith, powered by genuine concern. But they also endorsed one of the mistaken tenets of therapism: that people are fragile. And in their zeal to help, they underestimated our natural fortitude.

———

Therapism and the Nation's Future

Radio talk show host Don Imus and his wife Deirdre run a summer camp in New Mexico for children with cancer. The camp does not award stress badges and there are no "feelings dances." The kids spend very little time talking about themselves. In fact, it is against the rules to mention a child's disease at all. No one is pitied and no one is babied. According to Deirdre Imus, "The purpose here is for these kids to work hard, to learn to ride a horse, and to care for the animals—to take responsibility and recover their self-sufficiency."[1] By all accounts, especially the children's, the camp is an extraordinary success.

Mrs. Imus tells the story of a camp ranch hand, Jack, who was badly scratched when he tried to stop a fight between a dog and cat. When worried friends would ask if he was all right, he would say, "I just have to cowboy up."[2] Imus says, "It's one of the key concepts of Western life and an idea we live by on the Imus Ranch. I'd explain it this way: When you're ignoring pain, brushing past hardship, doing your best despite adversity— that's when you know what it means to 'cowboy up.' "[3]

The spirit of the Imus Ranch contrasts sharply with the spirit being encouraged in most of the nation's schools. Within weeks of the terrorist attack on September 11, then New York

City schools chancellor Harold O. Levy commissioned a tip sheet from "leading child-trauma experts" to give to the city's eighty thousand teachers. It offered educators the remarkable counsel to "avoid clichés such as 'Be strong.' "[4] Why shouldn't adults encourage children to be strong? Aren't courage and strength exactly what they needed in order to cope?

"Be strong" is a vital life lesson, not an insensitive cliché. Yet, child trauma experts, as well as New York City school officials who take them seriously, warn teachers against imparting this advice. Their anxiety exposes the paradox of therapism. In theory, therapism offers a compassionate and caring philosophy of life; in practice it enfeebles those it seeks to help. By treating them as fragile victims, therapism badly underestimates their natural strength and courage.

In his studies of national attitudes and mores, Alan Wolfe showed that a great many Americans embrace a therapeutic perspective because "they think of themselves as caring people just trying to be good to others."[5] We cited his example of Kelly Houston of Fall River who, referring to compulsive gamblers, alcoholics, and drug addicts, said, "I think there's an internal something within them that's drawing them to it. I don't think that a person's character is weak or anything."[6]

No reasonable person denies "there is an internal something" that makes some of us more vulnerable to addiction than others. Our society has made great progress since the days when addicts were dehumanized and reviled as "drunkards" and "dope fiends." Compassion and pragmatism have been important influences in encouraging treatment for substance abusers. But, as we have repeatedly pointed out, therapeutic "kindness" is inadvertently unkind and disrespectful when it regards addicts as passive and helpless.

At the heart of therapism is the revolutionary idea that psychology can and should take the place of ethics and religion. Recall Abraham Maslow's elated claim that the new psychologies of self-actualization were offering a "religion surrogate" that could change the world. He had "come to think of this humanist trend in psychology as a revolution in the truest, oldest sense of the word, the sense in which Galileo, Darwin, Einstein, Freud, and Marx made revolutions . . . new conceptions of ethics and values."[7] Carl Rogers then looked upon group therapy as a kind of earthly paradise—a "state where all is known and all accepted."[8] The sixties and seventies were heady times for Maslow and Rogers. They were promoting a visionary realignment of values, away from the Judeo-Christian ethic, in the direction of what they regarded as a science of self-actualization.

Despite its powerful appeal, and despite the good intentions of Maslow, Rogers, and their colleagues, the alternative "revolutionary" ethic of the human potential movement was built on grand theory and wishful thinking and could not achieve its promise. Early experiments at Esalen and Synanon "where all is known and all accepted" turned out neither happy nor good. The classical virtues and the precepts of Judeo-Christian ethics are informed by an understanding of human psychology, to be sure, but psychological gimmickry cannot replace them.

Sigmund Freud himself once said, referring to the fate of all false ideas, "The voice of the intellect is a soft one but it does not rest till it has gained a hearing."[9] Therapism falters under rational scrutiny; if Freud is right, its hold on the American mind cannot last. But a change in perspective will not come easily. Too many Americans have been convinced, for example, that self-expression is more important than self-control, that nonjudgmentalism is the essence of kindness, that psychic pain is a pathology in need of a cure.

Therapism will begin to recede when parents demand knowledge-based instead of feelings-centered classrooms. Its entrenched hold on the country will loosen when conscientious psychologists correct, rather than promulgate, the myth that we are a nation of afflicted Hamlets and Ophelias. It will be weakened when journalists report on post-traumatic growth at least as often as they highlight post-traumatic stress.

But most of all, therapism will lose credibility when more Americans come to understand how it fundamentally contradicts our ideals about character and about our national character. From the earliest days of its founding, the nation has been guided by a philosophy that social historians call the American Creed. The creed's paramount values are self-reliance, stoicism, courage in the face of adversity, and the valorization of excellence. Therapism is at odds with them all.

The British historian Paul Johnson concludes his magisterial *A History of the American People* with a tribute to the spirit of the American Creed.[10] His book is far too favorable to its subject to survive review by the bias and sensitivity committees that determine which textbooks are fit reading for American schoolchildren. Johnson is candid about America's many failings, but he unabashedly praises it as "a human achievement without parallel:"

> That achievement—the transformation of a mostly uninhabited wilderness into the supreme national artifact of history—did not come about without heroic sacrifice and great sufferings stoically endured. . . . There have indeed been many setbacks in 400 years of American history. . . . But the Americans are, above all, a problem-solving people. They do not believe that anything in this world is beyond human capacity to soar to and dominate. They will not give up.[11]

The American Creed that has sustained the nation is now under powerful assault by the apostles of therapism. The fateful question is: Will Americans actively defend the traditional creed of stoicism and the ideology of achievement, or will they continue to allow the nation to slide into therapeutic self-absorption and moral debility? Our very future depends on our answer.

Acknowledgments

We are enormously grateful to Keith Humphreys, Richard Mc-Nally, and Fred Sommers, who brought critical insight and vast stores of knowledge about psychology and philosophy to multiple drafts. No authors could wish for more devoted and scholarly readers.

Claudia Winkler and Tamler Sommers did meticulous and intelligent editing. Our esteemed AEI colleagues, Karlyn Bowman and Norman Ornstein, were unflagging in their enthusiasm and gave invaluable advice.

Howard Telson, a great friend, died before we completed the book. The chapters on trauma owe an immense debt to his experience as a psychiatrist working in New York City after September 11, his skeptical wisdom, and his playful sense of humor.

We enlisted a Rolodex' worth of researchers and clinicians for their expertise: Keith Bea, Joseph Boscarino, George Bonanno, Marilyn Bowman, David Brooks, Todd Buckley, John Winston Bush, Brad Bushman, Barrie Cassileth, Bennett Cohen, James Coyne, Grant Devilly, Wayne Fenton, Chris Frueh, Neil Genzlinger, Richard Gist, Elzbieta Gozdziak, George Hagman, Seth Hassett, James Herbert, Gene Heyman, Steve Hy-

man, Selby Jacobs, Ron Kessler, Michael Knable, Paul Lees-
Haley, Scott Lilienfeld, David Marlowe, Paul McHugh, William
Narrow, Kim Newbold, George Neugebauer, Carol North,
Mary Utne O'Brien, Anand Pandya, Loren Pankratz, Holly
Prigerson, Saul Raw, Richard Redding, James Rosack, George
Rosen, Robert Rosenheck, Marc Sageman, Wallace Sampson,
Paula Schnurr, Gilbert Sewall, Ben Shephard, Ned Shorter,
Roxane Cohen Silver, David Spiegel, Karen Seeley, Carol
Tavris, John Tuskan, Simon Wessely, Christine Whelan.

We appreciate the vast energy, good humor, and loyalty of
our research assistants, Erin Conroy and Nell Manning. Our
agents, Lynn Chu and Glen Hartley, have never failed to give
superb advice.

The manuscript benefited greatly from the sharp judgment
of our editor, George Witte, and the careful attention of Daniela
Rapp and Surie Rudoff, all of St. Martin's Press.

Our friend and benefactor Elizabeth Lurie has been steadfast
and unstintingly generous in her support of our work over
many years—now as scholars with the W. H. Brady Program in
Culture and Freedom at AEI.

Christina's son, David Sommers, and his delightful friends,
Haskell Garon, Mark Levy, and Elliott Stixrud, provided a sane
perspective and palpable anecdotal evidence that young Americans can indeed be psychologically healthy, whole, normal,
and—dare we say it?—happy.

Christopher DeMuth, president of AEI, is an ideal boss who
presides with vision, tact, and wisdom over a scholarly milieu
where intellectual freedom is respected and encouraged. We ded-
icate this book to him.

Notes

PREFACE: ONE NATION UNDER THERAPY.

1. Sarah E. Shea, et al., "Pathology in the Hundred Acre Wood: A Neurodevelopmental Perspective on A. A. Milne," *Canadian Medical Association Journal* 163, no. 12 (2000), pp. 1557–59.

2. Mary Pipher, *Reviving Ophelia: Saving the Selves of Adolescent Girls* (New York: Putnam, 1994), p. 12.

3. Ibid., p. 19.

4. William Pollack, *Real Boys: Rescuing Our Sons from the Myths of Boyhood* (New York: Henry Holt, 1999).

5. William Pollack, "Listening to Boys' Voices," May 22, 1998, study manuscript, p. 28. (Obtained through the McLean Hospital Department of Public Affairs, Belmont, Mass.)

6. William Pollack in Mary Jo Kochakian, "Psychologists Search for Ways to Help Boys in Distress," *Hartford Courant*, August 24, 1999, sec. F, p. 5.

7. Louis Harris and Associates, *Commonwealth Fund Survey of Women's Health* (New York: Commonwealth Fund, 1993).

8. Michael Posner, "Women & Depression Studied," *Reuters*, July 15, 1993. A Louis Harris vice president would later repudiate the study. See Christina Hoff Sommers, *Who Stole Feminism: How Women have Betrayed Women* (New York: Simon & Schuster) 1994, pp. 249–54.

9. Susan Faludi, *Stiffed: The Betrayal of the American Man* (New York: William Morrow, 1999), p. 39.

10. Daniel Goleman, *Emotional Intelligence: Why It Can Matter More than IQ* (New York: Bantam, 1995), p. x.

11. Jim Windolf, "A Nation of Nuts," *Wall Street Journal*, October 22, 1997.
12. The National Opinion Research Center at the University of Chicago, which has been tracking levels of general happiness and life satisfaction in the general population since 1957, consistently finds that close to 90 percent of Americans describe themselves as happy with their lives with no significant differences between men and women. National Opinion Research Center, see http://www.icpsr.umich.edu/gss99; see also David Myers and Ed Diener, "Who is Happy?" *Psychological Science* 6, no. 1 (1995). For data on adolescence, see Anne C. Petersen, et al. "Depression in Adolescence," *American Psychologist* 48, no. 2 (1993), p. 155; Daniel Offer and Kimberly A. Schonert-Reichl, "Debunking the Myths of Adolescence: Findings from Recent Research," *Journal of the American Adolescent Psychiatry* 31, no. 6 (1992), pp. 1003–14. See also chapter 1, pp. 19–23.
13. For list of members see, http://www.eiconsortium.org/members/membership_consortium.htm (accessed March 4, 2004).
14. See "Program Description" at http://www.eiconsortium.org/model_programs/emotional_competence_training.htm (accessed March 4, 2004).
15. See, for example, Anne M. Paul, "Promotional Intelligence," *Salon*, June 29, 1999; J. D. Mayer, P. Salovey, and D. Caruso, "Models of Emotional Intelligence," in *Handbook of Intelligence*, ed. Robert J. Sternberg (Cambridge: Cambridge University Press, 2000), pp. 396–420. These authors challenge Goleman's definition of emotional intelligence, suggesting that it represents little more than standard personality attributes. They also suggest that he overstates the degree to which these attributes predict success.
16. Goleman, *Emotional Intelligence*, p. 268.
17. Ibid., p. 261.
18. Ibid.
19. The term "therapism" was coined by the popular British satirist, Fay Weldon. "This is an era of therapism," she told an interviewer with dismay, "a drive towards the belief that talk is all we need," http://www.varsity.cam.ac.uk/VarsityOnline/Online2/Content/Life/Stories/030298_meetsFayWeldon.html (accessed April 20, 2004).
20. Neil Williams, "Eastern Connecticut State University physical education professor," in Tamala M. Edwards, "Scourge of the Playground," *Time*, May 21, 2001.
21. Merle Froschl, Barbara Sprung, and Nancy Mullin-Rindler, *Quit it! A Teacher's Guide on Teasing and Bullying for Use with Students in Grades K–3* (New York: Educational Equity Concepts, 1998), p. 86.
22. Diane Ravitch, *The Language Police: How Pressure Groups Restrict What Students Learn* (New York: Knopf, 2003), pp. 22, 197–200.
23. Ibid., p. 23.

24. See Brad J. Bushman and Roy F. Baumeister, "Threatened Egotism, Narcissism, Self-Esteem, and Direct and Displaced Aggression: Does Self-Love or Self-Hate Lead to Violence?" *Journal of Personality and Social Psychology* 75, no. 1 (1998), pp. 219–29; Roy F. Baumeister, Jennifer D. Campbell, Joachim I. Krueger, and Kathleen D. Vohs, "Does High Self-Esteem Cause Better Performance, Interpersonal Success, Happiness, or Healthier Lifestyles?," *Psychological Science in the Public Interest* 4, no. 1 (2003), pp. 1–44.

25. Alan Wolfe, *Moral Freedom: The Search for Virtue in a World of Choice* (New York: W. W. Norton, 2001), p. 79.

26. With the help of the *New York Times*, Wolfe conducted a survey on American values and reported the findings in the *New York Times Magazine* (March 18, 2001) and in his book *Moral Freedom* (2001). In addition to his scientific poll, Wolfe carried out in-depth interviews with a (somewhat) random selection of citizens from eight U.S. communities. The subjects came from both culturally liberal areas like the Castro district of San Francisco and more conservative areas like the farm town of Tipton, Iowa.

27. Nadya Labi, "The Grief Brigade," *Time*, May 17, 1999.

28. Viktor Frankl, *Man's Search For Meaning* (New York: Washington Square Press, 1984), p. 125.

29. Lance Morrow, "The Case For Rage and Retribution," *Time*, September 12, 2001.

30. Richard McNally, *Remembering Trauma* (Cambridge, Mass.: Belknap/Harvard University Press, 2003).

31. See for example, Eva S. Moskowitz, In *Therapy We Trust: America's Obsession with Self Fulfillment* (Baltimore, Md.: Johns Hopkins University Press, 2001).

32. Abraham Maslow in Edward Hoffman, *The Right To Be Human: A Biography of Abraham Maslow* (Los Angeles: Jeremy P. Tarcher, 1988), p. 207.

33. Philip Rieff, *The Triumph of the Therapeutic: Uses of Faith After Freud* (Chicago: University of Chicago Press, 1987); Christopher Lasch, *The Culture of Narcissism: American Life in An Age of Diminishing Expectations* (New York: Warner, 1979); Allan Bloom, *The Closing of the American Mind: How Higher Education Has Failed Democracy and Impoverished the Souls of Today's Students* (New York: Simon & Schuster, 1988); Charles J. Sykes, *A Nation of Victims: The Decay of the American Character* (New York: St. Martin's Press, 1993); Wendy Kaminer, *I'm Dysfunctional, You're Dysfunctional: The Recovery Movement and Other Self-Help Fashions* (New York: Vintage, 1993).

1. THE MYTH OF THE FRAGILE CHILD.

1. Girl Scouts of the USA, *Junior Girl Scout Badge Book* (New York: Girl Scouts of the USA, 2001), p. 87; Nicole C. Wong, "New Relaxation

Badge is a Hit With Preteen Scouts," Knight Ridder Newspapers, April 23, 2002.

2. Dr. Harriet S. Mosatche in Patricia Leigh Brown, "Cinematography and Chilling Out? That's Scouting," *New York Times*, May 13, 2002, sec. A, p. 10.

3. Lindsay Gray in Ibid.

4. Pat Samarge in Martin Miller, "Principal Says the Game of Tag Lowers Students' Self-Esteem," *Chicago Tribune*, June 26, 2002, sec. C, p. 5.

5. Sandy Coleman, "A Dodgy Issue: Traditional Phys-Ed Activity Sparks Debate in Schools Across the Nation," *Boston Globe*, March 29, 2001, sec. B, p. 1.

6. Thomas Murphy, physical education teacher at Tobin Elementary School, Ibid.

7. Paul Zientarski, department chairman for Naperville Central High School, in Karen Brandon, "Foul Ball: Childhood Game Picking Up More Enemies; Some PE Teachers Say Dodge Ball Sends Harmful Message," *Chicago Tribune*, March 18, 2001, sec. C, p. 1.

8. Rick Reilly, "The Weak Shall Inherit the Gym," *Sports Illustrated*, May 14, 2001, p. 96.

9. Neil F. Williams, "The Physical Education Hall of Shame," *The Journal of Physical Education, Recreation, & Dance* 63, no. 6 (1992), pp. 57–60.

10. Neil F. Williams, "The Physical Education Hall of Shame, Part II," *The Journal of Physical Education, Recreation & Dance* 65, no.2 (1994), p. 19.

11. Lee Sherman, "The Death of Dodge Ball: A Generation of High-Tech Couch Potatoes Meets a New Kind of PE," *Northwest Education Magazine* 6, no. 1 (2000).

12. Dave Finnegan, "Mr. Juggle Bug," in Patricia Ward Biederman, "Tossing Self-Esteem Into Mix; Calabasas Phys-Ed Teacher Uses Juggling as a Friendlier Fitness Tool," *Los Angeles Times*, May 9, 2001, sec. 2, p. 9.

13. Jim Clemmensen, Ibid.

14. John Leo, "Toward Mindless Inclusion," *Chattanooga Times Free Press*, June 27, 2001, sec. B, p. 9.

15. Merle Froschl, Barbara Sprung, and Nancy Mullin-Rindler, *Quit it! A Teacher's Guide on Teasing and Bullying for Use with Students in Grades K-3* (New York: Educational Equity Concepts, 1998), p. v.

16. Ibid., p. 86.

17. Ibid., pp. 86–87.

18. Anthony Pellegrini and Jane Perlmutter, "Rough-and-Tumble Play on the Elementary School Playground," *Young Children* (January 1998), pp. 14–17.

19. Ibid., p. 15.

20. Diane Ravitch, *The Language Police: How Pressure Groups Restrict What Students Learn* (New York: Knopf, 2003).
21. Ibid., p. 8.
22. Ibid., p. 9.
23. Sensitivity panel statement, Ibid., p. 13.
24. Ibid., p. 159.
25. Jonathan Yardley, "Read No Evil: A Textbook Case of Censorship," *Washington Post*, June 12, 2003, sec. C, p. 1.
26. Kevin Miller, "Only 55 More Shopping Days Before the Self-Esteem Holiday," Timely Snow: occasional observations by Kevin Miller, March 19, 2004, http://ruixue.cogsci.uiuc.edu/mt/snowtime/archives/000384.html (accessed March 23, 2004).
27. Rossella Santagata, "Running Head: Cultural Beliefs and Practices in Mistake-Handling," (paper on file with author, submitted for publication), p. 11.
28. Rossella Santagata, in discussion with authors.
29. See Alice! (Columbia University's Health Education Program) at Columbia University, http://www.alice.columbia.edu/; Healthy Devil at Duke University, http://healthydevil.studentaffairs.duke.edu/; University Health Services at the University of Wisconsin–Madison, http://www.uhs.wisc.edu/index.jsp; Student Health Services at the University of Kansas, http://www.ku.edu~shs/; Wellness Education Services at the University of Buffalo, http://www.livingwell.buffalo.edu/; Juliet Williams, "For Students in Finals, a New Degree of Stress Relief: Colleges Provide Food, Massage, Toys, and Entertainment to Make Exam Week Less Intense," *Washington Post*, December 12, 2002, sec. A, p. 13.
30. Rachel O'Kanis, "Napping Event to Help Students Relax," *News@UW-Madison*, December 9, 2002, http://www.news.wisc.edu/releases/8095.html (accessed October 12, 2003).
31. See "Relaxation and Stress Management: Massage for Massage" at Duke University, http://healthydevil.studentaffairsduke.edu/health_promotion/relaxation_and_stress_management.html (accessed October 14, 2003).
32. Mary Pipher, *Reviving Ophelia: Saving the Selves of Adolescent Girls* (New York: Putnam, 1994), p. 28.
33. Mary Pipher, "Your Child's Mental Health: a conversation with Mary Pipher," WebMD, November 4, 2003, http://my.webmd.com/content/Article/78/95678.htm (accessed June 29, 2004).
34. William Pollack, *Real Boys: Rescuing Our Sons from the Myths of Boyhood* (New York: Henry Holt, 1999), p. xxi.
35. William Pollack with Todd Shuster, *Real Boys' Voices* (New York: Random House, 2000), p. ix.

36. See, for example, J. H. Kashani, G. O. McGee, S. E. Clarkson, et al., "Depression in a Sample of 9-year-old Children: Prevalence and Associated Characteristics," *Archives of General Psychiatry* 40 (1983), pp. 1217–23; E. J. Costello, A. J. Costello, C. Edelbrock, et al., "Psychiatric Disorders in Pediatric Primary Care: Prevalence and Risk Factors," *Archives of General Psychiatry* 45 (1988), pp. 1107–16; R. McGee, M. Feehan, S. Williams, et al., "DSM-III Disorders in a Large Sample of Adolescents," *Journal of the American Academy of Child and Adolescent Psychiatry* 29 (1990), pp. 611–19; E. J. Costello, A. Angold and G. P. Keeler, "Adolescent Outcomes of Childhood Disorders: The Consequences of Severity and Impairment," *Journal of the American Academy of Child and Adolescent Psychiatry* 38 (1999), pp. 121–28; A. J. Oldehinkel, H. U. Wittchen, and P. Schuster, "Prevalence, 20-month Incidence, and Outcome of Unipolar Depressive Disorders in a Community Sample of Adolescents," *Psychological Medicine* 29 (1999), pp. 655–68. See also Linda J. Sax, Jennifer A. Lindolm, Alexander W. Astin, William S. Korn and Kathryn M. Mahoney. *The American Freshman: National Norms for Fall 2002* (Los Angeles: Higher Education Research Institute, UCLA, 2002), p. 12 and Sax et al., *The American Freshman: National Norms for Fall 2003* (Los Angeles: Higher Education Research Institute, UCLA, 2003); Sax et al., *The American Freshman: Thirty-five Year Trends, 1966–2001* (Los Angeles: Higher Education Research Institute, UCLA, 2001).

37. CDC, *Morbidity and Mortality Weekly Report*, 53, no. 22 (June 11, 2004), pp. 471–74; See also, Associated Press, "CDC: Suicide Rate for Children, Teens Drops," CNN.com, June 10, 2004, http://www.cnn.com/2004/HEALTH/06/10/suicide.cdc.ap/ (accessed June 30, 2004).

38. U.S. Department of Health and Human Services, *Mental Health: A Report of the Surgeon General* (Rockville, Md.: U.S. Department of Health and Human Services/Substance Abuse and Mental Health Services Administration/Center for Mental Health Services/National Institutes of Health/National Institute of Mental Health, 1999), pp. 123–24; E. B. Weller, R. A. Weller, and A. K. Danielyan, "Mood Disorders in Prepubertal Children," in *Textbook of Child and Adolescent Psychiatry*, 3rd ed., J. M. Wiener and M. K. Dulcan (Washington, D.C.: American Psychiatric Publishing, 2004).

39. Daniel Offer and Kimberly A. Schonert-Reichl, "Debunking the Myths of Adolescence: Findings from Recent Research," *Journal of the American Academy of Child and Adolescent Psychiatry* 31, no. 6 (1992), pp. 1003–14; For a "new generation" of studies, see for example: A. C. Petersen, B. E. Compas, J. Brooks-Gunn, et al., "Depression in Adolescence," *American Psychologist* 48 (1993), pp.155–68; L. A. Weithorn and S. B. Campbell, "The Competency of Children and Adolescents to Make Informed

Treatment Decisions," *Child Development* 53 (1982), pp. 1589–98; M. J. Quadrel, B. Fischhoff, and W. Davis, "Adolescent (in)Vulnerability," *American Psychologist* 48 (1993), pp. 102–16; T. Grisso et al., "Juvenile Competence to Stand Trial: A Comparison of Adolescents' and Adults' Capabilities as Trial Defendants," *Law & Human Behavior*, in press.

40. Jerald Bachman, Lloyd Johnston, and Patrick O'Malley, *Monitoring the Future: Questionnaire Responses from the Nation's High School Seniors, 2000* (Ann Arbor, Mich.: Survey Research Center, University of Michigan, 2001), p. 159.

41. Duane Alexander in Francine Kiefer, "U.S. Children Near Records for Well-Being," *Christian Science Monitor*, August 18, 2000.

42. Poverty rate for persons under 18 peaked in 1981–1982 at about 23 percent; in 1994 it was about 23 percent; in 2000 it was 16 percent, U.S. Census Bureau, Poverty 2000 Graphs, http://www.census.gov/hhes/poverty/poverty00/povage00.html.

43. According to *Monitoring the Future*, the annual survey of drug use by high schoolers conducted by the federal Substance Abuse and Mental Health Administration, illicit drug use has remained constant or declined over the last seven years. In particular, both annual and previous month use of marijuana, heroin, cocaine, ecstasy, inhalants, and hallucinogens stayed relatively steady since the midnineties and all (except inhalants) declined from 2002 to 2003, the last year for which there were data. Nonmedical use of pain relievers, by contrast, has increased measurably in the past decade from 1 percent in 1991 to 4 percent in 2003. See L. D. Johnston, P. M. O'Malley, and J. G. Bachman, "Ecstasy Use Falls for Second Year in a Row, Overall Teen Drug Use Drops," University of Michigan News and Information Services, December 19, 2003, http://www. monitoringthefuture.org (accessed January 15, 2004).

44. Howard N. Synder, "Juvenile Arrests 2001," *Juvenile Justice Bulletin*, December, 2003, http://www.ncjrs.org/html/ojjdp/201370/contents.html.

45. Horatio Alger Association, *The State of Our Nation's Youth: 2002–2003* (Alexandria, Va.: Horatio Alger Association of Distinguished Americans, 2002), pp. 6, 14.

46. Ibid., pp. 4, 41.

47. Ibid., pp. 3, 20, 46–47.

48. Ibid., pp. 23, 48.

49. Rachel Simmons, *Odd Girl Out: the Hidden Culture of Aggression in Girls* (New York: Harcourt, 2002); Rosalind Wiseman, *Queen Bees and Wannabes: Helping Your Daughter Survive Cliques, Gossip, Boyfriends, and Other Realities of Adolescence* (New York: Crown, 2002).

50. Susannah Meadows, "Meet the GAMMA girls," *Newsweek*, June 3, 2002.
51. *The Oprah Winfrey Show*, February 18, 2002; *The Oprah Winfrey Show*, May 15, 2002; *The Today Show*, April 16, 2002; *Talk of the Nation*, February 27, 2002.
52. ABC News *Nightline*, May 10, 2002.
53. William Damon, in discussion with authors.
54. Michael Lewis, "Coach Fitz's Management Theory," *New York Times Magazine*, March 28, 2004, p. 46.
55. Ibid.
56. Ibid., p. 49.
57. Unnamed mother, Ibid., p. 64.
58. Scott McLeod, Ibid., p. 44.
59. *CBS Evening News*, December 10, 2002.
60. Data as cited in Brown Center on Education Policy, "Part II: Do Students Have Too Much Homework?" in *Brown Center Report on American Education* (Washington, DC: 2003), pp. 19, 21.
61. Ibid., p. 19.
62. Ibid., p. 17.
63. See, for example, Gilbert T. Sewall, "Lost in Action: Are Time-Consuming, Trivializing Activities Displacing the Cultivation of Active Minds?" *American Educator*, Summer 2000.
64. Brown Center, "Do Students Have Too Much Homework?" p. 18.
65. Ibid., p. 24; The American Council on Education at the University of California, Los Angeles publishes an annual survey of attitudes and experiences of college freshman. It shows a steady decline in the amount of time students spend on homework and studying in their senior year of high school. For example, in 1987, 12 percent of college freshmen reported spending 11–15 hours studying during their senior year; by 2002 the number fell to 8 percent. See, *The American Freshman: National Norms for Fall 2002* (Los Angeles: University of California, Higher Education Research Institute, 2003). One explanation is that today's seniors have a lot of extracurricular activity. But if children are really overworked, it is not because of homework.
66. Jean Johnson and Steve Farkas, *Getting By: What American Teenagers Really Think About Their Schools* (New York: Public Agenda, 1997).
67. Ibid., p. 20.
68. Ibid., p. 15.
69. Ibid., p. 35.
70. Denise Clark Pope, *"Doing School:" How We Are Creating a Generation of Stressed Out, Materialistic, and Miseducated Students* (New Haven, Conn.: Yale University Press, 2001).

71. Endorsement, http://www.yale.edu/yup/books/090137.htm (accessed December 12, 2003); (Other leading education scholars agreed. A professor at Columbia found it "powerful . . . and deeply affecting." Another at the University of Wisconsin praises it for its "methodological innovativeness and interpretive sophistication.")

72. Denise Clark Pope, *"Doing School,"* p. 169.

73. Ibid., p. 174.

74. Ibid.

75. Ibid., p. 175.

76. Ibid., p. 6.

77. Ibid., p. 154.

78. Ibid., pp. 156–57.

79. Steve Farkas and Jean Johnson, *Different Drummers: How Teachers of Teachers View Public Education* (New York: Public Agenda, 1997), p. 13.

80. Ibid.

81. E. D. Hirsch Jr., *The Schools We Need: And Why We Don't Have Them* (New York: Doubleday, 1996), p. 245.

82. Suzanne Hidi and Judith M. Harackiewicz, "Motivating the Academically Unmotivated: A Critical Issue for the 21st Century," *Review of Educational Research* 70, no. 2 (2000), pp. 151–79.

83. Ibid.

84. Avi Kaplan and Michael J. Middleton, "Should Childhood Be a Journey or a Race?: Response to Harackiewicz et al.," *Journal of Education Psychology* 94, no. 3 (1994), pp. 646–48.

85. Judith Harackiewicz, in discussion with author Sommers.

86. Thomas D. Snyder with Charlene M. Hoffman and the National Center for Education Statistics, *Digest of Education Statistics, 2002, NCES* (Washington, D.C.: U.S. Department of Education, National Center for Education Statistics, 2003), pp. 222–23, 225.

87. Jean Johnson and Steve Farkas, *Getting By: What American Teenagers Really Think About Their Schools*, p. 13.

88. Roy F. Baumeister, "Violent Pride: Do People Turn Violent Because of Self-Hate, or Self-Love?" *Scientific American* 284, no. 4 (2001), pp. 96–101.

89. See for example Brad J. Bushman and Roy F. Baumeister, "Threatened Egotism, Narcissism, Self-Esteem, and Direct and Displaced Aggression: Does Self-Love or Self-Hate Lead to Violence?" *Journal of Personality and Social Psychology* 75, no. 1 (1998), pp. 219–29; Roy F. Baumeister, Jennifer D. Campbell, Joachim I. Krueger, and Kathleen D. Vohs, "Does High Self-Esteem Cause Better Performance, Interpersonal Success, Happiness, or Healthier Lifestyles?" *Psychological Science in the Public Interest* 4, no. 1 (May 2003), pp. 1–44.

90. Baumeister, et al.

91. Ibid., p. 20.
92. Ibid.
93. Ibid., p. 28.
94. Ibid., p. 25.
95. John Stuart Mill, *Utilitarianism* (Indianapolis: Bobbs-Merrill Company, 1957), pp. 12–14.
96. William James, *The Principles of Psychology, vol. 1* (New York: Dover Publications, 1950), p. 306.
97. John P. Hewitt, *The Myth of Self-Esteem: Finding Happiness and Solving Problems in America* (New York: St. Martin's Press, 1998).
98. Ibid., p. 79.
99. Ibid., p. 85.
100. Karen Stone McCown, Anabel L. Jensen, Joshua M. Freedman and Marsha C. Rideout, *Self-Science: The Emotional Intelligence Curriculum* (San Mateo, Calif.: Six Seconds, 1998).
101. Ibid., p. 64.
102. Ibid.
103. Ibid., p. 150.
104. Ibid., p. 152.
105. J. Bybee, A. Kramer, and E. Zigler, "Is Repression Adaptive? Relationships to Socioemotional Adjustment, Academic Performance, and Self-Image," *American Journal of Orthopsychiatry* 67, no. 1 (1997), pp. 59–69.
106. James Traub, "New York's New Approach," *New York Times*, August 2, 2003, sec. 4A, p. 20.
107. Lucy McCormick Calkins and Shelley Harwayne, *The Writing Workshop: A World of Difference—A Guide for Staff Development* (Portsmouth, N.H.: Heinemann, 1987), p. 21.
108. Ibid.
109. *The Writing Workshop: A World of Difference*, Lucy McCormick Calkins, Shelley Harwayne, and Alex Mitchell, forty min., pub: Heinemann, 1987. Videocassette.
110. Lucy McCormick Calkins and Shelley Harwayne, *The Writing Workshop: A World of Difference-A Guide for Staff Development*, p. 74.
111. Erica, Ibid., p. 85.
112. Jackie Bennett, "Lesson Plan: The World Beyond the Child," *New York Times*, August 9, 2003, sec. A, p. 10.
113. Curriculum Frameworks and Instructional Resources Division, California Department of Education, *Standards for Evaluating Instructional Materials for Social Content*, 2000 edition (Sacramento, Calif.: California Department of Education, 2001), p. iv.
114. Ibid., pp. 3, 4.

115. Gilbert T. Sewall, *Islam and the Textbooks* (New York: American Textbook Council, 2003), p. 30.

116. J. Martin Rochester, "The Training of Idiots: Civics Education in America's Schools," in *Where Did Social Studies Go Wrong?*, ed. James Leming, Lucien Ellington, and Kathleen Porter (Washington, D.C.: Fordham Foundation, 2003), p. 16.

117. Steve Farkas and Jean Johnson, *A Lot to Be Thankful For: What Parents Want Children To Learn About America* (Washington, D.C.: Public Agenda, 1998), p. 19.

118. Ibid., p. 21.

119. Benjamin R. Barber, "Constitutional Faith," in *For Love of Country?: In a New Democracy Forum on the Limits of Patriotism*, Martha C. Nussbaum (Boston: Beacon Press, 2000), p. 32.

120. Lewis Lapham, "The Loss of History: Experience Can't Bind Us if We Don't Remember," *Dallas Morning News*, December 10, 1995, sec. J, p. 5.

121. National Center for Education Statistics, "The Nation's Report Card 2001: U.S. History Highlights, NCES 2002-482," U.S. Department of Education, Office of Educational Research and Improvement, p. 1.

122. Ibid., p. 2.

123. Anne D. Neal and Jerry L. Martin, *Restoring America's Legacy: The Challenge of Historical Literacy in the 21st Century* (Washington, D.C.: American Council of Trustees and Alumni, 2002), Appendix A.

124. Anne D. Neal and Jerry L. Martin, *Restoring America's Legacy*, p. 1.

125. Ibid.

126. William Damon, "What Does Democracy Mean to the Young?," lecture delivered at conference, "Our Country and Our Future: Educating Citizens for Democracy," Washington, D.C., June 12–13, 2001, p. 3.

127. Gilbert T. Sewall, "The Classroom Conquest of World History," *Education Week*, June 13, 2001; Gilbert T. Sewall, *World History Textbooks: A Review* (New York: American Textbook Council, 2004).

128. Gary B. Nash, *American Odyssey: The United States in the Twentieth Century* (New York: Glencoe, 1999), pp. 23–24, in Diane Ravitch, *The Language Police*, p. 153.

129. Amelie A. Walker, "Newsbriefs: Anasazi Cannibalism?" *Archaeology* 50, no. 5 (1997).

130. California *Standards*, p. 5.

131. Connecticut Department of Education, "Fairness Review Criteria for the Connecticut Mastery Test," p. 2.

132. Thomas K. Hearn, "Charge to the Graduates: Truth With a Capital 'T'," speech delivered at the 2000 Wake Forest University Commencement, Winston-Salem, N.C., May 15, 2000.

133. Robert Simon, "Suspending Moral Judgment: The Paralysis of 'Absolutophobia,'" *Chronicle of Higher Education*, June 27, 1997, p. B5.

134. Kay Haugaard, "Suspending Moral Judgment: Students Won't Decry Evil—a Case of Too Much Tolerance?" *Chronicle of Higher Education*, June 27, 1997.

135. NAS/Zogby Poll of College Seniors, "Ethics, Enron, and American Higher Education," findings report, http://www.nas.org/reports/zogethics_poll/zogby_ethics_report.htm.

136. Vidiadhar S. Naipaul, "Our Universal Civilization," lecture delivered at the 1990 Wriston Lecture, The Manhattan Institute for Policy Research, New York City, October 30, 1990.

137. I am grateful to Professor Jeffrey Mirel for bringing the Counts' book to my attention in Jeffrey Mirel, "Defending Democracy," in William J. Bennett, Lamar Alexander, Erich Martel, et al., "How to Teach About Terrorism, Despotism, and Democracy," *Terrorists, Despots, and Democracy: What Our Children Need To Know* (Washington, D.C.: Thomas B. Fordham Foundation, 2003), pp. 53–56.

138. George S. Counts, *The Education of Free Men in American Democracy* (Washington, D.C.: Educational Policies Commission, 1941), p. 27.

139. Ibid., p. 68.

140. Ibid., p. 50.

141. National Education Association, "Remember September 11," http://neahin.org/programs/schoolsafety/september11/materials/lessonhome.htm (accessed September 9, 2002; March 16, 2004).

142. NEA, "Remember September 11: Facing Personal Feelings," Lesson Plan, http://neahin.org/programs/schoolsafety/september11/materials/rm01.htm, http://neahin.org/programs/schoolsafety/september11/materials/rm01/1plan168.htm (accessed March 16, 2004).

143. NEA, "Remember September 11: Sending Liberty and Faith Across the Nation," Lesson Plan, http://neahin.org/programs/schoolsafety/september11/materials/n18.htm (accessed March 20, 2004).

144. NEA, "Remember September 11: Circle of Feelings," Lesson Plan, http://www.neahin.org/programs/schoolsafety/september11/materials/n29.htm (accessed March 16, 2004).

145. Chester E. Finn, "Why This Report?: Introduction," in *Terrorists, Despots, and Democracy: What Our Children Need To Know*, p. 9.

146. Ellen Galinsky, "Preface: Understanding the Goals of *9/11 As History*," in *9/11: Looking Back, Moving Forward*, Lois Backon, Ellen Galinsky, Erin Brownfeld and Kelly Sakai (New York: Families and Work Institute, 2003), p. iii.

147. Families and Work Institute, "About 9/11 As History," http://www.familiesandwork.org/911ah/about911ah.html (accessed May 25, 2004).

148. Ellen Galinksy, "Preface: Understanding the Goals of *9/11 As History*," p. i.
149. This book was part of the Institute's effort to make the curriculum available to educators for future anniversaries and commemorations.
150. Ellen Galinksy, "Preface: Understanding the Goals of *9/11 As History*," p. i.
151. Families and Work Institute with the Anti-Defamation League, "All Kinds of Feelings," Lesson Plan, http://www.familiesandwork.org/911ah/lp_prek-2_adl.html.
152. Ibid.
153. Ibid.
154. Maureen Underwood and Nicci Spinazzola with Families and Work Institute, "Helping People Who Work With Kids Prepare for the 9/11 Anniversary," http://www.familiesandwork.org/911ah/preparation.html.
155. Families and Work Institute with Reading Rainbow, "Everyday Heroes," Lesson Plan, http://www.familiesandwork.org/911ah/lp_prek-2_rr.html.
156. Ibid.
157. Families and Work Institute with Families GOALS Project and Maureen Underwood, "What's Special About Me?" http://www.familiesandwork.org/911ah/lp_prek-2_mu.html.
158. Ibid.
159. Families and Work Institute with Robin Gurwitch, "Building Strength Through Knowledge," Lesson Plan, http://www.familiesandwork.org/911ah/lp_6-8_rg.html.
160. Ellen Galinksy, "Preface: Understanding the Goals of *9/11 As History*," p. ii.
161. Families and Work Institute with Do Something, Inc, "Community Citizens, Community Banner," Lesson Plan, http://www.familiesandwork, org/911ah/1p_6-8_ds.html.
162. Unnamed man in Sylvia Whitman, *Children of the World War II Home Front* (Minneapolis, Minn.: Carolrhoda Books, 2001), p. 29.

2. ESTEEM THYSELF.

1. Daniel Goleman, *Emotional Intelligence* (New York: Bantam, 1995), p. 46.
2. Karen Stone McCown, Anabel L. Jensen, Joshua M. Freedman, and Marsha C. Rideout, *Self-Science: The Emotional Intelligence Curriculum* (San Mateo, Calif.: Six Seconds, 1998), p. 3.
3. Plato, *Apology of Socrates*, ed., trans. Michael C. Stokes (Warminster, England: Aris & Phillips, 1997), pp. 65, 85–87.

4. Suppression is defined as deliberate withholding of emotional expression or tamping down thoughts or internal experience of feelings. Repression was used by Freud to indicate both deliberate and unconscious processes. Confusion stems from the fact that American psychoanalysts tend to use the word repression as an unconscious process. When we use the word repression, we qualify it as either unconscious or deliberate repression.

5. Postwar American psychoanalysis differed from prewar European analysis (which came to a standstill after WWII in Europe as analysts, primarily Jews, fled Germany or perished in concentration camps). European analysis focused on Freud's "id psychology." Id theory was largely focused on primitive sexual and aggressive instincts and frustrations and early traumatic experiences as causing adult problems. In America, the emphasis was on "ego psychology" which focused more intently on the mind's more mature apparatuses—defenses (e.g.: repression, denial, projection, regression, reaction-formation) and adaptation to the demands of society—and paid less attention to instinctual drives. The goal of ego-based psychoanalysis was the delineation and alteration of maladaptive defenses. See A. Cooper, A. Frances and M. Sacks, "The Psychoanalytic Model," in *Psychiatry vol. 1*, ed. R. Michels, J. Cavenar, A. Cooper, et al. (Philadelphia: J. B. Lippincott, 1988), pp. 1–16.

6. William Barrett, "Delmore: A 30's Friendship and Beyond," *Commentary* 58, no. 3 (1974), pp. 41–54.

7. Abraham Maslow in Edward Hoffman, *The Right To Be Human: A Biography of Abraham Maslow* (Los Angeles: Jeremy P. Tarcher, 1988), p. 254.

8. David Frum, *How We Got Here: The 70s—The Decade that Brought You Modern Life (For Better or Worse)* (New York: Basic Books, 2000), p. 101.

9. Abraham Maslow and colleague, in Edward Hoffman, *The Right To Be Human*, p. 206.

10. Abraham Maslow, Ibid., p. 207.

11. Abraham H. Maslow, *Toward A Psychology of Being*, 2nd ed. (New York: D. Van Nostrand, 1968), p. iv.

12. Edward Hoffman, *The Right to Be Human*, p. 258.

13. Abraham Maslow, *Toward A Psychology of Being*, p. iii.

14. Ibid., p. 196.

15. Edward Hoffman, *The Right To Be Human*, p. 155.

16. Abraham Maslow, Ibid., p. 185.

17. Abraham H. Maslow, *Toward A Psychology of Being*, 2nd ed., p. 4.

18. Ibid., p. 6.

19. Abraham Maslow in, Edward Hoffman, *The Right To Be Human*, p. 188.

20. Ibid.

21. Abraham Maslow, Ibid., p. 172.

22. Ibid.
23. Ibid., p. 298.
24. Abraham H. Maslow, *Toward A Psychology of Being*, 2nd ed., p. 3.
25. Abbie Hoffman, *The Autobiography of Abbie Hoffman* (New York: Four Walls Eight Windows, 2000), p. 26.
26. Abraham Maslow in Joyce Milton, *The Road to Malpsychia: Humanistic Psychology and Our Discontents* (San Francisco: Encounter Books, 2002), p. 170.
27. Ibid., p. 63.
28. Abraham Maslow in Edward Hoffman, *The Right To Be Human*, p. 266.
29. Nor did he publicly condemn Leary's proselytizing for drugs. In 1965, Leary and his associate Richard Alpert (later Baba Ram Dass) were charged with ethics violations for dispensing drugs in their experiments and threatened with expulsion from the American Psychological Association. Maslow, then president of the association, kept his distance from the proceedings. Eventually the charges were mysteriously dropped. In his journal, Maslow clearly took the side of Leary and Alpert as innovators: "Maybe I have to write a code of ethics for revolutionary science," he mused. As late as 1967, after the dangerous fatuity of such "revolutionary science" could no longer be denied, Maslow continued to defend the practice of experimenting with psychedelic drugs. See Ibid., p. 282.
30. Jane Howard, *Please Touch: A Guided Tour of the Human Potential Movement* (New York: Delta, 1970), p. 10.
31. Abraham Maslow in Edward Hoffman, *The Right To Be Human*, p. 293.
32. Ibid., p. 302.
33. Ibid., p. 312.
34. For an excellent history of Synanon see Rod A. Janzen, *The Rise and Fall of Synanon: A California Utopia* (Baltimore, Md.: Johns Hopkins University Press, 2001).
35. The bitten lawyer survived and in 1980 Dederich was forced to give up leadership of Synanon.
36. Abraham Maslow, Joyce Milton, *The Road to Malpsychia*, p. 175.
37. See for example, John P. Hewitt, *The Myth of Self-Esteem: Finding Happiness and Solving Problems in America* (New York: St. Martin's Press, 1998); Roy F. Baumeister, Jennifer D. Campbell, Joachim I. Krueger, and Kathleen D. Vohs, "Does High Self-Esteem Cause Better Performance, Interpersonal Success, Happiness, or Healthier Lifestyles?," *Psychological Science in the Public Interest* 4, no. 1 (2003), pp. 1–44; Joyce Milton, *Malpsychia*.
38. Carl R. Rogers, *On Becoming A Person: A Therapist's View of Psychotherapy* (Boston: Houghton Mifflin, 1995), p. 357.
39. Carl Rogers, *On Encounter Groups* (New York: Harrow, 1973), p. 121.
40. Carl R. Rogers, *On Becoming A Person*, p. 119.

41. Carl Rogers and H. Jerome Freiberg, *Freedom To Learn*, 3rd ed. (Upper Saddle River, N.J.: Merrill, 1994), p. 158.
42. Ibid., p. 215.
43. Carl R. Rogers, *On Becoming A Person*, pp. 74–75.
44. Carl Rogers, *On Encounter Groups*, p. 22.
45. Ibid.
46. Carl R. Rogers, *On Becoming A Person*, p. 15.
47. Carl Rogers, *On Encounter Groups*, p. 174.
48. Carl R. Rogers, *On Becoming A Person*, p. 194.
49. Frank Furedi, *Therapy Culture: Cultivating Vulnerability in an Uncertain Age* (London: Routledge, 2004), p. 107.
50. Carl Rogers, *On Encounter Groups*, p. 11.
51. Frank Furedi, *Therapy Culture*, p. 107.
52. Abraham H. Maslow, *Toward A Psychology of Being*, 2nd ed., p. 5.
53. Abraham H. Maslow, *Religions, Values, and Peak Experiences* (New York: Viking, 1970), p. 37.
54. Jane Howard, *Please Touch*, pp. 15–16.
55. George Leonard, *Education and Ecstasy With "The Great School Reform Hoax"* (Berkeley, Calif.: North Atlantic, 1987), pp. 193–211.
56. Ibid., pp. 207–9.
57. George Leonard, "Human Potential: The Movement, the Media, the Myth," *Noetic Sciences Review*, Autumn 1993.
58. Jean Huston in Kenneth L. Woodward, "Getting Your Head Together," *Newsweek*, September 6, 1976.
59. George Steiner in Jane Howard, *Please Touch*, p. 234.
60. Ibid.
61. Richard Dean Rosen, *Psychobabble: Fast Talk and Quick Cure in the Era of Feeling* (New York: Scribner, 1977); Martin L. Gross, *The Psychological Society: A Critical Analysis of Psychiatry, Psychotherapy, Psychoanalysis, and the Psychological Revolution* (New York: Random House, 1978).

3. SIN TO SYNDROME.

1. Mark Steyn, "Mohammed Atta and His Federal Loan Officer: No Matter How Dumb He Was, Officialdom Was Always Dumber," *National Post (Canada)*, June 10, 2002, sec. A, p. 18; John Leo, "Going Soft in the Head," *U.S. News & World Report*, June 24, 2002, p. 47.
2. ABC, *World News Tonight*, June 6, 2002.
3. Mohammed Atta, Ibid.
4. Steyn, "Mohammed Atta and His Federal Loan Officer."
5. Alan Wolfe, *Moral Freedom: The Search for Virtue in a World of Choice* (New York: W. W. Norton, 2001); Alan Wolfe, "The Final Freedom," *New York Times Magazine*, March 18, 2001, sec. 6, p. 48.

6. Alan Wolfe, *Moral Freedom*, p. 145.
7. Ibid., p. 190.
8. Kelly in Ibid., p. 87.
9. Rosalyn in Ibid.
10. Ibid., p. 83.
11. Alan Wolfe, "The Pursuit of Autonomy," *New York Times Magazine*, May 7, 2000, sec. 6, p. 53.
12. Interview with Frederick S. Berlin, M.D., Ph.D., United States Conference of Catholic Bishops, Office of Communications, http://www.usccb.org/comm/kit6.htm (accessed September 16, 2003).
13. *Boston Globe* investigative staff, *Betrayal: The Crisis in the Catholic Church* (Boston: Little, Brown, 2003), pp. 172–75.
14. Ibid., p. 173; "Catholic Clergy; Sins of the Fathers," *Economist*, July 18, 1992, p. 28.
15. Daniel J. Wakin, "Confronting His Abuser, on Tape; Voice of Anguish Demands Remorse of Priest and Bishop," *New York Times*, February 23, 2003, sec. 1, p. 35. According to Oathout, the abuse began when he was nine years old; Father Bentley claims that Oathout was ten or eleven.
16. Ibid.
17. For full report on the church crisis, especially the notorious Father Geoghan case, see *Boston Globe* investigative staff, *Betrayal: The Crisis in the Catholic Church*.
18. *Boston Globe* investigative staff, *Betrayal: The Crisis in the Catholic Church*, pp. 35, 51–52. See also Barry Werth, "Father's Helper: How the Church Used Psychiatry to Care For and Protect Abusive Priests," *The New Yorker* June 9, 2003, p. 61.
19. Michael Rezendes, "Spotlight: Geoghan Papers; Memos Offer Split View of Priest; Medical Records Contrast on Risk," *Boston Globe*, January 24, 2002, sec. A, p. 1.
20. Cardinal Bernard Law, "Cardinal Law's Pilot Column: Restoring Hope to Broken Hearts and Minds," *The Pilot*, July 27, 2001, http://www.rcab.org/pilotlaw/Column072701.html.
21. Richard John Neuhaus, "The Public Square: Scandal Time," *First Things* 122 (2002), http://www.firstthings.com/ftissues/ft0204/public.html#scandal.
22. Philip Jenkins, "Opinion: The Uses of Clerical Scandal," *First Things*, 60 (1996), http://www.firstthings.com/ftissues/ft9602/opinion/opinion.html.
23. Erica Noonan and Sacha Pfeiffer, "In Meeting With Victims, Law Begs Forgiveness; Private Talk Marked by Tears and Anger," *Boston Globe*, October 30, 2002, sec. A, p. 1.

24. Cardinal Bernard Law in David D. Haskell, "Cardinal Law Offers Sex-Abuse Apology," *United Press International*, November 4, 2002.
25. Charles Krauthammer, "Why Didn't the Church Call the Cops?" *Washington Post*, June 7, 2002, sec. A, p. 27.
26. Ibid.
27. Ibid.
28. William Donahue in *Boston Globe* investigative staff, *Betrayal: The Crisis in the Catholic Church*, p. 112.
29. Cardinal Law in Ibid., p. 14.
30. Father Geoghan in Ibid., p. 25.
31. Daniel Goleman, *Emotional Intelligence* (New York: Bantam, 1995), pp. 13–14.
32. Ibid., p. 14.
33. Theodore Dalrymple, *Life at the Bottom: The Worldview That Makes the Underclass* (Chicago: Ivan R. Dee, 2001), p. 9.
34. Ibid.
35. Ibid., p. 10.
36. Ibid.
37. Ibid., p. 8.
38. Harry Weber, "Lawyer to Argue Insanity for Suspect," *Associated Press*, November 30, 2001.
39. Kathryn Marchocki, "Parker Cuts Murder Deal: Teens' Defense Strategies Shed No Clues On 'Why?'" *Union Leader* (Manchester, N.H.), December 4, 2001, sec. A, p. 1.
40. Ron Powers, "The Apocalypse of Adolescence," *Atlantic Monthly*, March 2002.
41. Ibid.
42. U.S. Census Bureau, "Sex by Age [209]" for Vermont; Vermont Department of Corrections Report, "Age Distribution: Incarcerated Population Number by Age Cohort."
43. Ron Powers, "The Apocalypse of Adolescence."
44. Harry R. Weber, "Expert: New Details in Dartmouth Professor Slayings May Jeopardize Teen's Insanity Defense," Associated Press, February 20, 2001.
45. Dr. Deborah Yurgelin-Todd in Julie Blair and Debra Viadero, "Research Notes: Teenage Decisionmaking," *Education Week* 18, no. 2 (1998); http://www.edweek.org/ew/vol-18/02rnotes.h18 (accessed June 14, 2004).
46. Daniel R. Weinberger, "A Brain Too Young for Good Judgment," *New York Times*, March 10, 2001, sec. A, p. 13.
47. Ibid.

48. Steven Pinker, *The Blank Slate: The Modern Denial of Human Nature* (New York: Viking, 2002).

49. Ibid., p. 175.

50. Ibid., p. 176.

51. *King Lear* 1.2.107–115.

52. James Boswell, *Life of Samuel Johnson* (New York: Borzoi/Knopf, 1992), p. 833.

53. Sidney Hook, "Necessity, Indeterminism, and Sentimentalism," in *Determinsim and Freedom*, ed. Sidney Hook (New York: Collier, 1961), p. 189.

54. Cited in Steven Pinker, *The Blank Slate*, p. 179.

55. Steven Pinker, *The Blank Slate*, p. 180.

56. Ibid., p. 183.

57. Alan M. Dershowitz, *The Abuse Excuse: And Other Cop-outs, Sob Stories, and Evasions of Responsibility* (Boston: Little, Brown, 1994); James Q. Wilson, *Moral Judgment: Does the Abuse Excuse Threaten Our Legal System?* (New York: Basic Books, 1997).

58. Alan M. Dershowitz, *The Abuse Excuse*, pp. 321–41.

59. Ibid., title of Part One, p. 43.

60. James Q. Wilson, *Moral Judgment*, p. 2.

61. Ibid., p. 77.

62. Alan M. Dershowitz, *The Abuse Excuse*, p. 4.

63. James Q. Wilson, *Moral Judgment*, p. 43.

64. B. Vastag, "Addiction Poorly Understood by Clinicians—Experts Say Attitudes, Lack of Knowledge Hinder Treatment," *Journal of the American Medical Association* 290 (2003), pp. 1299–1303.

65. Ibid., p. 1299.

66. Alan I. Leshner, "Addiction is a Brain Disease," *The Addiction Recovery Guide*, http://www.addictionrecoveryguide.org/articles/article151.html (accessed September 18, 2003).

67. John Schwarzlose, president of the Betty Ford Center and member of the partnership for Recovery, a coalition of three of the nation's most respected nonprofit alcohol and drug dependency providers, claims that "People don't stay addicted because they choose to or somehow are weak-willed;" see http://partnershipforrecovery.org/who.htm (accessed September 15, 2003).

68. Committee to Identify Strategies to Raise the Profile of Substance Abuse and Alcoholism Research, *Dispelling the Myths About Addiction: Strategies to Increase Understanding and Strengthen Research* (Washington DC: National Academy of Science, 1997).

69. John Walters in Quynh-Giang Tran, "Drug Policy Chief Looks to the Root of Addiction: U.S. Eyes 10% Reduction in Abuse in Two Years," *Boston Globe*, July 10, 2002, sec. A, p. 3.

70. Bill Moyers Sr. in NBC News: *Meet the Press*, March 29, 1998.
71. *Interdiction and Incarceration Still Top Remedies* (Pew Research Center for People and the Press, March 21, 2001)—Question: All in all, should drug use be treated more like a crime or like a disease? Answer: 35 percent crime, 52 percent disease, 9 percent both, 4 percent don't know/neither. *Harvard School of Public Health/Robert Wood Johnson Foundation Study of Americans' Attitudes Toward Illicit Drugs Treatment and Alcohol Treatment*, July 15, 1999—Question: What do you think is the main reason people abuse alcohol/drugs? Answer: 31 percent/21 percent (alcohol percent/drug percent) physical or psychological disease, 18 percent/25 percent character or moral problem, 37 percent/37 percent social or economic condition, 10 percent/18 percent don't know or refused.
72. Ernest Kurtz, *Not God: A History of Alcoholics Anonymous* (Center City, Md.: Hazelden Information and Educational Services, 1998).
73. "How It Works" in *Alcoholics Anonymous Big Book* (New York: Alcoholics Anonymous World Services, 1991), ch. 5.
74. A. Leshner, "Addiction is a Brain Disease, and It Matters," *Science* 278 (1997), pp. 45–47.
75. Positron Emission Tomography (PET scan)
76. S. Satel and F. K. Goodwin, *Is Drug Addiction a Brain Disease?* (Washington D.C.: Ethics and Public Policy Center, 1998), p. 1.
77. Steven Hyman, M.D., in discussion with author Satel, April 14, 2004.
78. R. D. Weiss, M. L. Griffin, C. Mazurick, et al., "The Relationship Between Cocaine Craving, Psychological Treatment, and Subsequent Cocaine Use," *American Journal of Psychiatry* 160 (2003), pp. 1320–25.
79. Daniel Shapiro, Ph.D., presentation entitled "Addiction, Responsibility, and Drug Policy" at the University of Minnesota at Morris, May 1997.
80. William R. Uttal, *The New Phrenology: The Limits of Localizing Cognitive Processes in the Brain* (Cambridge, Mass.: MIT Press, 2003).
81. Gene M. Heyman, "Is Addiction a Chronic Relapsing Disease?" in *Drug Addiction and Drug Policy*, ed, Philip B. Heymann and William N. Brownsberger (Cambridge, Mass.: Harvard University Press, 2001), p. 82.
82. Ibid., pp. 81–99.
83. Nora Volkow in Guy Gugliotta, "Revolutionary Thinker; Leon Trotsky's Great-Granddaughter Is Following Her Own Path to Greatness," *Washington Post*, August 21, 2003, sec. C, p. 1.
84. Glen R. Hanson, "How Casual Drug Use Leads to Addiction—The "Oops" Phenomenon," *Atlanta Inquirer* 41, no. 5 (July 13, 2002), p. 4.
85. Jacob Sullum, *Saying Yes: In Defense of Drug Use* (New York: Tarcher-Putnam, 2003), p. 235.
86. A. T. McLellan, D. C. Lewis, C. P. O'Brien, and H. D. Kleber, "Drug Dependence—A Chronic Medical Disease: Implications for Treat-

ment, Insurance, and Outcome Evaluation," *Journal of the American Medical Association* 284, no. 3 (2000), pp. 1689–95.

87. D. B. Marlowe and D. S. DeMatteo, "Drug Policy by Analogy: Well, It's Like This . . . ," *Psychiatric Services* 54, no. 11 (2003), pp. 1455–56.

88. A. T. McLellan et al., "Drug Dependence—A Chronic Medical Disease: Implications for Treatment, Insurance, and Outcome Evaluation,"; R. Bonnie, "Addiction and Responsibility," *Social Research* 63, no. 3 (2001), pp. 813–35; Join Together Panel, *Ending Discrimination Against People with Drug and Alcohol Problems*, published by Join Together, a project of the Boston University School of Public Health, with the assistance of the American Bar Association's Standing Committee on Substance Abuse, April, 2003, http://www.jointogether. org/sa/files/pdf/discrimination.pdf (accessed January 20, 2004).

89. Jenifer Warren, "California Propositions; Vote Backing Treatment for Drug Offenders; Campaign Funding Limits are Winning. Retirement Benefits for Legislators are Headed for Defeat," *Los Angeles Times*, November 8, 2000, sec. A, p. 1.

90. Medication like methadone, which quell withdrawal symptoms from heroin such as nausea, muscle cramps, and chills, can be very helpful— but they involve the patient in the conscious decision to take it.

91. Kenneth J. Bender, "ASAM Conference Attendees Consider Addiction Treatment Developments," *Psychiatric Times*, February 1, 2003, p. 82.

92. Such common sense appears in a paper by two prominent clinician- researchers called "Cocaine Dependence: A Disease of the Brain's Reward System" yet it's a title that practically regards addiction as a neurological condition. The paper concludes with a thoughtful section on treatment that regards the patient as anything but passive; C. A. Dackis and C. P. O'Brien, "Cocaine Dependence: A Disease of the Brain's Reward System," *Journal of Substance Abuse Treatment*, 21, no. 3 (2001), pp. 111–117.

93. Herbert Fingarette, *Heavy Drinking: The Myth of Alcoholism as a Disease* (Berkeley, Calif.: University of California Press, 1989).

94. S. T. Higgins and K. Silverman, eds., *Motivating Behavior Change Among Illicit-Drug Abusers: Research on Contingency Management Interventions* (Washington, D.C.: American Psychological Association, 1999).

95. Steven Belenko, *Research on Drug Courts: A Critical Review, 2001 Update* (New York: The National Center on Addiction and Substance Abuse (CASA) at Columbia University, 2001), http://www.casacolumbia. org/absolutenm/articlefiles/researchondrug.pdf (accessed April 15, 2004).

96. L. N. Robins, J. E. Helzer, M. Hesselbrock, and E. Wish, "Vietnam Veterans Three Years After Vietnam: How Our Study Changed Our View of Heroin," in *The Yearbook of Substance Use and Abuse, Vol. 2*, ed.

Leon Brill and Charles Winick (New York: Human Sciences Press, 1980), pp. 213–30.

97. Jane E. Brody, "Addiction: A Brain Ailment, Not a Moral Lapse," *New York Times*, September 30, 2003, sec. F, p. 8.

98. D. Marlowe "Integrating Substance Abuse Treatment and Criminal Justice Supervision." *Science and Practice Perspectives* August 2, no. 1 (2003), pp. 4–14; George E. Vaillant "If Addiction is Involuntary, How Can Punishment Help?" in *Drug Addiction and Drug Policy*.

99. A. Leshner, "Addiction is a Brain Disease, and It Matters," p. 47. Steven Belenko, *Research on Drug Courts: A Critical Review* (New York: The National Center on Addiction and Substance Abuse at Columbia University, 2001). A. Harrell, "Drug Courts and the Role of Graduated Sanctions," Research in Progress Seminar Series (Washington, D.C.: National Institute of Justice, 1998). S. T. Higgins and K. Silverman, ed., *Motivating Behavior Change Among Illicit-Drug Abusers: Research on Contingency Management Interventions* (Washington, D.C.: American Psychological Association, 1999).

4. EMOTIONAL CORRECTNESS.

1. Molly Ivins, "Who Needs Breasts, Anyway?" *Time*, February 18, 2002, p. 58.

2. Wendy Kaminer, *I'm Dysfunctional, You're Dysfunctional: The Recovery Movement and Other Self-Help Fashions* (New York: Vintage Books, 1993), p. 30.

3. Ibid., p. 31.

4. Lauren Slater, "Repress Yourself," *New York Times Magazine*, February 23, 2003.

5. Slater uses the term "repression" to refer to the conscious tamping down of particular thoughts and feelings rather than to a defensive process that operates outside of awareness. Freud used the term interchangeably. Slater might have used the word suppression (which refers to a conscious process only), but the article made her meaning clear.

6. *New York Times Magazine* discussion forum, entry 38 of 135, dated February 23, 2003.

7. *Ibid.*, entry 30 of 135.

8. J. R. Marshall, "The Expression of Feelings," *Archives of General Psychiatry* 27, no. 6 (1972), pp. 786–90.

9. Ibid., p. 786.

10. Charles Darwin, *The Expression of the Emotions in Man and Animals*, 3rd ed. (New York: Oxford University Press, 1998), pp. 359–60.

11. Almost fifty years ago psychologist Seymour Feshbach encouraged a

group of normal little boys to kick furniture and play with toy guns and generally run wild. Subsequently, they behaved much more aggressively during their free play times than they did before permission to run amok; see S. Feshbach, "The Catharsis Hypothesis and Some Consequences of Interaction with Aggression and Neutral Play Objects," *Journal of Personality and Social Psychology* 24 (1956), pp. 449–62; Shahbaz Khan Mallick and Boyd R. McCandless, "A Study of Catharsis Aggression," *Journal of Personality and Social Psychology* 4 (1966), pp. 591–96. A few years later psychologist R. Hornberger examined anger in adults. His subjects were insulted by a designated provoker and half of them instructed to pound nails into an object for about ten minutes. The other subjects did nothing. Next, all participants were given a chance to criticize the person who taunted them. Unexpectedly, the pounders, presumably having "released" their anger, were more hostile toward the person who insulted them than the nonpounders; see R. Hornberger, "The Differential Reduction of Aggressive Responses as a Function of Interpolated Activities," *American Psychology* 14 (1959), p. 354, abstract.

12. Albert Bandura in B. J. Bushman, "Does Venting Anger Feed or Extinguish the Flame? Catharsis, Rumination, Distraction, Anger, and Aggressive Responding," *Personality and Social Psychology Bulletin* 28 (2002), pp. 724–31.

13. Leonard Berkowitz, "The Case for Bottling Up Rage," *Psychology Today*, July 1973, p. 31; Leonard Berkowitz, "Experimental Investigations of Hostility Catharsis," *Journal of Consulting and Clinical Psychology* 35 (1970), pp. 1–7.

14. Carol Tavris, *Anger: The Misunderstood Emotion* (New York: Touchstone Books, 1989).

15. Jon G. Allen, *Coping with Trauma: A Guide to Self-Understanding* (Washington, D.C.: American Psychiatric Press, 1995), p. 237.

16. S. M. Southwick, C. A. Morgan III, and R. Rosenberg, "Social Sharing of Gulf War Experiences. Association with Trauma-Related Psychological Symptoms," *Journal of Nervous and Mental Disease* 188 (2000), pp. 695–700.

17. S. Nolen-Hoeksema and J. Morrow, "A Prospective Study of Depression and Posttraumatic Stress Symptoms After A Natural Disaster: The 1989 Loma Prieta Earthquake," *Journal of Personality and Social Psychology* 61, no. 1 (1991), pp. 115–21.

18. T. D. Borkovec and E. Costello, "Efficacy of Applied Relaxation and Cognitive Behavioral Therapy in the Treatment of Generalized Anxiety Disorder," *Journal of Consulting and Clinical Psychology* 61 (1993), pp. 611–19; Bernard Rime, "Mental Rumination, Social Sharing, and the Recovery From Emotional Exposure," in *Emotion, Disclosure, and Health*, ed. James W. Pennebaker (Washington, D.C.: American Psychological

Association, 1995), pp. 271–92; P. P. Schnurr, J. D. Ford, M. J. Friedman et al., "PTSD in Word War II Mustard Gas Test Participants: A Preliminary Report," *Annals of the New York Academy of Science* 821 (1997), pp. 425–29; R. Tait and R. C. Silver, "Coming to Terms with Major Negative Life Events," in *Unintended Thought*, ed. John A. Bargh and James S. Uleman (New York: Guilford Press 1989), pp. 351–82.

19. John Stuart Mill, *Autobiography* (New York: Penguin, 1989), pp. 117–18.
20. Notably, Mill biographers believe that his encounter with depression created a need to reconcile the intellectual, rational self with the feeling self and thus led to a broader definition of liberalism. See Bruce Mazlish, *James and John Stuart Mill* (New York: Basic Books, 1975); J. Geller, "A Crisis in My Mental History," *Psychiatric Services* 54, no. 10 (2003), pp. 1347–49.
21. D. Spiegel, H. Kraemer, J. Bloom, and E. Gottheil, "Effect of Psychosocial Treatment on Survival of Patients With Metastatic Breast Cancer," *Lancet* 2 (1989), pp. 888–91.
22. Ralph W. Moss, *Cancer Therapy: The Independent Consumer's Guide to Non-Toxic Treatment and Prevention* (New York: Equinox, 1993), pp. 448–50; Margie Levine, *Surviving Cancer: One Woman's Story and Her Inspiring Program for Anyone Facing a Cancer Diagnosis* (New York: Broadway, 2001), p. 100; Dean King and Jonathan Pearlroth, *Cancer Combat: Cancer Survivors Share Their Guerrilla Tactics to Help You Win the Fight of Your Life* (New York: Bantam Doubleday Dell, 1998), p. 332; David Simon, *Return to Wholeness: Embracing Body, Mind, and Spirit in the Face of Cancer* (New York: John Wiley & Sons, 1999); Natalie Davis Spingarn, *New Cancer Survivors: Living with Grace, Fighting with Spirit* (Baltimore: Johns Hopkins University Press, 1999), p. 110; John W. Diamond, Burton Goldberg, and Lee W. Cowlden, *Cancer Diagnosis: What to do Next* (Berkeley, Calif.: Ten Speed Press, 2000), p. 30; Barbara Leckritz, *Adult Leukemia: A Comprehensive Guide For Patients and Families* (New York: O'Reilly & Associates, 2001), p. 327.
23. Marlene McKenna and Tom Monte, *When Hope Never Dies* (New York: Kensington Publishing, 2000), p. 208; also note that Spiegel's study said nothing about women who "avoid" therapy; all subjects in the Spiegel study were willing to be randomly assigned to therapy. In fact, the initial study was conducted in the mid-1970s, before participation in group therapy was part of the popular medical ethos. Thus, there is little reason to assume that patients randomized to the control group were distressed or feeling they were missing out because they were not assigned to the groups. Spiegel had even noted that his team had to work to encourage the group therapy patients to participate. See B. Fox, "A Hypothesis About Spiegel et al.'s 1989 Paper on Psychosocial Intervention and Breast Cancer Survival," *Psycho-oncology* 7 (1998), pp. 361–70.
24. Daniel Goleman, *Emotional Intelligence: Why it Can Matter More Than IQ*

(New York: Bantam, 1995), p. 180; According to Goleman, Dr. Jimmie Holland, the chief of psychiatric oncology at Sloan-Kettering told him "Every cancer patient should be in a group like this." See Ibid., p. 181. When we asked Dr. Jimmie Holland about her quotations, she said "I don't recall telling anyone that everyone should have been in a group like Spiegel's." Holland, in discussion with author Satel, July 1, 2003.

25. Goleman, *Emotional Intelligence*, p. 181.
26. It is not clear that the women in the therapy group lived especially long compared to expected longevity; if anything, members of the control group may have suffered unusually quick demise relative to expected longevity. Some oncologists think that the significant result came about because the controls died very quickly, much more rapidly than most breast cancer patients at their stage, according to epidemiological data. This suggests that Spiegel's control group was an unrepresentative sample of patients with metastatic breast cancer; see W. Sampson, "Inconsistencies and Errors in Alternative Medicine Research," *Skeptical Inquirer* 21, no. 5 (1997), pp. 35–38; B. Fox, "A Hypothesis about Spiegel et al.'s 1989 Paper on Psychosocial Intervention and Breast Cancer Survival," pp. 361–70; W. Sampson, "Controversies in Cancer and the Mind: Effects of Psychosocial Support," *Seminars in Oncology* 29, no. 6 (2002), pp. 595–600.
27. A. S. Relman, and M. Angell, "Resolved: Psychosocial Interventions Can Improve Clinical Outcomes in Organic Disease (Con)," *Psychosomatic Medicine* 64 (2002), pp. 558–63; Relman also discussed a study by I. F. Fawzy et al. on the effects of group therapy on longevity in patients with malignant melanoma. Fawzy did find a life-prolonging effect, but his sample was relatively small (thirty-four patients per group), there were relatively few deaths and, more important, his group did not report data on patients who dropped out of the study, thus making it difficult to interpret. See I. F. Fawzy, N. W. Fawzy, C. S. Hyun, et al., "Malignant Melanoma: Effects of Early Structured Psychiatric Intervention, Coping, and Affective State on Recurrence and Survival Six Years Later," *Archives of General Psychiatry* 50 (1993), pp. 681–89.
28. P. Goodwin, M. Leszcz, M. Ennis, et al., "The Effect of Group Psychosocial Support on Survival in Metastatic Breast Cancer," *New England Journal of Medicine* 345 (2001), pp. 1719–26.
29. Certain imbalances emerged later in the study (e.g.: progesterone receptor–positive tumors) but they favored longer survival in the intervention group.
30. P. Goodwin et al., "The Effect of Group Psychosocial Support on Survival in Metastatic Breast Cancer," p. 1721.
31. Note that all women in the study were agreeable to being in a therapy

group but knew they might not be assigned to it once randomization procedure took place. The study says nothing about the outcomes of women who refused to enter the study: either they did not want to be in a group at all, or they insisted on being in a group and did not want to risk randomization to the no-therapy condition. In any case, we know from Goodwin's study that women who were interested in being in group therapy benefited in terms of pain and emotional distress if they were assigned to therapy. If a woman was not bothered by much pain or was not significantly distressed, her pain and mood ratings did not change no matter which group she was assigned to.

32. C. Classen, L. Butler, C. Koopman, et al., "Supportive-Expressive Group Therapy and Distress in Patients with Metastatic Breast Cancer," *Archives of General Psychiatry* 58 (2001), pp. 494–501; B. L. Andersen, "Biobehavioral Outcomes Following Psychological Interventions for Cancer Patients," *Journal of Consulting and Clinical Psychology* 70 (2002), pp. 590–610.

33. T. Kuchler, D. Henne-Burns, S. Rappat, K. Holst, et al., "Impact of Psychotherapeutic Support on Gastrointestinal Cancer Patients Undergoing Surgery: Survival Results of a Trial," *Hepatogastroenterology* 46 (1999), pp. 322–35; R. McCorkle, N. E. Strumpf, I. F. Nuamah et al., "A Specialized Home Care Intervention Improves Survival Among Older Post-Surgical Cancer Patients," *Journal of the American Geriatrics Society*, 48 (2000), pp. 1707–13; J. L. Richardson, D. R. Shelton, M. Krailo, et al., "The Effect of Compliance with Treatment on Survival Among Patients with Hematologic Malignancies," *Journal of Clinical Oncology* 8 (1990), pp. 356–64.

34. There were no important differences in resource utilization (treatment, diagnostic tests, palliation) between the study groups, Pamela Goodwin, in discussion with author Satel; data presented at the annual meeting of American Society of Clinical Oncologists, June 3–8, 2004, New Orleans, Louisiana.

35. Two other studies on metastatic breast cancer published in the journal *Psycho-oncology* several years prior to the Goodwin study also found no effect on survival. Though informative, they received less notice because they were smaller studies and did not take similar pains to replicate the much-touted 1989 Spiegel study. These were: A. Cunningham, C. Edmonds, G. Jenkins, et al., "A Randomized Controlled Trial of the Effects of Group Psychological Therapy on Survival in Women with Metastatic Breast Cancer," *Psycho-oncology* 7 (1998), pp. 508–17; S. Edelman, D. Bell, and A. Kidman, "A Group Cognitive Behaviour Therapy Programme with Metastatic Breast Cancer Patients," *Psycho-oncology* 8 (1999),

pp. 295–305; see also L. Ross, E. Boesen, S. Dalton, and C. Johanson, "Mind and Cancer: Does Psychosocial Intervention Improve Survival and Psychological Well-being?" *European Journal of Cancer* 38, no. 11 (2002), pp. 1447–57, ("the question of whether psychosocial intervention among cancer patients has a beneficial effect remains unresolved," Ibid., p. 1447.) Dr. Spiegel has speculated that the failure of Goodwin to find an effect is due to improvements in chemotherapy, radiation, and hormonal treatments that have accrued since his data were collected in the 1970s and which may overwhelm any life-prolonging effects of emotional support from group therapy. Also, he suggests, the climate of stigma against cancer has also declined greatly since the 1970s such that women get support from friends and family even if they do not go to groups—support that could even out survival effects in experimental and control subjects. See D. Spiegel, "Effects of Psychotherapy on Cancer Survival," *Nature Reviews* 2 (2002), pp. 1–7.

36. Gina Kolata, "Cancer Study Finds Support Groups Do Not Extend Life," *New York Times*, December 13, 2001, sec. A, p. 36.

37. S. Newell, R. Sanson-Fisher and N. Savolainen, "Systematic Review of Psychological Therapies for Cancer Patients: Overview and Recommendations for Future Research Should be Required in this Field," *Journal of the National Cancer Institute* 94, no. 8 (2002), pp. 558–84. A substantial minority of cancer patients now seek psychosocial treatment with the belief that an improvement in their survival time will be the result. See M. Miller, M. J. Boyer, P. N. Butow, et al., "The Use of Unproven Methods of Treatment by Cancer Patients: Frequency, Expectations, and Cost," *Support Care Cancer* 6 (1998), pp. 337–47.

38. Sharon Sorenson and Suzanne Metzger, *The Complete Idiot's Guide to Living with Breast Cancer* (Indianapolis: Alpha Books, 2000), p. 209.

39. N. Frasure-Smith, F. Lespérance, G. Gravel, et al., "Long-Term Survival Differences Among Low-Anxious, High-Anxious, and Repressive Copers Enrolled in the Montreal Heart Attack Readjustment Trial," *Psychosomatic Medicine* 64 (2002), pp. 571–79.

40. Jimmie Holland in Kathy LaTour, "Breast Cancer and Support Groups: Balancing Facts," *Cure*, Summer 2002, pp. 44–49.

41. J. Holland and S. Lewis, *The Human Side of Cancer: Living With Hope, Coping With Uncertainty* (New York: Quill, 2001).

42. Ibid., p. 148.

43. Kolata, "Cancer Study Finds Support Groups Do Not Extend Life," sec. A, p. 36.

44. Ibid.

45. S. C. Palmer, J. C. Coyne, "Examining the Evidence that Psychotherapy Improves the Survival of Cancer Patients," *Biological Psychiatry* 56, no. 1 (2004), pp. 61–62.

46. S. Green, "Can Alternative Treatments Induce Immune Surveillance Over Cancer in Humans?" *Scientific Review of Alternative Medicine* 4 (2000), pp. 6–9; B. R. Cassileth, W. P. Walsh, E. J. Lusk, et al., "Psychosocial Correlates of Survival in Advanced Malignant Disease," *New England Journal of Medicine* 312 (1985), pp. 1551–55; S. Tross, J. Herndon II, A. Korzun, et al., "Psychological Symptoms and Disease-Free and Overall Survival in Women with Stage II Breast Cancer. Cancer and Lukemia Group B," *Journal of the National Cancer Institute* 88 (1996), pp. 66–71; B. R. Cassileth, "Stress and the Development of Cancer: A Persistent and Popular Link Despite Contrary Evidence," *Cancer* 77 (1996), pp. 1015–16; D. Protheroe, K. Turvey, K. Horgan, et al., "Stressful Life Events and Difficulties and Onset of Breast Cancer: A Case Control Study," *British Medical Journal* 319 (1999), pp. 1027–30; M. Petticrew, R. Bell, and D. Hunter, "Influence of Psychological Coping on Survival and Recurrence in People with Cancer: Systematic Review," *British Medical Journal* 325 (2002), pp. 1066–75, "People with cancer should not feel pressured into adopting particular coping styles to improve survival or reduce the risk of recurrence," Ibid., p. 1066; Of course, a coping style marked by complete refusal to take any treatments (denial) likely does shorten life, but this is not a matter of psychological processes acting on endocrine or immune function—the mechanisms by which mood could, at least theoretically, operate on the malignancy itself; P. Schofield, D. Ball, J. G. Smith, et al., "Optimism and Survival in Lung Carcinoma Patients," *Cancer* 100 (2004), pp. 1276–82.

47. S. Nolen-Hoeksema and J. Morrow, "A Prospective Study of Depression and Posttraumatic Stress Symptoms After A Natural Disaster: The 1989 Loma Prieta Earthquake," pp. 115–21; Typically, studies of coping rely on subjects' postdisaster reports of how they were feeling before the event took place; but frightening experiences can color the way people recall their earlier moods and attitudes, and this distorts before-and-after-disaster comparisons.

48. Ruminating about one's anger made an angry mood even worse. Psychologist Cheryl Rusting of the University of Michigan encouraged her subjects to recall their angriest recent experience. She instructed half of them to "overthink" their anger by going over and over the resentful and bitter thoughts and feelings. The other subjects were told to distract themselves by (define). Members of the first group reported feeling angrier than their self-distracted counterparts; see C. Rusting and S. Nolen-Hoeksema, "Regulating Responses to Anger: Effects of

Rumination and Distraction on Angry Mood," *Journal of Personality and Social Psychology* 74 (1998), pp. 790–803.

49. S. Nolen-Hoeksema and J. Morrow, "A Prospective Study of Depression and Posttraumatic Stress Symptoms After A Natural Disaster: The 1989 Loma Prieta Earthquake," p. 120.

50. Ibid., p. 340; R. Ingram, A. Lumry, D. Cruet and W. Sieber, "Attentional Processes in Depressive Disorders," *Cognitive Therapy and Research* 11 (1987), pp. 351–60; R. Larsen and G. Cowan, "Internal Focus of Attention and Depression: A Study of Daily Experience," *Motivation and Emotion* 12 (1988), pp. 237–49; T. Smith, R. Ingram, and L. Roth, "Self-Focused Attention and Depression: Self-Evaluation, Affect and Life Stress," *Motivation and Emotion* 9 (1985), pp. 381–89.

51. Individuals termed repressors are people who claim to be largely unaffected by negative events and seem less interested in their internal states than ruminators. In this context, repression refers to the absence of particular thoughts rather than to a defensive process that operates outside of awareness. The latter reflects the classic Freudian notion of the dynamic unconscious; see G. A. Bonanno, P. J. Davis, J. L. Singer, and G. E. Schwartz, "A Repressor Personality and Avoidant Information Processing: A Dichotic Listening Study," *Journal of Research in Personality* 25 (1991), pp. 386–401; D. A. Weinberger and M. N. Davidson, "Styles of Inhibiting Emotional Expression: Distinguishing Repressive Coping and Impression Management," *Journal of Personality* 62, no. 4 (1994), pp. 587–613.

52. D. A. Weinberger, "The Construct Validity of Repressive Coping Style," in *Repression and Dissociation Implications for Personality Theory, Psychopathology, and Health*, ed. Jerome L. Singer (Chicago: University of Chicago Press, 1990).

53. Yet they seem to fare well, report less internal conflict, test better at solving problems, exhibit better social skills, and have higher education performance. Repressors report less depression, are more popular with peers, are given higher teacher ratings, and report better self-image. See V. J. Tempone and W. Lamb, "Repression-Sensitization and its Relations to Measures of Adjustment and Conflict," *Journal of Consulting and Clinical Psychology* 31 (1967), pp. 131–36; L. D. Young and J. M. Allin, "Repression-Sensitization Differences in Recovery from Learned Helplessness," *Journal of General Psychology* 119 (1992), pp. 135–39; J. Bybee, A. Kramer, and E. Zigler, "Is Repression Adaptive? Relationships to Socioemotional Adjustment, Academic Performance, and Self-Image," *American Journal of Orthopsychiatry* 67, no. 1 (1997), pp. 59–69; On the downside, repressors are less likely to go to the doctor when ill and, some speculate, may encounter problems in

intimate relationships if they seem too emotionally distant. See D. A. Weinberger, G. E. Schwartz, and R. J. Davidson, "Low-Anxious, High-Anxious and Repressive Coping Styles: Psychometric Patterns and Behavioral and Physiological Responses to Stress," *Journal of Abnormal Psychology* 88 (1979), pp. 369–80; Repressors also display poorer recall of details and emotions surrounding threatening events than those less estranged from their inner life. See B. Thornton, "Repression and Its Mediating Influence on the Defensive Attribution of Responsibility," *Journal of Research in Personality* 26 (1992), pp. 44–57; T. Holtgraves and R. Hall, "Repressors: What Do They Repress and How Do They Repress It?" *Journal of Research in Personality* 29 (1995), pp. 306–17; also repressors may suffer in intimate relationships because they are uneasy sharing innermost feelings and thoughts. Though they perceive themselves as unruffled, they tend to register more physiological arousal when stressed (a potential risk for future cardiovascular disease). Finally, repressors tend to be inattentive to physical problems and may not seek timely medical attention.

54. K. Ginzburg, Z. Solomon, and A. Bleich, "Repressive Coping Style, Acute Stress Disorder, and Posttraumatic Stress Disorder After Myocardial Infarction," *Psychosomatic Medicine* 64 (2002), pp. 748–57.

55. Karni Ginzberg, "Repressing Anxiety May Protect Against Stress Disorders," http://www.eurekalert.org/pub_releases/2002—09/cfta—ram092302.php (accessed December 19, 2003).

56. Frasure-Smith, F. Lesperance, G. Ravel, et al., "Long-Term Survival Differences Among Low-Anxious, High-Anxious and Repressive Copers Enrolled in the Montreal Heart Attack Readjustment Trial," *Psychosomatic Medicine* 64 (2002), pp. 571–79.

57. Ibid., p. 571.

58. S. Lyubomirsky, N. Caldwell, and S. Nolen-Hoeksema, "Effects of Ruminative and Distracting Responses to Depressed Mood on Retrieval of Autobiographical Memories," *Journal of Personality and Social Psychology* 75, no. 1 (1998), pp. 166–77.

59. J. Teasdale, "Negative Thinking in Depression: Cause, Effect, or Reciprocal Relationship?" *Advances in Behavior Research and Therapy* 5 (1983), pp. 3–26.

60. Christopher R. Martell, Michael E. Addis and Neil S. Jacobson, *Depression in Context: Strategies For Guided Action* (New York: W. W. Norton, 2001); C. W. LeJuez, D. R. Hopko, J. LePage, et al., "A Brief Behavioral Activation Treatment for Depression," *Cognitive and Behavioral Practice* 8 (2001), pp. 164–75; N. S. Jacobson, K. S. Dobson, P. A. Truax, et al., "A Component Analysis of Cognitive-Behavioral Treatment for Depression," *Journal of Consulting and Clinical Psychology* 64 (1996), pp. 295–304.

61. These behaviors may be secondary to the depression (it is well known that people may act and feel certain ways only during a bout of depression) or they may cause it, but this is irrelevant in behavioral activation therapy. When people may act and feel certain ways only during a bout of depression, this is called state-dependent thinking or acting.

62. S. Lyubomirsky and S. Nolen-Hoeksema, "Self-Perpetuating Properties of Dysphoric Rumination," *Journal of Personality and Social Psychology* 65 (1993), pp. 339–49; S. Nolen-Hoeksema, L. Parker, and J. Larson, "Ruminative Coping with Depressive Mood Following Loss," *Journal of Personality and Social Psychology* 67 (1994), pp. 92–104.

63. Susan Nolen-Hoeksema, "Gender Differences in Depression," in *Handbook of Depression*, ed. Ian H. Gotlib and Constance L. Hammen (New York: Guilford, 2002); Susan Nolen-Hoeksema, *Women Who Think Too Much: How To Break Free of Overthinking and Reclaim Your Life* (New York: Henry Holt, 2003), p. 5.

64. Some psychologists have suggested that people who are beset by depressive thoughts are actually more realistic ("depressive realism") and that better humored individuals are those who innately practice microdistractions routinely. Cognitive psychologist Eric Stone (see http://psych.wfu.edu/psychology/faculty/stone.htm) states that the depressive realism hypothesis remains difficult to resolve. He writes, "The concept of depressive realism suggests that depressed people have more accurate perceptions of the world than nondepressed people do. Recent research we have conducted on the decision making of depressed vs. nondepressed people, however, suggests that findings taken as support for depressive realism may be the result of a pessimism bias, rather than due to depressive realism per se. In future research, we hope to extend our results with undergraduate students to a clinical setting, as well as gain a better understanding of precisely what distinguishes depressed from nondepressed people at a cognitive level."

65. S. Nolen-Hoeksema, *Women Who Think Too Much*, p. 15; B. Fredrickson, "What Good are Positive Emotions?" *Review of General Psychology* 2 (1998), pp. 300–19; S. Folkman and T. Moskowitz, "Stress, Positive Emotion, and Coping," *Current Directions in Psychological Science* 9 (2000), pp. 115–18.

66. Ibid., p. 117.

67. R. Davidson, "Affective Style, Psychopathology, and Resilience: Brain Mechanisms and Plasticity," *American Psychologist* 55 (2000), pp. 1196–1214.

68. Ibid., p. 1198.

69. For example, writing exercises can be used to "reframe" experience and structure an emotional event by defining the emotional content more clearly. Psychologist James Pennebaker at the University of

Texas, Austin, has used this technique successfully to help reduce distress and enhance an individual's sense of self-control. See James W. Pennebaker, *Opening Up: The Healing Power of Expressing Emotion* (New York: Guilford Press, 1997).

70. Susan Cohen, "Rage Makes Me Strong," *Time*, July 29, 1996.

71. Ibid.

72. Cheney cartoon, *The New Yorker*, June 7, 1999, p. 34.

73. Charles Krauthammer, "The Grief Racket," *Washington Post*, May 7, 1999, sec. A, p. 39.

74. Jonathan Yardley, "Vultures Over Littleton," *Washington Post*, April 26, 1999, sec. C, p. 2.

75. A grief counselor is someone certified by a proprietary bereavement agency; he may have a college or postgraduate degree or none at all.

76. R. S. Lazarus, "The Trivialization of Distress," in *Prevention in Health Psychology*, ed. J. C. Rose and L. J. Solomon (Hanover, N.H.: University Press of New England, 1985), pp. 279–98.

77. J. Pennebaker and K. Harber, "A Social Stage Model of Collective Coping: the Loma Prieta Earthquake and the Persian Gulf War," *Journal of Social Issues* 49, no. 4 (1993), pp. 125–45; In his book *The Careless Society— Community and Its Counterfeits*, John McKnight of the Institute for Policy Research at Northwestern University paints a dystopian vision of life in the age of the grief counselor. He fears that communities will lose cohesion and self-sufficiency as they come to believe that counselors are essential. See John McKnight, *The Careless Society—Community and Its Counterfeits* (New York: Basic Books, 1995); "Finally one day the aged father of a local woman will die. And the next-door neighbor will not drop by because he doesn't want to interrupt the bereavement counselor. The woman's kin will stay home because they will have learned that only the bereavement counselor knows how to process grief in the proper way. . . . It will only be one generation between the time the bereavement counselor arrives and the disappearance of the community of mourners. The counselor's new tool will cut through the social fabric, throwing aside kinship, care, neighborly obligations, and community ways of coming together and going on."; Ibid., pp. 6–7; McKnight's vision may be too dark but there is little question that many people think they'll need some kind of guidance. Remarking upon the plethora of books on death and dying, the late physician Lewis Thomas once said, "You'd think [dying] was a new sort of skill which all of us our now required to learn. . . . Proper dying has become an extraordinary, exotic experience, something only the specially trained get to do."; see Lewis Thomas, *The Medusa and the Snail* (New York: Gale Group, 1979), p. 102.

78. Victor Lewis-Smith, "Grief Relief? It's a Joke, Bernard," *Daily Mirror*, March 2, 1996, p. 7.

79. Frank Furedi, *Therapy Culture: Cultivating Vulnerability in an Uncertain Age* (London: Routledge, 2003), p. 14.

80. California Association of School Psychologists, "Schoolyard Tragedies: Coping with the Aftermath," http://www.nasponline.org/NEAT/neat_school.html (accessed May 28, 2003); A friend tells an especially unnerving account after an Illinois eighth grader was killed in a car accident. Some of his classmates went to see the grief counselor posted on duty in the school library even though they did not particularly like the child, who was considered a bully. When the kids were asked why they visited the counselor, they said because it got them out of class and there were donuts and orange juice. See also Kim Newbold, in discussion with Satel, May 28, 2003.

81. Office of Safe and Drug-Free Schools, U.S. Department of Education, *Practical Information on Crisis Planning: Guide for Schools and Communities* (Washington, D.C.: U.S. Department of Education, 2003), p. 79.

82. "Secretary Paige Unveils New Guide to Help Schools Plan for Crises," May 16, 2003, http://www.ed.gove/print/news/pressreleases/2003/05/05162003.html (accessed September 30, 2003).

83. Allyson O'Sullivan of the Employee Assistance Programs Association (5,000 members), in discussion with author Satel, September 30, 2003; Bill Bowler, also of the EAPA, says 93 percent of members offer grief counseling, in discussion with author Satel, September 30, 2003.

84. M. Prince, "Employers Deploy Grief Counselors," *Crain Communication*, February 10, 2003.

85. Anne Kadet, "Good Grief," *Smart Money*, May 2002, pp. 110–14.

86. Ibid., p. 113.

87. Megan Rosenfeld, "Profits of Loss; The Bereavement Business Is Booming as Grief Counselors Attempt to Fill the Void," *Washington Post*, June 25, 1997, sec. D, p. 1.

88. Jessica Mitford, *The American Way of Death Revisited* (New York: Vintage Books, 1998), p. 64.

89. "Grief Recovery Certification Training," The Grief Recovery Institute, http://www.grief.net/Certification/Certification.htm (accessed August 14, 2002).

90. Lyn Prashant, "Published Writings," Degriefing Counseling & Education, http://www.degriefing.com/published.html (accessed May 29, 2003).

91. Association for Death Education and Counseling, "About ADEC," http://www.adec.org/about/index.htm (accessed October 6, 2003).

92. ADEC, "Certification Program: Certified in Thanatology, Death, Dying, and Bereavement (CT)," http://www.adec.org/cert/index.htm (accessed August 28, 2002).

93. American Academy of Grief Counseling, http://www.aihcp.org/aagc.htm (accessed September 25, 2003).

94. G. Hagman, "Beyond Cathexis: Towards A New Psychoanalytic Understanding of Treatment of Mourning," in *Meaning Reconstruction and the Experience of Loss*, ed. Robert A. Neimeyer (Washington, D.C.: American Psychological Association, 2000).

95. Elizabeth Large, "Grieving is an Individual Process," *Baltimore Sun*, April 6, 2003.

96. E. Nussbaum, "Good Grief: The Case for Repression," *Lingua Franca* October 1997, pp. 49–51.

97. Selby Jacobs, in discussion with Satel, August 28, 2002.

98. A social psychologist is a researcher who examines the psychological impact of social forces on the behavior of individuals, he does not see patients; clinical psychologists see patients and many of them conduct clinical research as well. An experimental psychologist does experiments using healthy people (often college students) and the purpose is to elucidate normal mental and behavioral processes, not develop treatments.

99. C. Wortman and R. C. Silver, "The Myths of Coping With Loss," *Journal of Clinical and Consulting Psychology* 57 (1998), pp. 349–57; follow-up article, C. Wortman and R. C. Silver, "Myths of Coping With Loss Revisited," in *Handbook of Bereavement: Consequences, Caring, and Coping*, ed. M. Stroebe, R. Hansson, and H. Schut (Washington, D.C.: American Psychological Association, 2001), pp. 405–29; R. A. Neimeyer, "Grief Therapy and Research as Essential Tensions: Prescriptions for a Progressive Partnership," *Death Studies* 24 (2000), pp. 603–10; J. R. Jordan, "Research that Matters: Bridging the Gap Between Research and Practice in Thanatology," *Death Studies* 24 (2000), pp. 457–68.

100. Brendan Maher, in discussion with author Satel, July 4, 2003.

101. M. Bruce, K. Kim, P. Leaf, and S. Jacobs, "Depressive Episodes and Dysphoria Resulting From Conjugal Bereavement in a Prospective Community Sample," *American Journal of Psychiatry* 147, no. 5 (1990), pp. 608–11; it is possible, of course, that subjects who do not report intense levels of distress and depression are still suffering with milder forms of depression. When Bruce and colleagues at Yale specifically inquired about low levels of depression called dysphoria (two or more weeks of feeling sad, blue, or loss of interest or pleasure in the things one generally enjoys) within a one-year study period, they found that 61.5 percent were dysphoric, 30.8 percent were diagnosed with major

depression, and about 8 percent did not report significant depressive symptoms; see also C. Mendes de Leon, S. Kasl, and S. Jacobs, "A Prospective Study of Widowhood and Changes in Symptoms of Depression in a Community Sample of the Elderly," *Psychological Medicine* 24, no. 3 (1994), pp. 613–24; C. Wortman and R. C. Silver, "The Myths of Coping With Loss," pp. 349–57. To be sure, one would expect to find higher levels of intense reactions closer to the time of the loss and when the death was unexpected. Indeed, that is the case. For example, within four months after the traumatic death of a child and within three weeks of loss of a baby to Sudden Infant Death Syndrome about 70 percent of the mothers reported depression, according to studies by Shirley Murphy, Ph.D., at the University of Washington (as cited in C. Wortman and R. C. Silver, "Myths of Coping With Loss Revisited,") and Wortman and Silver, respectively, in C. Wortman and R. C. Silver, "Coping With Irrevocable Loss," in *Cataclysms, Crises, and Catastrophes: Psychology in Action, Master Lecture Series*, ed. Gary R. VadenBos and Brenda K. Bryant (Washington, DC: APA, 1987), pp. 189–235. Similarly, one month after the death of a lover to AIDS, Folkman found that up to 80 percent reported clinically significant depression. Even so, Wortman and Silver found that 29 percent of the mothers experienced only low levels of depression at one month after the loss. Folkman and colleagues noted that nearly 25 percent reported relatively low levels of depressive mood within one month as well; see S. Folkman, M. Chesney, L. Collette, et al., "Post-Bereavement Depressive Mood and Its Pre-Bereavement Predictors in HIV+ and HIV− Gay Men," *Journal of Personal and Social Psychology* 70 (1996), pp. 336–48; S. A. Murphy, "A Bereavement Intervention for Parents Following the Sudden, Violent Deaths of Their 12–28 Year Old Children: Description and Applications to Clinical Practice," *Canadian Journal of Nursing Research* 29, no. 4 (1997), pp. 51–72; C. Wortman and R. C. Silver, "Coping with Irrevocable Loss," pp. 189–235.

102. G. A. Bonanno and C. S. Kaltman, "Varieties of Grief Experience," *Clinical Psychology Review* 21 (2001), pp. 705–34.

103. S. Zisook, M. Paulus, S. Shuchter and L. Judd, "The Many Faces of Depression Following Spousal Bereavement," *Journal of Affective Disorders* 45 (1997), pp. 85–94.

104. J. Bodnar and J. Kielcolt-Glaser, "Caregiver Depression After Bereavement: Chronic Stress Isn't Over When It's Over," *Psychology and Aging* 9 (1994), pp. 372–80; D. Cohen and C. Eisendorfer, "Depression In Family Members Caring for A Relative with Alzheimer's Disease," *Journal of the American Geriatric Society* 36 (1988), pp. 885–89; A. Horowitz, "Sons and Daughters as Caregivers to Older Parents: Differ-

ences In Role Performance and Consequences," *Gerontologist* 25 (1985), pp. 612–17; B. Wheaton, "Life Transitions, Role Histories, and Mental Health," *American Sociological Review* 55 (1990), pp. 209–23; Susan Folkman and her colleagues at the University of California at San Francisco followed over two hundred gay men whose lovers were dying of AIDS. The researchers were surprised to find that the majority of the bereaved derived positive meanings from the death—enhanced feelings of self-worth, of personal strength, and wisdom. Some of the lovers reported both positive and negative emotions and a minority reported negative only; those reporting the most positive attitudes, Folkman found, enjoyed better psychological adjustment. See S. Folkman, "Revised Coping Theory and the Process of Bereavement," in *Handbook of Bereavement: Consequences, Caring, and Coping.*

105. G. A. Bonanno, C. B. Wortman, D. Lehman, et al., "Resilience to Loss and Chronic Grief: A Prospective Study From Pre-Loss to 18 Months Post-Loss," *Journal of Personality and Social Psychology* 83, no. 5 (2002), pp. 1150–64.

106. D. Carr, J. House, R. Kessler, et al. "Marital Quality and Psychological Adjustment to Widowhood Among Older Adults: A Longitudinal Analysis," *The Journals of Gerontology, Series B: Psychological Sciences and Social Sciences* 55, no. 4 (2000), pp. S197–207. This study followed the same Detroit sample for a total of forty-eight months.

107. Stanley W. Jackson, *Melancholia and Depression: From Hippocratic Times to Modern Times* (New Haven, Conn.: Yale University Press, 1990).

108. E. Lindemann, "Symptomatology and Management of Acute Grief," *American Journal of Psychiatry* 101 (1944), pp. 141–48.

109. Therese A. Rando, *Grief, Dying, and Death: Clinical Interventions for Caregivers* (Champaign, IL: Research Press, 1984); Marian Osterweis, Frederic Solomon, and Morris Green, eds., *Bereavement Reactions: Consequences and Care* (Washington, D.C.: National Academies Press, 1984).

110. H. Deutsch, "Absence of Grief," *Psychoanalytic Quarterly* 6 (1937), pp. 12–22; These concepts still hold considerable sway. A survey of bereavement experts found that 66 percent claimed psychoanalytic theory to be a useful model. See W. Middleton, A. Moylan, B. Raphael, et al., "An International Perspective on Bereavement Related Concepts," *Australian and New Zealand Journal of Psychiatry* 27 (1993), pp. 457–63; The latest edition of *Psychoanalytic Terms and Concepts*, published by the American Psychoanalytic Association, defines mourning very much as Freud did, emphasizing a loss of interest in the outside world and the need to "decathect," or release emotional ties to the dead. See American Psychological Association, *Psychoanalytic Terms and Concepts*, 1990 ed. (Washington, D.C.: APA, 1990), p. 122.

111. Geraldine M. Humphrey and David G. Zimpfer, *Counselling for Grief and Bereavement* (Thousand Oaks, Calif.: Sage, 1996), p. 152.

112. C. B. Wortman, K. Wolff, and G. A. Bonanno, "Loss of an Intimate Partner Through Death," in *Handbook of Closeness and Intimacy*, ed. Debra J. Mashek and Arthur Aron (Mahwah, N.J.: Erlbaum, 2004).

113. W. Middleton, A. Moylan, B. Raphael, et al., "An International Perspective on Bereavement Related Concepts," *Australian and New Zealand Journal of Psychiatry* 27 (1993), pp. 457–63.

114. Robert A. Neimeyer and Heidi Levitt, "Coping and Coherence: A Narrative Perspective on Resilience," in *Coping With Stress*, ed. C. R. Snyder (New York: Oxford University Press, 2001), pp. 47–67; W. Middleton, P. Burnett, B. Raphael, and N. Martinek, "The Bereavement Response: A Cluster Analysis," *British Journal of Psychiatry* 169 (1996), pp. 167–71; G. Bonanno and N. Field, "Evaluating the Delayed Grief Hypothesis Across Five Years of Bereavement," *American Behavioral Scientist* 44 (2001), pp. 798–816; M. Vachon, J. Rogers, W. Lyall, et al., "Predictors and Correlates of Adaptation to Conjugal Bereavement," *American Journal of Psychiatry* 139 (1982), pp. 998–1002.

115. C. Wortman and R. C. Silver, "The Myths of Coping With Loss Revisited," pp. 405–29.

116. G. Bonanno and N. Field, "Evaluating the Delayed Grief Hypothesis Across Five Years of Bereavement," pp. 798–816; G. Bonanno and S. Kaltman, "The Varieties of Grief Experience," *Annals of Psychological Review* 20 (2001), pp. 1–30.

117. W. Middleton, P. Burnett, B. Raphael, et al., "The Bereavement Response: A Cluster Analysis," *British Journal of Psychiatry* 169 (1996), pp. 167–71; full quote: "no evidence was found for the pattern of response which might be expected for delayed grief," Ibid., p. 169.

118. Simon Shimshon Rubin, "The Wounded Family: Bereaved Parents and the Impact of Adult Child Loss," in *Continuing Bonds: New Understandings Of Grief*, ed. Dennis Klass, Steven L. Nickman, and Phyllis R. Silverman (Washington, D.C.: Taylor & Francis, 1996), pp. 217–35; Susan Nolen-Hoeksema and Judith Larson, *Coping With Loss* (Mahwah, N.J.: Erlbaum, 1999).

119. M. Cleiren, *Bereavement and Adaptation: A Comparative Study of the Aftermath of Death* (Philadelphia, Pa.: Hemisphere, 1993); S. Lepore, R. Silver, C. Wortman, and H. Wayment, "Social Constraints, Intrusive Thoughts, and Depressive Symptoms Among Bereaved Mothers," *Journal of Personal and Social Psychology* 70 (1996), pp. 271–82; J. Pennebaker, "Traumatic Experience and Psychosomatic Disease," in *Advances In Experimental Social Psychology*, vol. 22, ed. L. Berkowitz (New York: Academic Press, 1989), pp. 211–14.

120. http://www.fema.gov/rrr/bereave.shtm (accessed September 8, 2004).

121. Elizabeth Kübler-Ross, *On Death and Dying* (New York: Simon & Schuster, 1997).

122. C. M. Parkes, "A Historical Overview of the Scientific Study of Bereavement," in *Handbook of Bereavement Research*, ed. M. S. Stroebe, R. O. Hansson, W. Stroebe, and H. Schut (Washington, D.C.: American Psychological Association, 2001), pp. 25–46.

123. Ibid., p. 30.

124. James William Worden, *Grief Counseling and Grief Therapy: A Handbook for the Mental Health Practioner*, 2nd ed. (New York: Springer Publishing, 1991).

125. C. Wortman and R. C. Silver, "The Myths of Coping With Loss Revisited," p. 423.

126. M. Stroebe and W. Stroebe, "Does 'Grief Work' Work?" *Journal of Consulting and Clinical Psychology* 59 (1991), pp. 479–82; M. Stroebe, W. Stroebe, H. Schut, et al., "Does Disclosure of Emotion Facilitate Recovery for Bereavement? Evidence from Two Prospective Studies," *Journal of Consulting and Clinical Psychology* 70, no. 1 (2002), pp. 169–78. (The researchers asked bereaved spouses a number of questions including, "Do you avoid anything that would be too painful a reminder?" "During pangs of grief, do you pull yourself together or let yourself go?" and "Is any activity a welcome distraction?" Responses could range from "never" to "always.")

127. G. Downey, R. C. Silver, and C. B. Wortman, "Reconsidering the Attribution—Adjustment Relation Following a Major Negative Event: Coping with the Loss of a Child," *Journal of Personality and Social Psychology* 59 (1990), pp. 925–40; D. N. McIntosh, R. C. Silver, and C. B. Wortman, "Religion's Role in Adjustment to a Negative Life Event: Coping with the Loss of a Child," *Journal of Personality and Social Psychology* 65 (1993), pp. 812–21. Similarly, researchers find that individuals who focus repetitively on their distress and the circumstances surrounding those symptoms have higher levels of depression symptoms and physical complaints months later, independent of their mood at baseline. By contrast, those who deliberately sought to distract themselves when they felt bad and those less likely to talk about their low mood exhibit lower rates of depressed mood about a year later. See S. Nolen-Hoeksema, L. Parker, and J. Larson, "Ruminative Coping With Depressed Mood Following Loss," *Journal of Personal and Social Psychology* 67 (1994), pp. 92–104; L. Capps and G. Bonanno, "Narrating Bereavement: Thematic and Grammatical Predictors of Adjustment to Loss," *Discourse Processes* 30 (2000), pp. 1–25.

128. Hanna Kaminer and Peretz Lavie, "Sleep and Dreams in Well-adjusted and Less Adjusted Holocaust Survivors," in *Handbook of Bereavement— Theory, Research, and Intervention,* ed. Margaret S. Stroebe, Wolfgang Stroebe, and Robert O. Hanssen (New York: Cambridge University Press, 1999), pp. 331–45; R. L. Silver, C. Boon, and M. H. Stones, "Searching For Meaning in Misfortune: Making Sense of Incest," *Journal of Social Issues* 39 (1983), pp. 81–102; S. Nolen-Hoeksema, A. McBride, and J. Larson, "Rumination and Psychological Distress Among Bereaved Partners," *Journal of Personal and Social Psychology* 72 (1997), pp. 855–63.

129. Therese A. Rando, *How to Go On Living When Someone You Love Dies* (New York: Bantam, 1988), pp. 248, 254, 256; Although Rando's book was published in 1988, she still promotes these ideas.

130. Janice L. Genevro, Tracy Marshall, and Tess Miller, "Interventions," *Report on Bereavement and Grief Research* (Washington, D.C.: Center for the Advancement of Health, 2003), pp. 65–71, http://www.cfah.org/pdfs/griefreport.pdf; Robert O. Hansson and Margaret Stroebe, "Grief, Older Adulthood," in *Encyclopedia of Primary Prevention and Health Promotion,* ed. Thomas P. Gullotta and Martin Bloom (New York: Kluwer Academic Publishing, 2003), pp. 515–21; H. Schut, M. Stroebe, J. van den Bout, and M. Terheggen, "The Efficacy of Bereavement Intervention—Who Benefits?" *Handbook of Bereavement Research,* p. 731; L. Sabatini, "Evaluating a Treatment Program for Newly Widowed People," *Omega* 19 (1988), pp. 229–36; F. Tudiver, J. Hilditch, J. Permaul, and D. McKendree, "Does Mutual Help Facilitate Newly Bereaved Widowers? Report of a Randomized Controlled Trial," *Evaluation and the Health Professions* 15 (1992), pp. 147–62; M. Lieberman and I. Yalom, "Brief Group Psychotherapy for the Spousally Bereaved: A Controlled Study," *International Journal of Group Psychotherapy* 42, no. 1 (1992), pp. 117–32.

131. D. L. Allumbaugh and W. J. Hoyt, "Effectiveness Of Grief Therapy: A Meta-Analysis," *Journal of Counseling Psychology* 46 (1999), pp. 370–80; P. M. Kato and T. Mann, "A Synthesis of Psychological Interventions for the Bereaved," *Clinical Psychology Review* 19 (1999), pp. 275–96; J. R. Jordan and R. A. Neimeyer, "Does Grief Counseling Work?" *Death Studies* 27 (2003), pp. 765–86.

132. R. Neimeyer, "Searching for the Meaning of Meaning: Grief Therapy and the Process of Reconstruction," *Death Studies* 24 (2000), pp. 541–58.

133. Ibid., p. 541.

134. N. Farberow, "The Los Angeles Survivors After Suicide Program: An Evaluation," *Crisis* 13 (1992), pp. 23–34; G. A. Bonanno, "Emotional

Dissociation, Self-Deception, and Adaptation to Loss," in *Traumatology of Grieving*, ed. C. R. Figley (Philadelphia, Pa.: Taylor & Francis, 1999), pp. 89–105; L. Mastrogianis and M. A. Lumley, "Aftercare Services From Funeral Directors to Bereaved Men: Surveys of Both Providers and Recipients," *Omega* 45 (2002), pp. 167–85; S. A. Murphy, L. C. Johnson, and J. Lohan, "Finding Meaning in a Child's Violent Death: A Five-Year Prospective Analysis of Parents' Personal Narratives and Empirical Data," *Death Studies* 27 (2003), pp. 381–404.

135. J. R. Jordan and R. A. Neimeyer, "Does Grief Counseling Work?" pp. 765–86; C. M. Parkes, "Grief: Lessons From the Past, Visions for the Future," *Death Studies* 26 (2002), pp. 367–86; H. Schut, M. Stroebe, J. van den Bout and M. Terheggen, "The Efficacy of Bereavement Intervention—Who Benefits?" *Handbook of Bereavement Research*, pp. 705–38.

136. H. G. Prigerson, "Traumatic Grief as a Risk Factor for Mental and Physical Morbidity," *American Journal of Psychiatry* 154 (1997), pp. 616–23; C. H. Ott, "The Impact of Complicated Grief on Mental and Physical Health at Various Points in The Bereavement Process," *Death Studies* 27 (2003), pp. 249–72.

137. H. G. Prigerson and S. G. Jacobs, "Perspectives on Care at the Close of Life: Caring for Bereaved Patients: 'All the Doctors Just Suddenly Go,'" *Journal of the American Medical Association* 286 (2001), pp. 1369–76; H. G. Prigerson, M. K. Shear, S. C. Jacobs, et al., "Consensus Criteria for Traumatic Grief. A Preliminary Empirical Test," *British Journal of Psychiatry* 174 (1999), pp. 67–73; H. A. Schut, M. S. Stroebe, J. van den Bout, and J. de Keijser, "Intervention for the Bereaved: Gender Differences in the Efficacy of Two Counselling Programmes," *British Journal of Clinical Psychology* 36 (1997), pp. 63–72. (In this meta-analysis the authors looked at seven studies in which the subjects were already suffering from clinical levels of depression, anxiety, and other bereavement-induced disorders at the time of entry into the study. They found that patients benefited significantly.)

138. Typically considered about six months from loss; Selby Jacobs, M.D., in discussion with author Satel, January 16, 2004.

139. Janice L. Genevro, Tracy Marshall, and Tess Miller, *Report on Bereavement and Grief Research*, http://www.cfah.org/pdfs/griefreport.pdf (accessed February 21, 2004).

140. "Grief Counseling Not Always Effective, New Report Concludes," Center for the Advancement of Health, http://www.cfah.org/pdfs/grief_pressrelease.pdf (accessed February 21, 2004).

141. John Stuart Mill, *On Liberty* (New York: W. W. Norton, 1975), p. 14.

5. FROM PATHOS TO PATHOLOGY.

1. Anna Freud and Dorothy T. Burlingham, *War and Children* (New York: Medical War Books, 1943), p. 21; See also Norman G. Garmezy, "Stressors of childhood," in *Stress, Coping, and Development in Children,* ed. Norman G. Garmezy and Michael Rutter (New York: McGraw Hill, 1983).

2. See A, Masten "Ordinary Magic: Resilience Processes in Development," *American Psychologist* 56 (2001), pp. 227–38 for discussion of how "psychology has neglected important phenomena in human adaptation." Masten notes that "resilience does not come from rare and special qualities [but from] . . . ordinary normative resources in the minds, brains, and bodies of children."; G. Bonanno, "Loss, Trauma, and Human Resilience: Have We Underestimated the Human Capacity to Thrive After Extremely Aversive Events?" *American Psychologist* 59 (2004): 20–28.

3. Barbara E. Harrell-Bond, *Imposing Aid: Emergency Assistance to Refugees* (New York: Oxford University Press, 1986).

4. R. C. Kessler, A. Sonnega, E. Bromet et al., "Posttraumatic Stress Disorder in the National Comorbidity Survey," *Archives of General Psychiatry* 52, no. 12 (1995), pp. 1048–60; J. E. Helzer, L. N. Robins, and L. McEvoy, "Posttraumatic Stress Disorder in the General Population. Findings of the Epidemiological Catchment Area Study," *New England Journal of Medicine* 317, no. 26 (1987), pp. 1630–34; J. R. Davidson, D. Hughes, D. G. Balzer, and L. K. George, "Posttraumatic Stress Disorder in the Community: An Epidemiological Study," *Psychological Medicine* 21, no. 3 (1991), pp. 713–21.

5. A word about definitions. We use the term "mental health professional" to refer to anyone, no matter his credentials, who performs an intervention to ameliorate distress or to prevent the development of distress or mental illness. A counselor is someone with either a bachelor's or master's level degree in counseling. A trauma counselor is someone who is certified by a proprietary trauma services organization, typically the International Critical Incident Stress Foundation; he or she may have a college or postgraduate degree or none at all. The term traumatologist refers to any mental health professional who specializes in research or treatment of trauma. Generally, we refer to individuals by their highest degree; for example, someone who is a doctoral-level psychologist (Ph.D.) or a psychiatrist (M.D.) is described as such. Researchers and investigators are typically trained at the Ph.D. or M.D. level.

6. C. Shatan, "The Grief of Soldiers: The Vietnam Veteran and the Self-Help Movement," *American Journal of Orthopsychiatry* 43 (1973) pp. 640–53, 650–51.
7. Jon Nordheimer, "Postwar Shock Is Found to Beset Veterans Returning From the War in Vietnam," *New York Times*, August 28, 1972.
8. Chaim F. Shatan, "Post-Vietnam Syndrome," *New York Times*, May 6, 1972.
9. C. Shatan, "The Grief of Soldiers: The Vietnam Veteran and the Self-Help Movement," pp. 640–53.
10. Robert J. Lifton, "The Scars of Vietnam," *Commonweal* 20, February, 1970, pp. 554–56; see also Tom Wicker, "The Vietnam Disease," *New York Times*, May 27, 1975.
11. Jerry Lembcke, "The Spitting Image: Myth, Memory, and the Legacy of Vietnam," paper presented at the Research Libraries Group 1999 Annual Membership Meeting, http://www.rlg.org/annmtg/lembcke99.html (accessed October 26, 2003).
12. Eric T. Dean, *Shook Over Hell: Post-Traumatic Stress, Vietnam, and the Civil War* (Cambridge, Mass.: Harvard University Press, 1997), p. 5.
13. For histories of PTSD see Wilbur J. Scott, *The Politics of Readjustment: Vietnam Veterans Since The War* (New York: Aldine De Gruyter, 1993); Allan Young, *The Harmony of Illusions: Inventing Post-Traumatic Stress Disorder* (Princeton, N.J.: Princeton University Press, 1995); Mardi Jon Horowitz, *Stress Response Syndromes* (Northvale, N.J.: Jason Aronson, 1978). The Horowitz book is considered the first scholarly analysis of the phenomenon; it played an important role in adoption of PTSD.
14. Judith Lewis Herman, *Trauma and Recovery: The Aftermath of Violence—from Domestic Abuse to Political Terror* (New York: Basic Books, 1992).
15. In the first two editions of the *Diagnostic and Statistical Manual*, war-related pathology would have fallen under one of two formal diagnostic categories. In the first edition (1952) "Gross Stress Reaction" and in the second edition (1968) "Adjustment Reaction to Adult Life" were the diagnostic entities within which an acute PTSD-like syndrome could be subsumed. Gross Stress Reaction, which could be caused by combat, the manual specifically indicated, had no provision for delayed or chronic stress-related symptoms. Adjustment Reaction to Adult Life also presumed that the symptoms would disappear when the stress was removed. Both editions asserted that if conditions persisted in time, then another mental disorder should be diagnosed. See E. A. Brett "The Classification of Posttraumatic Stress Disorder," in *Traumatic Stress: The Effects of Overwhelming Experience on Mind, Body, and Society*, ed. Bessel A. van der Kolk, Alexander C. McFarlane, and Lars Weisaeth (New York: Guilford Press, 1996), pp. 117–28.

16. T. Van Putten and W. H. Emory, "Traumatic Neurosis in Vietnam Returnees. A Forgotten Diagnosis?" *Archives of General Psychiatry* 29, no. 5 (1973), pp. 695–98; Roy R. Grinker and John P. Spiegel, *Men Under Stress* (New York: McGraw-Hill, 1963).

17. The Veterans Administration was reluctant to grant this benefit in the early years of the war. Also, the VA did not consider symptoms that emerged one year after return to be service-related; see Wilbur J. Scott, *The Politics of Readjustment*, p. 52.

18. Ibid., p. 238.

19. Charles R. Figley and Seymour Leventman, *Strangers At Home: Vietnam Veterans Since the War* (Westport, Conn.: Greenwood Group, 1980), p. 363; R. J. Lifton, "The Scars of Vietnam," pp. 554–56.

20. Executions for desertion and "cowardice" did occur. According to Ben Shephard perhaps 30–40 of 306 military executions carried out by the British may have suffered war trauma, Ben Shephard, in discussion with author Satel, March 22, 2004.

21. Elliot G. Smith and T. H. Pear, *Shell Shock and its Lessons* (Manchester: Manchester University Press, 1918), pp. 87–88.

22. N. Q. Brill and G. W. Beebe, "Follow-up Study of Psychoneuroses: Preliminary Report," *American Journal of Psychiatry* 108, no. 6 (1951), pp. 417–25; William Sargant, *The Unquiet Mind* (London: Heinemann, 1967), pp. 86–87; W. Sargant and E. Slater, "Acute War Stress," *Lancet* 1 (1940); for review see D. H. Marlowe, *Psychological and Psychosocial Consequences of Combat and Deployment with Special Emphasis on the Gulf War* MR-1018/11-OSD (RAND, 2000), http://www.gulflink.osd.mil/library/randrep/marlowe_paper/ (accessed December 26, 2003).

23. R. Yehuda and A. C. McFarlane, "A Conflict Between Current Knowledge About Posttraumatic Stress Disorder and its Original Conceptual Basis," *American Journal of Psychiatry* 152, no. 12 (1995), pp. 1705–13, 1708.

24. Ben Shephard, *A War of Nerves* (Cambridge, Mass.: Harvard University Press, 2001), p. 355.

25. R. Yehuda and A. C. McFarlane, "A Conflict Between Current Knowledge About Posttraumatic Stress Disorder and its Original Conceptual Basis," pp. 1705–13, 1706; The 2000 DSM IV-R states that "The severity, duration, and proximity of an individual's exposure to the traumatic event are the most important factors affecting the likelihood of developing this disorder," p. 466.

26. D. Summerfield, "The Invention of PTSD and the Social Usefulness of a Psychiatric Category," *British Medical Journal* 322, no. 7278 (2001), pp. 95–98.

27. If development of PTSD or related symptoms depends solely upon the characteristics of the traumatic event (independent of the characteris-

tics of the victim), we would expect a direct relationship between severity of the event and mental state. Yet this correlation is not reliably observed. For review see Richard McNally, *Remembering Trauma* (Cambridge, Mass.: Belknap Press/Harvard University Press, 2003), pp. 79–84; see also M. Sabin, B. Lopes Cardozo, L. Nackerud, R. Kaiser and L. Varese, "Factors Associated with Poor Health Among Guatemalan Refugees Living in Mexico 20 Years after Civil Conflict," *Journal of the American Medical Association* 290, no. 5 (2003), pp. 635–42; A. Bleich, M. Gelkopf and Z. Solomon, "Exposure to Terrorist Attacks, Stress-Related Mental Health Symptoms, and Coping Behaviors Among a Nationally Representative Sample in Israel," *Journal of the American Medical Association* 290, no. 5 (2003), pp. 612–20.

28. C. Brewin, B. Andrews and J. Valentine, "Meta-analysis of Risk Factors for Posttraumatic Stress Disorder in Trauma-Exposed Adults," *Journal of Consulting and Clinical Psychology* 68, no. 5 (2000), pp. 748–66; D. King, L. King, D. Foy, and D. Gudanowski, "Prewar Factors in Combat-Related Posttraumatic Stress Disorder. Structural Equation Modeling with a National Sample of Female and Male Vietnam Veterans," *Journal of Consulting and Clinical Psychology* 64, no. 3 (1996), pp. 520–31; S. Rabinowitz, C. Margalit, M. Mark, Z. Solomon, and A. Bleich, "Debate Reawakened: Premorbid Factors for Soldiers with Refractory Posttraumatic Stress Disorder," *Psychological Reports* 67, no. 3, pt. 2 (1990), pp. 1363–66; E. Bromet, A. Sonnega, and R. Kessler, "Risk factors for DSM-III-R Posttraumatic Stress Disorder: Findings from the National Comorbidity Survey," *American Journal of Epidemiology* 147, no. 4 (1998), pp. 353–61; E. J. Ozer, S. R. Best, T. L. Lipsey, and D. S. Weiss, "Predictors of Posttraumatic Stress Disorder and Symptoms in Adults: A Meta-Analysis," *Psychological Bulletin* 129, no. 1 (2003), pp. 52–73; N. Breslau, G. C. Davis, P. Andreski, and E. Peterson, "Traumatic Events and Posttraumatic Stress Disorder in an Urban Population of Young Adults," *Archives of General Psychiatry* 48, no. 3 (1991), pp. 216–22; A. C. McFarlane, "Post-Traumatic Morbidity of a Disaster. A Study of Cases Presenting for Psychiatric Treatment," *Journal of Nervous and Mental Disease* 174, no. 1 (1986), pp. 4–14; B. L. Green, M. C. Grace, J. D. Lindy, et al., "Risk Factors For Posttraumatic Stress Disorder and Other Diagnoses in a General Sample of Vietnam Veterans," *American Journal of Psychiatry* 147, no. 6 (1990), pp. 729–33; J. E. Helzer, L. N. Robins, and L. McElvoy, "Posttraumatic Stress Disorder in the General Population. Findings of the Epidemiological Catchment Area Survey," pp. 1630–34; J. L. Escobar, E. T. Randolph, G. Puente, et al., "Posttraumatic Stress Disorder in Hispanic Vietnam Veterans. Clinical Phenomenology and Socio-

cultural Characteristics," *Journal of Nervous and Mental Disease* 171, no. 10 (1983), pp. 585–96; R. K. Pitman, S. P. Orr, M. J. Lowenhagen, et al., "Pre-Vietnam Contents of PTSD Veterans' Service Medical and Personnel Records," *Comprehensive Psychiatry* 32, no. 5 (1991), pp. 416–22; L. A. Champion, G. Goodall, and M. Rutter, "Behaviour Problems in Childhood and Stressors in Early Adult Life: I. A 20-Year Follow-Up of London School Children,"*Psychological Medicine* 25, no. 2 (1995), pp. 231–46.

29. N. Breslau et al, "Risk Factors for PTSD-Related Traumatic Events," pp. 529–35; E. Bromet, A. Sonnega, and R. Kessler, "Risk factors for DSM-III-R Posttraumatic Stress Disorder: Findings from the National Comorbidity Survey," *American Journal of Epidemiology* 147, no. 4 (1998), pp. 353–61; A. Y. Shalev, T. Sahar, S. Freedman, et al., "A Prospective Study of Heart Rate Response Following Trauma and the Subsequent Development of Posttraumatic Stress Disorder," *Archives of General Psychiatry* 55, no. 6 (1998), pp. 553–59; R. Yehuda, "Current Concepts: Post-Traumatic Stress Disorder," *New England Journal of Medicine* 346 (2002), pp. 108–14; I. Bamsen, A. Dirkzwager, and H. M. van der Ploeg, "Predeployment Personality Traits and Exposure to Trauma as Predictors of Posttraumatic Stress Symptoms: A Prospective Study of Former Peacekeepers," *American Journal of Psychiatry* 157, no. 7 (2000), pp. 1115–19; B. I. O'Toole, R. P. Marshall, R. J. Schureck, and M. Dobson, "Risk Factors for Posttraumatic Stress Disorder in Australian Vietnam Veterans," *Australian and New Zealand Journal of Psychiatry* 32, no. 1 (1998), pp. 21–31; P. P. Schnurr, M. J. Friedman, and S. D. Rosenberg, "Premilitary MMPI Scores as Predictors of Combat-related PTSD Symptoms," *American Journal of Psychiatry* 150, no. 3 (1993), pp. 479–83; K. A. Lee, G. E. Valliant, W. C. Torrey, and G. H. Elder, "A 50-year Prospective Study of the Psychological Sequelae of World War II Combat," *American Journal of Psychiatry* 152, no. 4 (1995), pp. 516–22; R. R. Silva, M. Alpert, D. M. Munoz, et al., "Stress and Vulnerability to Posttraumatic Stress Disorder in Children and Adolescents," *American Journal of Psychiatry* 157, no. 8 (2000), pp. 1229–35; N. Breslau, G. Davis, E. Peterson, and L. Schultz, "A Second Look at Comorbidity in Victims of Trauma: The Posttraumatic Stress Disorder–Major Depression Connection," *Biological Psychiatry* 48 (2000), pp. 902–9.

30. A. Ehlers and D. M. Clark, "A Cognitive Model of Posttraumatic Stress Disorder," *Behaviour Research and Therapy* 38, no. 4 (2000), pp. 319–45; See also J. J. Vasterling, L. M. Duke, K. Brailey, et al., "Attention, Learning, and Memory Performances and Intellectual Resources in Vietnam Veterans: PTSD and No Disorder Comparisons,"

Neuropsychology 16, no. 1 (2002), pp. 5–14; for correlation between level of education and likelihood of PTSD (negative correlation) and also for review establishing that PTSD is not only associated with less native intelligence but is probably associated with select post-event cognitive deficits. A prospective study by Michael Macklin of Harvard and colleagues examined predeployment intelligence test scores of Vietnam combat veterans. They found that average IQ for veterans diagnosed with PTSD at the time of the study was normal, about 106, but the average for the men without the condition was 119. Notably, the lower the IQ score among those with PTSD, the more severe the symptoms, even when accounting for the extent of combat exposure. See M. L. Macklin, L. J. Metzger, B. T. Litz, et al., "Lower Precombat Intelligence is a Risk Factor for Posttraumatic Stress Disorder," *Journal of Consulting and Clinical Psychology* 66, no. 2 (1998), pp. 323–26; (Finally, any disparity between pre- and postcombat IQ was unrelated to PTSD severity. "Stated differently," McNally says in his review of the Macklin study, "above-average cognitive ability may enhance a soldier's ability to cope with stressors, thereby buffering him against developing PTSD," in R. J. McNally, "Progress and Controversy in the Study of Posttraumatic Stress Disorder," *Annual Review of Psychology* 54 (2003), pp. 229–52; Another prospective report from Israeli researchers who examined the premilitary testing of over nine hundred Israeli soldiers revealed that below average intelligence was a strong predictor of later PTSD in Z. Kaplan, M. Weiser, A. Reichenberg et al., "Motivation to Serve in the Military Influences Vulnerability to Future Post Traumatic Stress Disorder," *Psychiatry Research* 109, no. 1 (2002), pp. 45–49; McNally notes that when the authors controlled for motivation to serve, the inverse relationship between PTSD and intelligence disappeared, but since lower intelligence was correlated with lower motivation, the adjustment inappropriately discounts the relationship between intelligence and PTSD. See Richard McNally, *Remembering Trauma*, p. 92; a retrospective study of trauma-exposed children in New York City found that children and adolescents with below-average intelligence were considerably more likely to have PTSD than their brighter counterparts. See R. R. Silva, M. Alpert, D. M. Munoz, et al, "Stress and vulnerability to posttraumatic stress disorder in children and adolescents," pp. 1229–35.

31. Marilyn L. Bowman, *Individual Differences in Posttraumatic Respons: Problems With the Adversity-Distress Connection*, (Mahwah, N.J.: Lawrence Erlbaum Associates: 1997), p. vii.

32. A. S. Blank, "Irrational Reactions to Posttraumatic Stress Disorder and Vietnam Veterans," in *The Trauma of War: Stress and Recovery in*

Vietnam Veterans, ed. Stephen M. Sonnenberg, Arthur S. Blank Jr., and John A. Talbott (Washington, D.C.: American Psychiatric Press, 1985).

33. Richard McNally, *Remembering Trauma*, p. 89.

34. American Psychiatric Association, *DSM IV-TR 2000* (Washington, D.C.: American Psychiatric Publishing, 2000), pp. 467–68.

35. J. LeDoux, "Emotion Circuits in the Brain," *Annual Review of Neuroscience* 23 (2000), pp. 155–84; D. S. Charney, "Psychobiological Mechanisms of Resilience and Vulnerability: Implications for Successful Adaptation to Extreme Stress," *American Journal of Psychiatry* 161 (2004), pp. 195–216.

36. D. A. Tomb, "The Phenomenology of Posttraumatic Stress Disorder," *The Psychiatric Clinics of North America* 17, no. 2 (1994), pp. 237–50; N. Breslau, G. C. Davis, P. Andreski, and E. Peterson, "Traumatic Events and Posttraumatic Stress Disorder in an Urban Population of Young Adults," pp. 216–22; F. Norris, "Epidemiology of Trauma: Frequency and Impact of Different Potentially Traumatic Events on Different Demographic Groups," *Journal of Consulting and Clinical Psychology* 60 (1992), pp. 409–18.

37. C. North, S. Nixon, S. Shariat, et al., "Psychiatric Disorders Among Survivors of the Oklahoma City Bombing," *Journal of the American Medical Association* 282 (1999), pp. 755–62.

38. R. C. Kessler, A. Sonnega, E. Bromet, et al., "Posttraumatic Stress Disorder in the National Comorbidity Survey," pp. 1048–60; B. O. Rothbaum, E. B. Foa, D. Riggs, et al., "A Prospective Examination of Post Traumatic Stress Disorder in Rape Victims," *Journal of Traumatic Stress* 5 (1992), pp. 455–75; A. McFarlane and G. De Girolamo, "The Nature of Traumatic Stressors and Epidemiology of Posttraumatic Reactions," in *Traumatic Stress: The Effects of Overwhelming Experience on Mind, Body, and Society*, pp. 129–54.

39. Fran H. Norris, "50,000 Disaster Victims Speak: An Empirical Review of the Empirical Literature, 1981–2001," Prepared for The National Center for PTSD and The Center for Mental Health Services (SAMHSA), September 2001, http://www.istss.org/terrorism/victims_speak.htm (accessed December 1, 2003).

40. L. E. Beutler and M. L. Malik, eds., *Rethinking the DSM: A Psychological Perspective* (Washington, D.C.: American Psychological Association, 2002); J. H. Ehrenreich, "Understanding PTSD: Forgetting 'Trauma,'" *Analyses of Social Issues and Public Policy* 3 (2003), pp. 15–28.

41. Richard McNally, *Remembering Trauma*.

42. American Psychological Association, *DSM-III: 1980*, p. 238.

43. S. Reisner, "Trauma: The Seductive Hypothesis," *Journal of the American Psychoanalytic Association* 51, no. 2 (2003), pp. 51, 381–414.

44. Marilyn L. Bowman, *Individual Differences in Posttraumatic* Response, p. 104.
45. Jon Nordheimer, "Postwar Shock Besets Ex-GIs," *New York Times*, August 21, 1972.
46. J. I. Walker and J. O. Cavenar Jr., "Vietnam Veterans. Their problems continue," *Journal of Nervous and Mental Disease* 170, no. 3 (1982), pp. 174–80.
47. Eric T. Dean, *Shook Over Hell*, p. 15.
48. J. F. Borus, "Incidence of Maladjustment in Vietnam Returnees," *Archives of General Psychiatry* 30 (1974), pp. 554–57; B. Gerson and I. Carlier, "PTSD: The History of a Recent Concept," *British Journal of Psychiatry* 161 (1992), pp. 742–48; R. Fleming, "Post Vietnam Syndrome: Neurosis or Sociosis?" *Psychiatry* 48 (1985), pp. 122–39; E. R. Worthington, "Post-Service Adjustment and Vietnam Era Veterans," *Military Medicine* 142 (1977), pp. 865–66 (concludes that "post-service adjustment problems could be attributed to social, education, or vocational problems not connected with military service," p. 866).
49. Richard A. Kulka, Daniel Weiss, John A. Fairbank, and B. Kathleen Jordan, *Trauma and the Vietnam Generation: Report of Findings from the National Vietnam Veterans Readjustment Study* (New York: Brunner-Mazel, 1990).
50. Partial PTSD was defined as the presence of three-to-five symptoms of PTSD; see Ibid., p. 282.
51. Ibid., p. 53.
52. P. G. Bourne "Military Psychiatry and the Vietnam Experience," *American Journal of Psychiatry* 127 (1970), pp. 481–88.
53. W. J. Tiffany Jr. and W. S. Allenton, "Army Psychiatry in the Mid-60s," *American Journal of Psychiatry* 123 (1967), pp. 810–21; W. J. Tiffany Jr., "The Mental Health of Army Troops in Vietnam," *American Journal of Psychiatry* 123 (1967), pp. 1585–6; F. J. Braceland, "Psychiatry, Hospital Ships, and Vietnam," *American Journal of Psychiatry* 124 (1967), pp. 377–79; R. E. Huffman, "Which Soldiers Break Down: A Survey of 610 Psychiatric Patients in Vietnam," *Bulletin of the Menninger Clinic* 34 (1970), pp. 343–51; D. R. Bey, "Division Psychiatry in Vietnam," *American Journal of Psychiatry* 127 (1970), pp. 228–32; R. E. Strange, "Combat Fatigue Versus Pseudo Combat Fatigue in Vietnam," *Military Medicine* 133 (1968), pp. 823–26; L. N. Robins, J. E. Helzer and D. H. Davis, "Narcotic Use in Southeast Asia and Afterward: An Interview Study of 898 Vietnam Returnees," *Archives of General Psychiatry* 32 (1975), pp. 955–61; see also E. P. Nace, A. Meyers, C. P. O'Brien, et al., "Depression in Veterans Two Years After Viet Nam," *American Journal of Psychiatry* 134 (1977), pp. 167–70; C. P.

O'Brien, E. P. Nace, et al., "Follow-Up of Vietnam Veterans. I. Relapse to Drug Use After Vietnam Service," *Drug and Alcohol Dependence* 5 (1980), pp. 333–40; E. Jones and S. Wessely, "Psychiatric Battle Casualties: An Intra- and Interwar Comparison," *British Journal of Psychiatry* 178 (2001), pp. 242–7; R. H. Fleming, "Post Vietnam Syndrome: Neurosis or Sociosis?" *Psychiatry* 48, no. 2 (1985), pp. 122–39, 128–29.

54. P. G. Bourne, "Psychiatric Casualties in Vietnam, Lowest Ever for Combat Zone Troops," *U.S. Medicine*, May 15, 1969, p. 10; E. M. Colbach and M. D. Parrish, "Army Mental Health Activities in Vietnam: 1965–1970," *Bulletin of the Menninger Clinic* 34 (1970), pp. 333–42.

55. The Centers for Disease Control Vietnam Experience Study, "Health Status of Vietnam Veterans. I. Psychosocial Characteristics," *Journal of the American Medical Association* 259, no. 18 (1988), pp. 2701–7; J. Helzer and L. Robins, "The Prevalence of Posttraumatic Stress Disorder," *New England Journal of Medicine* 318 (1988), p. 1692; T. Keane and W. Penk, "Prevalence of Posttraumatic Stress Disorder," *New England Journal of Medicine* 318 (1988), pp. 1690–91.

56. The Centers for Disease Control Vietnam Experience Study, "Post-Service Mortality Among Vietnam Veterans," *Journal of the American Medical Association* 257, no. 6 (1987), pp. 790–95; The Centers for Disease Control Vietnam Experience Study, "Health Status of Vietnam Veterans. I. Psychosocial Characteristics," pp. 2701–7 (the study did find higher rates of depression, anxiety and alcohol abuse and dependence); D. A. Pollock, P. Rhodes, C. A. Boyle, et al., "Estimating the Number of Suicides Among Vietnam Veterans," *American Journal of Psychiatry* 147, no. 6 (1990), pp. 772–76; Bureau of Labor Statistics, "News Release (USDL 86-125)," U.S. Department of Labor, Washington, D.C., March 31, 1986 (non-veterans 35–44 years old had 5.4 percent unemployment; Vietnam era veterans had 4.6 percent unemployment, Vietnam theatre veterans had 6.3 percent unemployment; non-veterans 45 and over had 5.5 percent unemployment, Vietnam era 2.5 percent and Vietnam-theater 3.1 percent.)

57. D. G. Kikpatrick, H. S. Resnick, J. R. Freedy, D. Pelcovitz, et al., "Report of Findings From the DSM-IV PTSD Field Trial: Emphasis on Criterion A and Overall PTSD Diagnosis," Unpublished paper prepared for the DSM-IV Workgroup on PTSD, 1991.

58. C. S. North, E. L. Spitznagel and E. M. Smith, "A Prospective Study of Coping After Exposure to a Mass Murder Episode," *Annals of Clinical Psychiatry* 13, no. 2 (2001), pp. 81–87; C. North, S. Nixon, S. Shariat, et al., "Psychiatric Disorders Among Survivors of the Oklahoma City Bombing," pp. 755–62; S. D. Johnson, C. S. North, and E. M. Smith, "Psychiatric Disorders Among Victims of a Courthouse Shooting

Spree: A Three-Year Follow-Up Study," *Community Mental Health Journal* 38, no. 3 (2002), pp. 181–94; L. Weisaeth, "Torture of a Norwegian Ship's Crew: The Torture, Stress Reactions and Psychiatric After-Effects," *Acta Psychiatrica Scandnavica* supplement 355 (1989), pp. 63–72; L. Weisaeth "The Stressors and the Post-traumatic Stress Syndrome After an Industrial Disaster," *Acta Psychiatrica Scandanavica* supplement 355 (1989), pp. 25–37; P. Stallard, R. Velleman, and S. Baldwin, "Recovery from Posttraumatic Stress Disorder in Children Following Road Traffic Accidents: The Role of Talking and Feeling Understood," *Journal of Community & Applied Social Psychology* 11, no. 1 (2001), pp. 37–41.

59. A. C. McFarlane, "The Longitudinal Course of Posttraumatic Morbidity: The Range of Outcomes and Their Predictors," *Journal of Nervous and Mental Disease* 176, no. 1 (1988), pp. 30–39; D. Koren, I. Arnon, and E. Klein, "Acute Stress Response and Posttraumatic Stress Disorder in Traffic Accident Victims: A One-Year Prospective, Follow-up Study," *American Journal of Psychiatry* 156, no. 3 (1999), pp. 367–73, R. A. Mayou, A. Ehlers and B. Bryant, "Posttraumatic Stress Disorder After Motor Vehicle Accidents: Three-Year Follow-up of a Prospective Longitudinal Study," *Behaviour, Research and Therapy* 40, no. 6 (2002), pp. 665–75.

60. M. M. Green, A. C. McFarlane, C. E. Hunter, and W. M. Griggs, "Undiagnosed Post-traumatic Stress Disorder Following Motor Vehicle Accidents," *Medical Journal of Australia* 159, no. 8 (1993), pp. 529–34; R. S. Epstein, "Avoidant Symptoms Cloaking the Diagnosis of PTSD in Patients with Severe Accidental Injury," *Journal of Traumatic Stress* 6 (1993), pp. 451–58; T. C. Buckley, E. B. Blanchard, and E. J. Hickling, "A Prospective Examination of Delayed Onset PTSD Secondary to Motor Vehicle Accidents," *Journal of Abnormal Psychology* 105, no. 4 (1996), pp. 617–25; R. A. Bryant and A. G. Harvey, "Delayed-Onset Posttraumatic Stress Disorder: A Prospective Evaluation," *Australian and New Zealand Journal of Psychiatry* 36, no. 2 (2002), pp. 205–9.

61. C. L. Port, B. Engdahl, and P. Frazier, "A Longitudinal and Retrospective Study of PTSD Among Older Prisoners of War," *American Journal of Psychiatry* 158, no. 9 (2001), pp. 1474–79; J. C. Kluznik, N. Speed, C. Van Valkenburg, and R. Magraw, "Forty-Year Follow-up of United States Prisoners of War," *American Journal of Psychiatry* 143, no. 11 (1986), pp. 1443–46; A. Burstein, "How Common is Delayed Posttraumatic Stress Disorder?" *American Journal of Psychiatry* 142, no. 7 (1985), p. 887; N. Breslau, G. C. Davis, P. Andreski, and E. Peterson, "Traumatic Events and Posttraumatic Stress Disorder in an Urban

Population of Young Adults," pp. 216–22; J. D. Bremner, S. M. Southwick, A. Darnell, and D. S. Charney, "Chronic Posttraumatic Stress Disorder In Vietnam Combat Veterans: Course of Illness and Substance Abuse," *American Journal of Psychiatry* 153, no. 3 (1996), pp. 369–75; Z. Solomon, M. Kotler, A. Shalev and R. Lin, "Delayed Onset PTSD Among Israeli Veterans of the 1982 Lebanon War," *Psychiatry* 52, no. 4 (1989), pp. 428–36.

62. H. G. Prigerson, P. K. Maciejewski, and R. A. Rosenheck, "Combat Trauma: Trauma With Highest Risk of Delayed and Unresolved Posttraumatic Stress Disorder Symptoms, Unemployment, and Abuse Among Men," *Journal of Nervous and Mental Disease* 189, no. 2 (2001), pp. 99–108; P. P. Schnurr, C. A. Lunney, A. Sengupta, and L. C. Waelde, "A Descriptive Analysis of PTSD Chronicity in Vietnam Veterans," *Journal of Traumatic Stress* 16, no. 6 (2003), pp. 545–53.

63. C. Van Dyke, N. J. Zilberg, and J. A. McKinnon, "Posttraumatic Stress Disorder: A Thirty-Year Delay in a World War II Veteran," *American Journal of Psychiatry* 142, no. 9 (1985), pp. 1070–3; A. Pomerantz "Delayed Onset of PTSD: Delayed Recognition or Latent Disorder?" *American Journal of Psychiatry* 148 (1991), p. 1609; R. Pary, D. Turns and C. R. Tobias, "A Case of Delayed Recognition of Posttraumatic Stress Disorder," *American Journal of Psychiatry* 143, no. 7 (1986), p. 941; N. Herrmann and G. Eryavec "Delayed Onset Posttraumatic Stress Disorder in World War II Veterans," *Canadian Journal of Psychiatry* 39 (1994), pp. 439–41; W. G. Niederland, "Clinical Observations on the 'Survivor Syndrome,'" *International Journal of Psychoanalysis* 49 (1968), pp. 313–15; L. C. C. Lim, "Delayed Emergence of Posttraumatic Stress Disorder," *Singapore Medical Journal* 32 (1991), pp. 92–93.

64. A. D. Macleod, "The Reactivation of Post-Traumatic Stress Disorder in Later Life," *Australian and New Zealand Journal of Psychiatry* 28 (1994), pp. 625–34.

65. The DSM III, which formed the basis for clinical interviews of the NVVRS, did not require presence of impairment or great suffering. In DSM IV this requirement is known as "Criterion F."

66. R. L. Spitzer and J. C. Wakefield, "DSM-IV Diagnostic Criterion for Clinical Significance: Does It Help Solve the False Positives Problem?" *American Journal of Psychiatry* 156 (1999), pp. 1856–64.

67. Charles C. Myers, *Shellshock in France 1914–1918, Based on a War Diary Kept by Charles S. Myers*, (Cambridge, England: Cambridge University Press, 1940), pp. 12–13, 92–97; Ben Shephard, *A War of Nerves*, pp. 53–71.

68. T. W. Salmon, "The Care and Treatment of Mental Disease and War Neuroses ('Shell Shock') in the British Army," *Mental Hygiene* 1 (1917), pp. 509–47; E. Jones and S. Wessely, "Psychiatric Battle Casualties: An Intra- and Interwar Comparison," *British Journal of Psychiatry* 178 (2001), pp. 242–47; R. E. Strange, "Combat Fatigue Versus Pseudo Combat Fatigue in Vietnam," *Military Medicine* 133 (1968), pp. 823–26; J. Herbert and M. Sageman " 'First Do No Harm:' Emerging Guidelines for the Treatment of Posttraumatic Reactions," in *Posttraumatic Stress Disorder: Issues and Controversies*, ed. G. Rosen (West Sussex, UK: John Wiley & Sons, in press).

69. A. J. Glass, "Psychotherapy in the Combat Zone," *American Journal of Psychiatry* 110 (1954), pp. 725–31; N. L. Rock, J. W. Stokes, R. J. Koshes, et al., "U.S. Army Combat Psychiatry," in *Textbook of Military Psychiatry: War Psychiatry*, ed. R. Zajtchuk and R. F. Bellamy (Washington, D.C.: Office of the Surgeon General of the United States, 1995), ch. 7.

70. E. Schwarz, J. Kowalski, and R. McNally, "Malignant Memories: Post-traumatic Changes in Memory in Adults after a School Shooting," *Journal of Traumatic Stress* 6 (1993), pp. 545–53; D. King, L. King, D. Erickson, et al., "Posttraumatic Stress Disorder and Retrospectively Reported Stressor Exposure: A Longitudinal Prediction Model," *Journal of Abnormal Psychology* 109 (2000), pp. 624–33; S. Southwick, A. Morgan, A. Nicolau, and D. Charney, "Consistency of Memory for Combat-related Traumatic Events in Veterans of Operation Desert Storm," *American Journal of Psychiatry* 154 (1997), pp. 173–77; S. Wessely, C. Unwin, M. Hotopf et al., "Stability of Recall of Military Hazards over Time: Evidence from the Persian Gulf War of 1991," *British Journal of Psychiatry* 183 (2003), pp. 314–22; L. Roemer, B. Litz, S. Orsillo, et al., "Increases in Retrospective Accounts of War Zone Exposure over Time: The Role of PTSD Symptom Severity," *Journal of Traumatic Stress* 11 (1998), pp. 597–605; A. G. Harvey and R. A. Bryant, "Memory for Acute Stress Disorder Symptoms: A Two-year Prospective Study," *Journal of Nervous and Mental Disease* 188, no. 9 (2000), pp. 602–7; I. Bramsen, A. J. Dirkzwager, S. C. van Esch, and H. M. van der Ploeg, "Consistency of Self-reports of Traumatic Events in a Population of Dutch Peacekeepers: Reason for Optimism?" *Journal of Traumatic Stress* 14 (2001), pp. 733–40 (McNally claims that there is little reason for optimism since the "magnitude of the relation between PTSD symptoms and increase in remembered trauma from first to second assessment" revealed that severity of PTSD symptoms that follow-up predicted the

magnitude of memory inflation, "implying that current clinical state distorts memory for stressors;" see McNally, *Remembering Trauma*, pp. 82–83.)

71. Terence Keane, Ph.D. (consultant to NVVRS), "Testimony at the House Veterans Affairs Committee, Subcommittee on Health," Congressional hearing, Washington, D.C., March 11, 2004.

72. McNally, *Remembering Trauma*, p. 279.

73. T. Van Putten and W. H. Emory, "Traumatic Neurosis in Vietnam Returnees. A Forgotten Diagnosis?" pp. 695–98.

74. D. R. Johnson, S. C. Feldman, S. M. Southwick, and D. S. Charney, "The Concept of the Second Generation Program in the Treatment of Posttraumatic Stress Disorder among Vietnam Veterans," *Journal of Traumatic Stress* 7, no. 2 (1994), pp. 217–35, 226.

75. T. Van Putten and W. H. Emory, "Traumatic Neurosis in Vietnam Returnees. A Forgotten Diagnosis?" pp. 695–98.

76. Roy R. Grinker and John P. Spiegel, *War Neuroses* (Philadelphia: Blakiston, 1945). Therapists did not believe that all war recollections were banished completely from awareness, or repressed, like Freud's childhood sexual traumas, but that the mind had obscured them for the sake of its own preservation. Some thoughts and memories were painful because they represented tension between diverging drives. Imagine, for example, the intense shame felt by a soldier who wanted to act bravely but whose fear kept him from engaging the enemy. While he cowered, his buddy was killed.

77. Abram Kardiner, *The Traumatic Neuroses of War* (New York: P. B. Hoeber, 1941); The book formed the basis for DSM III formulation of the PTSD diagnosis. See also A. J. Glass, "Psychotherapy in the Combat Zone," *American Journal of Psychiatry* 110 (1954), pp. 725–31; F. D. Jones and R. E. Hales, "Military Combat Psychiatry: An Historical Review," *Psychiatric Annals* 17 (1987), pp. 525–27.

78. Allan Young, *The Harmony of Illusions*.

79. R. H. Fleming, "Post Vietnam Syndrome: Neurosis or Sociosis?" pp. 122–39; Joel Osler Brende and E. R. Parson, *Vietnam Veterans: The Road to Recovery* (New York: Perseus, 1985), pp. 185–86.

80. S. A. Haley, "When the Patient Reports Atrocities: Specific considerations of the Vietnam Veteran," *Archives of General Psychiatry* 30, no. 2 (1974), pp. 191–96.

81. Allan Young, *The Harmony of Illusions*, p. 233.

82. P. Cohen and J. Cohen, "The Clinician's Illusion," *Archives of General Psychiatry* 41 (1984), pp. 1178–82.

83. D. R. Johnson, R. Rosenheck, A. Fontana, et al., "Outcome of Inten-

sive Inpatient Treatment for Combat-related Posttraumatic Stress Disorder," *American Journal of Psychiatry* 153, no. 6 (1996), pp. 771–77.

84. D. R. Johnson, S. C. Feldman, S. M. Southwick, and D. S. Charney, "The Concept of the Second Generation Program in the Treatment of Posttraumatic Stress Disorder Among Vietnam Veterans," p. 231.

85. D. R. Johnson and H. Lubin, "Treatment Preferences of Vietnam Veterans with Posttraumatic Stress Disorder," *Journal of Traumatic Stress* 10, no. 3 (1997), pp. 361–76; R. Johnson, H. Lubin, R. Rosenheck, et al., "The Impact of the Homecoming Reception on the Development of Posttraumatic Stress Disorder: The West Haven Homecoming Stress Scale," *Journal of Traumatic Stress* 10, no. 2 (1997), pp. 259–77.

86. D. R. Johnson, A. Fontana, H. Lubin, et al., "Long-term Course of Treatment-Seeking Vietnam Veterans with Posttraumatic Stress Disorder: Mortality, Clinical Condition, and Life Satisfaction," *Journal of Nervous and Mental Disease* 192 (2004), pp. 35–41.

87. Z. Solomon, A. Bleich, S. Shoham, C. Nardi, and M. Kotler, "The 'Koach' Project for Treatment of Combat-related PTSD: Rationale, Aims, and Methodology," *Journal of Traumatic Stress* 5 (1992), pp. 175–93; Z. Solomon, A. Shalev, S. E. Spiro, et al., "Negative Psychometric Outcomes: Self-Report Measures and a Follow-up Telephone Survey," *Journal of Traumatic Stress* 5 (1992), pp. 225–46; M. Hammarberg and S. Silver, "Outcome of Treatment for Posttraumatic Stress Disorder in a Primary Care Unit Serving Vietnam Veterans," *Journal of Traumatic Stress* 7 (1994), pp. 195–216; M. Creamer, P. Morris, D. Biddle, and P. Elliott, "Treatment Outcome in Australian Veterans With Combat-Related Posttraumatic Stress Disorder: A Cause for Cautious Optimism?" *Journal of Traumatic Stress* 12 (1999), pp. 545–58.

88. A. Fontana and R. Rosenheck, "Effectiveness and Cost of the Inpatient Treatment of Posttraumatic Stress Disorder: Comparison of Three Models of Treatment," *American Journal of Psychiatry* 154, no. 6 (1997), pp. 758–65; in contrast, inpatient care organized around cognitive behavioral therapy was more promising, see L. Humphreys, J. Westerink, L. Giarrantano, and R. Brooks, "An Intensive Treatment Program for Chronic Posttraumatic Stress Disorder: 2-Year Outcome Data," *Australian and New Zealand Journal of Psychiatry* 33 (1999), pp. 848–54.

89. R. Rosenheck, A. Fontana and P. Errera, "Inpatient Treatment of War-Related Post Traumatic Stress Disorder: a 20 Year Perspective," *Journal of Traumatic Stress* 10, no. 3 (1997), pp. 407–13, 409; The Veteran's Affairs Chief Medical Director's Special Committee on PTSD declared in 1991 that veterans required specialized services that

delved deeply into their war zone experiences, a prescription based on almost no systematic evidence of their effectiveness. Chief Medical Director's Special Committee on PTSD (1991) Program Guide: Specialized PTSD Inpatient Units, Washington, D.C.: DAV, cited in R. Rosenheck, A. Fontana and P. Errera, "Inpatient Treatment of War-Related Post Traumatic Stress Disorder: a 20 Year Perspective."

90. In the latter instance, parallels can be found in the forensic arena wherein trauma-induced distress is often refractory to treatment— that is, until the case is resolved in the plaintiff's favor. See B. Aronson, L. Rosenwald, and G. Rosen, "Attorney-client confidentiality and the assessment of claimants who allege post traumatic stress," *Washington Law Review* 76 (2001), pp. 313–47.

91. P. R. McHugh and G. Treisman, "PTSD: A Misconception and its Consequences," Manuscript on file with author Satel, p. 8.

92. Douglas Mossman, "At the VA it Pays to be Sick—Department of Veterans Affairs," *The Public Interest* 114 (1994), pp. 35–47.

93. Paul R. McHugh, "How Psychiatry Lost its Way," *Commentary* 1 (1999), pp. 32–38.

94. L. Sparr and L. D. Pankratz, "Factitious Posttraumatic Stress Disorder," *American Journal of Psychiatry* 140, no. 8 (1983), pp. 1016–19; Pankratz in discussion with author Satel, November 14, 2002.

95. Pankratz's observation is widely reiterated in the literature, see P. S. Calhoun, K. S. Earnst, D. D. Tucker, A. C. Kirby, and J. C. Beckham, "Feigning Combat-Related Posttraumatic Stress Disorder on the Personality Assessment Inventory," *Journal of Personality Assessment 75*, no. 2 (2000), pp. 338–50; L. Hyer, P. Boudewyns, W. R. Harrison, et al., "Vietnam Veterans: Overreporting Versus Acceptable Reporting of Symptoms," *Journal of Personality Assessment* 52, no. 3 (1988), pp. 475–86; P. R. Lees-Haley and J. T. Dunn, "The Ability of Naïve Subjects to Report Symptoms of Mild Brain Injury, Post-traumatic Stress Disorder, Major Depression, and Generalized Anxiety Disorder," *Journal of Clinical Psychology* 50, no. 2 (1994), pp. 252–56; E. J. Lynn and M. Belza, "Factitious Posttraumatic Stress Disorder: The Veteran Who Never Got to Vietnam," *Hospital and Community Psychiatry* 35, no. 7 (1984), pp. 697–701; M. T. Orne, "On the Social Psychology of the Psychological Experiment: with Particular Reference to Demand Characteristics and their Implications," *American Psychologist* 17 (1962), pp. 776–83; M. Pendergrast, "Response to Karon and Widener (1997)," *Professional Psychology: Research and Practice* 29 (1998), pp. 479–81; N. Schwarz, "How the Questions Shape the Answers," *American Psychologist* 54 (1999), pp. 93–105; L. Sparr and L. D. Pankratz, "Factitious posttraumatic Stress Disorder," pp. 1016–19.

96. Pankratz in discussion with Satel, May 1, 2003.
97. Allan Young, *The Harmony of Illusions*, p. 229.
98. B. C. Frueh, M. B. Hamner, S. P. Cahill, et al., "Apparent Symptom Overreporting Among Combat Veterans Evaluated for PTSD," *Clinical Psychology Review* 20 (2000), pp. 853–85; A. Fontana and R. Rosenheck, "Effects of Compensation-Seeking on Treatment Outcomes Among Veterans With Posttraumatic Stress Disorder," *Journal of Nervous and Mental Disease* 186 (1998), pp. 223–30.
99. One-hundred-percent-service-connection payment is $2,193 per month, Department of Veterans Affairs, "Compensation and Pension Benefits: Compensation Rate Table," http://www.vba.va.gov/bln/21/Rates/comp01.htm (accessed December 1, 2003).
100. B. G. Burkett and Glenna Whitley, *Stolen Valor: How The Vietnam Generation Was Robbed of its Heroes and its History* (Dallas: Verity Press, 1998).
101. Vietnam Doorgunners Association, *100% PTSD Compensation Booklet* (Lee's Summit, Mo.: Privately published, 1995), pp. 11, 12 copyright Roxanne Hill (on file with authors); B. G. Burkett and G. Whitley, *Stolen Valor*, pp. 234–53; Doorgunner book quoted in *Stolen Valor*, p. 243; Loren Pankratz cites Roxanne Hill, *How to Apply for 100% Total Disability Rating* (Lee's Summit, Mo.: Privately Published, 1995) in Loren Pankratz, "The Misadventures of Wanderers and Victims of Trauma," in *Malingering And Illness Deception*, ed. Peter W. Halligan, Christopher Bass and David Oakley (Oxford: Oxford University Press, 2003); The Armed Forces Vietnam Network spiral-bound book is available for order at www.afvn.net/ptsd.htm (accessed July 15, 2003); text reads: "We highly recommend you answer questions such as the ones below with the answer that follows the question. Do not volunteer any information about childhood, your brother(s), sister(s) or your parents." [When asked the following questions, answer "no" or "normal"]: the questions are 'How was your childhood? Did your parents drink a lot? Did your parents fight a lot? Did you use drugs as a teenager? Did your dad get fired from different jobs? Were you ever sexually abused as a child? Were you in a serious accident as a child?' You need to always keep the appearance of your lifestyle before Vietnam as average and normal. This will help keep the VA from trying to say your problems are due to your lifestyle before you entered the Armed Forces."
102. Northport, New York, VAMC Substance Abuse/Post-traumatic Stress Treatment Program, "Referral Summary Form," obtained April 5, 2004, on file with author.
103. D. Mossman, "At the VA It Pays to be Sick; Department of Veterans Affairs," pp. 35–47; W. H. Campbell and M. J. Tueth, "Misplaced Re-

wards: Veterans' Administration System and Symptom Magnifica-
tion," *Clinical Orthopsychiatry* 336 (1997), pp. 42–46; N. A. Sayer and P.
Thuras, "The Influence of Patients' Compensation-Seeking Status on
the Perception of Veterans Affairs Clinicians," *Psychiatric Services* 53,
no. 2 (2002), pp. 210–12; A. Fontana and R. Rosenheck, "Effects of
Compensation-Seeking on Treatment Outcomes among Veterans with
Posttraumatic Stress Disorder," *Journal of Nervous and Mental Disease*
186, no. 4 (1998), pp. 223–30.

104. C. Frueh, J. Elhai, A. L. Grubaugh, et al., "Documented Combat Exposure of Veterans Seeking Treatment for Combat-Related Posttraumatic Stress Disorder: Review of Records from the U.S. National
Personnel Records Center," accepted for publication, September 2004,
in *British Journal of Psychiatry*. In an effort to bypass the ambiguity of
self-reports, other researchers have tried to identify veterans with
PTSD by measuring physiological responses to combat cues such as
images of firefights. But these data are difficult to interpret as well—a
fact dramatically underscored when a group of (unverified) combat
veterans asked to do mental arithmetic scored higher on physiological
arousal measures (e.g., heart rate, blood pressure, muscle tension) than
they did when presented with a script describing combat scenarios accompanied by still visual images and sounds of helicopters, small arms
fire, and explosions. See T. M. Keane, L. C. Kolb, D. G. Kaloupek, et al.,
"Utility of Psychophysiological Measurement in the Diagnosis of Posttraumatic Stress Disorder: Results From a Department of Veterans Affairs Cooperative Study," *Journal of Consulting and Clinical Psychology* 66,
no. 6 (1998), pp. 914–23.

105. American Psychological Assocation, *DSM-IV Revised 2000*, pp. 467, 487.

106. B. C. Frueh, M. B. Hamner, S. P. Cahill, et al., "Apparent Symptom
Overreporting Among Combat Veterans Evaluated for PTSD,"
pp. 853–85; B. C. Frueh, P. B. Gold and M. A. de Arellano, "Symptom
Overreporting in Combat Veterans Evaluated for PTSD: Differentia-
tion on the Basis of Compensation Seeking Status," *Journal of Personality Assessment* 68, no. 2 (1997), pp. 369–84; B. C. Freuh, D. W. Smith,
and S. E. Barker, "Compensation Seeking Status and Psychometric Assessment of Combat Veterans Seeking Treatment for PTSD," *Journal
of Traumatic Stress* 9, no. 3 (1996), pp. 427–39; P. B. Gold, and B. C.
Freuh, "Compensation-Seeking and Extreme Exaggeration of Psychopathology Among Combat Veterans Evaluated for Posttraumatic
Stress Disorder," *Journal of Nervous and Mental Disease* 187, no. 11
(1999), pp. 680–84; B. C. Frueh, J. D. Elhai, P. B. Gold, et al., "Disability Compensation Seeking Among Veterans Evaluated for Posttraumatic Stress Disorder," *Psychiatric Services* 54 (2003), pp. 84–91.

107. Cited in B. Shephard " 'Pitiless Psychology'—The Role of Prevention in British Military Psychiatry in the Second World War," *History of Psychiatry*, vol. x (1999), pp. 491–524, 503.

108. B. Shephard, "Risk Factors and PTSD; A Historian's Perspective" in *Posttraumatic Stress Disorder:Issues and Controversies*.

109. Paul R. McHugh, "How Psychiatry Lost its Way," pp. 32–38.

110. E. M. Gozdziak and J. Tuskan Jr., "Operation Provide Refuge: The Challenge of Integrating Behavioral Science and Indigenous Approaches to Human Suffering," in *Rethinking Refuge and Displacement, Selected Papers on Refugees and Immigrants Vol. VIII*, ed. E. M. Gozdziak and D. J. Shandy (Arlington, Va.: American Anthropological Association, 2000), pp. 194–222, 205.

111. E. Gozdziak, in discussion with Satel, October 16, 2002.

112. P. Wiles et al., *Independent Evaluation of Expenditure of DEC Kosovo Appeal Funds. Phases I and II, April 1999–January 2000, Vol II* (London: ODI/VALID, 2000), p. 122.

113. I. Agger and J. Mimica, *Psychosocial Assistance to Victims of War in Bosnia-Herzogovenia and Croatia: An Evaluation* (Brussels: European Community Humanitarian Office and European Community Task-Force; Pycho-Social Unit, 1996), pp. 96–97.

114. D. Summerfield, "The Social Experience of War and Some Issues for the Humanitarian Field," in *Rethinking the Trauma of War*, ed. P. J. Bracken and C. Petty (London: Free Association Books, 1998) p. 29; see also V. Pupavac, "Therapeutic Governance: Psychosocial Intervention and Trauma Risk Management," *Disasters* 25, no. 4 (2001), pp. 358–72.

115. Stephen Kinzer, "In Croatia, Minds Scarred by War," *New York Times*, January 9, 1995, sec. A, p. 6 (quotation from Soren Buus Jensen, at the time a World Health Specialist based in Zagreb, Croatia).

116. U.S. Committee for Refugees, "A Cry For Help: Refugee Mental Health in The United States," *Refugee Reports* 18, no. 9 (1997) http://www.refugees.org/world/articles/mentalhlth_rr97_9.htm; K. Miller, "Rethinking a Familiar Model: Psychotherapy and the Mental Health of Refugees," *Journal of Contemporary Psychotherapy* 29, no. 4 (1999), pp. 283–306, 284; Vancouver Community Network, "Refugee Mental Health: Moving Ahead Survey and Symposium Report," June 2002   http://www.vcn.bc.ca/vrhb/Down_loads/RefugeeMental-Health/RefugeeMentalHealthRprt_Jun-2001.pdf (accessed October 16, 2002); also see Doctors Without Borders, http://www.doctorswithoutborders.org and Immigration and Refugee Services of America, http://www.refugeesusa.org.

117. CARE, *CARE International Psychosocial Training and Support Program* (Kosovo: Care International, 1999), p. 5.

118. The term *PTSD movement* was used by Paul Stubbs of the Globalism and Social Policy Programme, Zagreb, in a paper presented to the Research Symposium on Critical and Interdisciplinary Approaches to the Mental Health of Asylum Seekers, Refugees, and Displaced Persons, Utrecht, Netherlands, April 24, 1999.

119. "Introduction" in *Rethinking the Trauma of War*, p. 4.

120. D. Summerfield, "A Critique of Seven Assumptions Behind Psychological Trauma Programmes in War-Affected Areas," *Social Science and Medicine* 48, no. 10 (1999), pp. 1449–62; D. Summerfield, "The Social Experience of War and Some Issues for the Humanitarian Field," in *Rethinking The Trauma of War*, pp. 9–37.

121. A. Kleinman, "Anthropology and Psychiatry: The Role of Culture in Cross-Cultural Research on Illness," *British Journal of Psychiatry* 151 (1987), pp. 447–54; N. Higginbotham and A. J. Marsella, "International Consultation and the Homogenization of Psychiatry in Southeast Asia," *Social Science and Medicine* 27, no. 5 (1988), pp. 553–61; The study of Turkish victims by Bosaglu revealed a relatively low percentage; others have found rates of PTSD in over three quarters of those examined; see R. F. Mollica, K. McInnes, T. Pham, et al., "The Dose-effect Relationships Between Torture and Psychiatric Symptoms in Vietnamese Ex-political Detainees and a Comparison Group," *Journal of Nervous and Mental Disease* 186, no. 9 (1998), pp. 543–53; S. M. Weine, D. Vojvoda, D. F. Becker, et al., "PTSD symptoms in Bosnian Refugees 1 Year After Resettlement in the United States," *American Journal of Psychiatry* 155, no. 4 (1998), pp. 562–64.

122. As cited by Summerfield 1999 as personal communication with D. Shuey; M. Hollifield, T. D. Warner, N. Lian, et al., "Measuring Trauma and Health Status in Refugees: A Critical Review," *Journal of the American Medical Association* 288, no. 5 (2002), pp. 611–21.

123. P. J. Bracken, J. E. Giller, and D. Summerfield, "Psychological Responses to War and Atrocity: The Limitations of Current Concepts," *Social Science Medicine* 40, no. 8 (1995), pp. 1073–82, 1078.

124. W. H. Sack, G. Clarke, C. Him, et al., "A Six-Year Follow-up Study of Cambodian Refugee Adolescents Traumatized as Children," *Journal of the American Academy of Child and Adolescent Psychiatry* 32, no. 2 (1993), pp. 431–37.

125. J. Giller, "Caring for Victims of Torture in Uganda," in *Rethinking the Trauma of War*, pp. 136, 142; M. Hollifield, T. D. Warner, N. Lian, et al., "Measuring Trauma and Health Status in Refugees: A Critical Re-

view," *Journal of the American Medical Association* 288 (2002), pp. 611–21.

126. H. M. Weinstein, J. G. Lipson, R. Sarnoff, and E. Gladstone, "Rethinking Displacement: Bosnians Uprooted in Bosnia and California," in *Selected Papers on Refugees and Immigrants, Vol. VII*, ed. J. G. Lipson and L. A. McSpadden (Arlington, Va.: American Anthropological Association, 1999), p. 69.

127. Ibid., p. 65; R. Neugebauer, "School-based Interventions for Children Exposed to Violence," *Journal of the American Medical Association* 290 (2003), pp. 2541–42; (Neugebauer writes "[Rwandan] children uncomfortable with emotional self-disclosure have been included and sometimes pressed to participate. Perhaps not surprisingly, uncontrolled trials of these interventions found that a substantial proportion of children experienced symptom exacerbation, rather than alleviation.")

128. Ibid., p. 64.

129. C. Merridale, "The Collective Mind: Trauma and Shell-Shock in Twentieth-Century Russia," *Journal of Contemporary History* 35, no. 1 (2000), pp. 39–55, 48.

130. C. Eyber and A. Ager, "Conselho: Psychological Healing in Displaced Communities in Angola," *Lancet* 360, no. 9336 (2002), p. 871.

131. S. Eppel, "Reburial Ceremonies for Health and Healing after State Terror in Zimbabwe," *Lancet* 360 (2002), pp. 369–70.

132. C. Gorst-Unsworth and E. Goldenberg, "Psychological Sequelae of Torture and Organised Violence Suffered by Refugees from Iraq: Trauma-related Factors Compared with Social Factors in Exile," *British Journal of Psychiatry* 172 (1998), pp. 90–94; R. Pernice and J. Brook, "Refugees' and Immigrants' Mental Health: Association of Demographic and Post-Immigration Factors," *Journal of Social Psychology* 136, no. 4 (1996), pp. 511–19; L. Swartz and A. Levett, "Political Repression and Children in South Africa: The Social Construction of Damaging Effects," *Social Science Medicine* 28, no. 7 (1989), pp. 741–50; J. D. Kinzie, W. Sack, R. Angell, et al., "The Psychiatric Effects of Massive Trauma on Cambodian Children: I. The Children," *Journal of the American Academy of Child Psychiatry* 25 (1986), pp. 370–76.

133. P. J. Bracken and C. Petty, eds., *Rethinking the Trauma of War*, p. 142.

134. P. Bracken, *Trauma: Culture, Meaning and Philosophy* (London: Whurr Publications Ltd., 2002).

135. M. Eastmond, L. Ralphsson and B. Alinder, "The Psychological Impact of Violence and War: Bosnian Refugees and Coping Strategies,"

Refugee Participation Network 16 (Oxford: Refugee Studies Programme, 1994), p. 9.

136. E. M. Gozdziak and J. Tuskan Jr., "Operation Provide Refuge: The Challenge of Integrating Behavioral Science and Indigenous Approaches to Human Suffering," p. 207.

137. L. Swartz and A. Levett, "Political Repression and Children in South Africa: The Social Construction of Damaging Effects," *Social Science Medicine* 28, no. 7 (1989), pp. 741–50.

138. Derek Summerfield, speaking at the Therapy Culture: Cultivating Vulnerability in an Uncertain Age conference, King's College London, the Strand, London, November 22, 2003.

139. C. Watters, "Emerging Paradigms in the Mental Health Care of Refugees," *Social Science Medicine* 52, no. 11 (2001), pp. 1709–18.

140. G. M. Rosen, "Malingering and the PTSD Data Base," in *Posttraumatic Stress Disorder: Issues and Controversies*; see also G. Eldridge, "Contextual Issues in the Assessment of Posttraumatic Stress Disorder," *Journal of Traumatic Stress* 4 (1991), pp. 7–23; L. F. Sparr and R. M. Atkinson, "Posttraumatic Stress Disorder as an Insanity Defense: Medicolegal Quicksand," *American Journal of Psychiatry* 143, no. 5 (1986), pp. 608–12; P. R. Lees-Haley, "Pseudo Post-Traumatic Stress Disorder," *Trial Diplomacy* Winter (1986), pp. 17–20; G. M. Rosen, "The *Aleutian Enterprise* Sinking and Posttraumatic Stress Disorder: Misdiagnosis in Clinical and Forensic Settings," *Professional Psychology: Research and Practice* 1 (1995), pp. 82–87 (Rosen documents that the very high rate of PTSD among the survivors—nine of twenty-two crew perished—could be explained, in part, by attorney advice to the twenty out of twenty-two survivors involved in litigation. Advice included instructions not to go back to work, to see a doctor frequently, and what symptoms to report.); Edward J. Hickling, Edward B. Blanchard, Elizabeth Mundy, and Tara E. Galovski, "Detection of Malingered MVA Related Posttraumatic Stress Disorder: An Investigation of the Ability to Detect Professional Actors by Experienced Clinicians, Psychological Tests, and Psychophysiological Assessment," *Journal of Forensic Psychology Practice* 2, no. 1 (2002), pp. 33–53.

141. N. Breslau and R. C. Kessler, "The Stressor Criterion in DSM-IV Posttraumatic Stress Disorder: An Empirical Investigation," *Biological Psychiatry* 50, no. 9 (2001), pp. 699–704; A. Young, *Harmony of Illusions*, pp. 288–89; Thomas A. Widiger, Allen J. Frances, Harold Alan Pincus, et al., *DSM-IV Sourcebook* (Washington, D.C.: American Psychiatric Association Press, 1994), vol. 2, pp. 594, 844–49 and vol. 4, pp. 806–7, 839–44.

142. D. Shuman, "Persistent Reexperiences in Psychiatry and Law: Current and Future Trends for the Role of PTSD in Litigation," in *Posttraumatic Stress Disorder in Litigation: Guidelines for Forensic Assessment*, ed. Robert I. Simon (Washington, D.C.: American Psychiatric Press, 2003), pp. 1–18.

143. A. A. Stone, "PTSD and the Law: Critical Review of the New Frontier," *Bulletin of the American Academy of Psychiatry the Law* 21, no. 1 (1993), pp. 23–36.

144. R. Slovenko, "Legal Aspects of Post–traumatic Stress Disorder," *The Psychiatric Clinics of North America* 17, no. 2 (1994), pp. 439–46, 441; G. Rosen, *Posttraumatic Stress Disorder: Issues and Controversies*.

145. California Trial Lawyers as noted by Kutchins and Kirk, the following citation is provided; J. von Tagle, "The New DSM-IV: Is it Easier to Prove Damages?" *California Trial Lawyers Association Forum* 25, no. 1 (1995), pp. 13–19.

146. Andrew Malleson, *Whiplash and Other Useful Illnesses* (Montreal: McGill-Queens University Press, 2002).

147. P. Lees-Haley and S. Anderson, "What PTSD is Not," *Claims*, April (1995), pp. 25–28.

148. Michael Rowett, "Wal-Mart Loses Appeal of $840,000 Wrong-Drug Verdict," *Arkansas Democrat-Gazette*, February 26, 2004.

149. James J. McDonald Jr., "Posttraumatic Stress Dishonesty," *Employee Relations Law Journal* 28 (2003), pp. 93–111; McDonald states that the Michigan Court of Appeals upheld a recent jury verdict against DaimlerChrysler in which a woman sued the auto company for $140 million dollars because she developed chronic PTSD and depression after having been traumatized by overhearing foul language in the workplace and being exposed to practical jokes over the course of several years. The court, however, thought awarding the plaintiff $140 million was a bit too much; the plaintiff received only $21 million.

150. Tara George, "Paula Trauma Unlikely—Docs," *Daily News*, March 15, 1998.

151. J. McDonald, "Posttraumatic Stress Dishonesty," p. 94.

152. C. Avina and W. O'Donohue, "Sexual Harassment and PTSD: Is Sexual Harassment Diagnosable Trauma?" *Journal of Traumatic Stress* 15, no. 1 (2002), pp. 69–75.

153. Ibid., 74.

154. Ted Conover, *Newjack: Guarding Sing Sing* (New York: Vintage, 2001), p. 371.

155. Eric T. Dean, *Shook Over Hell*, p. 23.

156. Marcella Bombardieri, "Theory Links Slavery, Stress Disorder. Proponents Make Case for a New Diagnosis," *Boston Globe*, November 12, 2002, sec. B, p. 1.

157. James Taranto, "Just What the Doctor Ordered," *Opinionjournal.com*, November 25, 2002, http://www.opinionjournal.com/best/?id=110002682 (accessed December 9, 2002).

158. Louis B. Hobson, "The Talented Ms. Paltrow," *Calgary Sun*, December 26, 1999, sec. R, p. 2.

159. Andy Borowitz, "Small Children May Be Traumatized by Ann Coulter, Psychologist Says: Few Coping Strategies for Exposure to Banshee-like Pundit," *Borowitz Report*, June 29, 2003, http://www.borowitzreport.com/archive_rpt.asp?rec=630 (accessed June 29, 2003).

160. Ibid.

161. "VA Struggles to Treat Iraq Veterans," *All Things Considered*, NPR, February 25, 2004; "No Forgetting," *NewsHour with Jim Lehrer*, PBS, January 15, 2004.

162. C. W. Hoge, C. A. Castro, S. C. Messer, et al. "Combat Duty in Iraq and Afghanistan, Mental Health Problems, and Barriers to Care," *New England Journal of Medicine* 351 (2004): 13–23.

163. *Operation Iraqi Freedom: Analysis of VA Healthcare Utilization—Report 4*, The VHA Office of Public Health and Environmental Hazards, Table 11 (March 9, 2004).

164. M. J. Friedman, "Acknowledging the Psychiatric Cost of War," *New England Journal of Medicine* 315 (2004): 75–79.

165. Eric T. Dean, *Shook Over Hell*, p. 9.

6. SEPTEMBER 11, 2001: THE MENTAL HEALTH
CRISIS THAT WASN'T.

1. James Herbert, Ph.D. of Drexel University posted the letter on the listserve of the Society for the Science of Clinical Psychology (SSCP-NET) on Friday September 14, 2001. It was simultaneously submitted for publication in the American Psychological Association's "Monitor on Psychology," appearing in print in the November 2001 issue, Richard McNally, one of the nineteen signatories, in discussion with author Satel, August 22, 2002.

2. Primum Non Nocere, *APA Monitor*, November 2001, letters section.

3. Erica Goode, "After The Attacks: Counseling: Some Therapists Fear Services Could Backfire," *New York Times*, September 16, 2001, sec. 1, p. 21.

4. Charles Fishman, "Business Fights Back: Crisis and Confidence at Ground Zero," *Fast Company* 53 (2001), p. 108.
5. Anne Kadet, "Good Grief," *Smart Money*, June 2002, pp. 108–14; (Kadet, in discussion with author Satel, April 3, 2003; Kadet arrived at a total of nine thousand by adding up the estimates she obtained from the following major aid organizations: Crisis Management International, Atlanta, Ga.; the American Psychological Association, Washington, D.C.; Center for Mental Health Services, Disaster Mental Health Division, Crisis Counseling Training and Assistance Program, Rockville, Md.; International Critical Incident Stress Foundation, Baltimore, Md.; International Society for Traumatic Stress Studies, Dr. John Briere president, based at U. of Southern Calif.; Scientologists Volunteer Ministers; Rev. John Carmichael, President, Church of Scientology of N.Y.; Red Cross, Washington, D.C.; Project Liberty, Albany, N.Y.; EMDR Humanitarian Assistance Program, Philadelphia, Pa.; Association of Traumatic Stress Specialists in Austin, Tx.; Green Cross, c/o Dr. Charles Figley at University of South Florida).
6. Maggie Farley and Charles Ornstein, "After The Attack: U.S. Mental Health Suffers a Major Blow," *Los Angeles Times*, September 22, 2001, sec. A, p. 27.
7. Arline Kaplan, "Anticipated Mental Health Consequences of the Sept. 11 Attacks: What Can We Do Now?" *Psychiatric Times* 18, no. 11 (2001), http://www.psychiatrictimes.com/p0111exc.html.
8. Neal H. Cohen, in testimony before the U.S. Health Education Labor Pensions Committee, Washington, D.C., September 27, 2001.
9. J. Stephenson, "Medical, Mental Health Communities Mobilize to Cope With Terror's Psychological Aftermath," *Journal of the American Medical Association* 286 (2001), p. 1825.
10. James Nininger, "A Monument to the Towers of Pain and Might; We Will Recover," *New York Times*, September 30, 2001, sec. 4, p. 12.
11. FEMA, "FEMA-Funded Program Reaches Out to New Yorkers—Largest Crisis Counseling Grant In FEMA's History," FEMA press release #1391DRNY PR118, May 21, 2002 (coming close to the $148 million spent on Regular Service Crisis Grants since 1974); According to Chip Felton, Project Liberty director, formal debriefing was not part of the counseling, Felton in discussion with author Satel, March 27, 2003.
12. Catherine May, "President's Column," *Washington Psychiatric Society News*, Sept–Oct 2002, p. 2.
13. Sandra G. Boodman, "The Vulnerable; For Others, Exposure to Horrific Events Can Trigger Serious Mental Disorders," *Washington Post*, September 18, 2001, sec. F, p. 1.

14. Karen S. Peterson, "Getting Into Hurt Minds," *USA Today*, September 27, 2001, sec. D, p. 1.

15. Edward Linenthal, *The Unfinished Bombing: Oklahoma City in American Memory* (Oxford: Oxford University Press, 2001), p. 90.

16. Nadya Labi, "The Grief Brigade," *Time*, May 17, 1999.

17. David Brown, "Counselors En Masse Invade Littleton Scene," *Washington Post*, May 3, 1999, sec. A, p. 1.

18. R. J. Koshes, S. A. Young, and J. W. Stokes, "Debriefing Following Combat," in *Textbook of Military Psychiatry: War Psychiatry*, ed. R. Zajtchuk and R. F. Bellamy (Washington, D.C.: Office of the Surgeon General of the United States, 1995), p. 277.

19. Police officers in the Netherlands are by law offered debriefing after a dangerous or gruesome incident. Carlier is reported to say this is her work; from Richard McNally, in discussion with author Satel.

20. Richard K. McGee, *Crisis Intervention in the Community* (Baltimore, Md.: University Park Press, 1974); see also Julian Rappaport, *Community Psychology: Values, Research, and Action* (New York: Holt, 1977).

21. Sally Satel attended a training session run by Dr. Jeffrey Mitchell on Critical Incident Stress Debriefing, May 30, 2002, vicinity of Baltimore, Md.

22. "There's a Need for Therapists who Treat Workplace Trauma," *Psychotherapy Finances* 25 (1999), pp. 6–7.

23. Michelle McPhee and Alice McQuillan, "Counselors Go to Firehouse Mocked by Post," New York *Daily News*, December 4, 2003, p. 6.

24. L. Sparr, "Review of Psychological Debriefing: Theory, Practice, and Evidence," *Journal of the American Medical Association* 286 (2001), pp. 604–5.

25. Karen A. Sitterle and John E. Deleray, "Facing Employee Trauma Without Warning," http://www.drj.com/special/wtc/w3_019.htm (accesssed April 22, 2004).

26. G. Devilly and P. Cotton, "Psychological Debriefing and the Workplace: Defining a Concept, Controversies and Guidelines for Intervention," *Australian Psychologist* 38 (2003), pp. 144–50.

27. "Judgement," Brendan Wood v. State of New South Wales, http://www.findlaw.com.au/cases/docs/201189.rtf (accessed June 2, 2004).

28. Simon Jeffery, "War Veterans Lose Stress Compensation Battle," *The Guardian*, May 21, 2003, http://www.guardian.co.uk/military/story/0,11816,960711,00.html.

29. "Soldiers Joining in What They Call Unprecedented Lawsuit Against the Military," *Canadian Press*, May 26, 2003, http://www.

psycport.com/stories/canadianp_eng_2003_05_26_eng-canadianp_
national_eng-canadianp_national_183958_6862378639823863600.xml.
html (accessed August 20, 2003).

30. Bruce Blythe, CEO of Crisis Management International, in discussion
with author Satel, June 21, 2004; according to Anne Kadet, Crisis
Management International, a firm based in Atlanta, sent 350 therapists, booking every room in one of New York's prominent hotels. As
reported by Richard McNally, in discussion with author Satel, June
17, 2003.

31. Justin A. Kenardy and Vaughan J. Carr, "Debriefing Post Disaster:
Follow-up After a Major Earthquake," in *Psychological Debriefing: The-
ory, Practice, and Evidence,* ed. Beverley Raphael and John P. Wilson
(New York: Cambridge University Press, 2000), p. 180.

32. S. Wessely and M. Deahl, "Psychological Debriefing is a Waste of
Time," *British Journal of Psychiatry* 183 (2003), pp. 12–14.

33. B. Bledsoe, "CISM: Possible Liability for EMS Services?" *Best Practices
in Emergency Medical Services* 5 (2002), pp. 66–67; Devilly and Cotton,
"Psychological Debriefing and the Workplace," pp. 144–50.

34. Sharon Begley, "Is Trauma Debriefing Worse Than Letting Victims
Heal Naturally?" *Wall Street Journal,* September 12, 2003, sec. B,
p. 1.

35. R. M. Yarnick, "Traumatic Event Debriefings Getting Second
Thoughts," *HR Magazine,* June 2003, pp. 32–34.

36. Tonya T. Slawinski and Bruce T. Blythe, "When Doing the Right
Thing Might Be Wrong: Research Questions the value of Critical Incident Stress Debriefings (CISD)," http://www.cmiatl.com/news_arti-
cle55.html (accessed September 14, 2003).

37. Anne Kadet, in discussion with author Satel, March 29, 2002.

38. J. T. Mitchell and G. S. Everly, *The Basic Critical Incident Stress Management Course: Basic Group Crisis Intervention* 3rd ed (Ellicott City, Md.: International Critical Incident Stress Foundation, Inc., 2001).

39. ICISF, "Who We Are: ICISF Proudly Announces the Formation of
Liaisons to the Office of the Executive Director," http://www.icisf.org/
about/liaisoncoord.htm (accessed April 22, 2004).

40. M. Deahl, "Psychological Debriefing: Controversy and Challenge,"
Australian and New Zealand Journal of Psychiatry 34 (2000), pp. 929–39;
Jennifer Bryne, interviewer, "Curse or Cure?" Lateline: Australian
Broadcasting Company, September 30, 1998, http://www.abc.net.au/
lateline/stories/s13123.htm.

41. "United Nations Recognizes ICISF," *LIFE NET* 8, no. 3 (1997), p. 1.

42. Jeffrey Mitchell course lecture in Basic Critical Incident Management,
May 30, 2002, attended by author Satel.

43. Steve Southwick M.D., associate professor of Psychiatry, Yale School of Medicine, in discussion with author Satel, August 6, 2002.

44. Richard Gist, Joseph Woodall and Lynn K. Magenheim, "And Then You Do the Hokey-Pokey and You Turn Yourself Around . . ." in *Response to Disaster: Psychosocial, Community, and Ecological Approaches*, ed. Richard Gist and Bernard Lubin (Philadelphia: Brunner, 1999), pp. 269–90.

45. S. Boschert, "Patients' Predisaster Problems Affect Response to Trauma," *Clinical Psychiatry News*, November, 2002.

46. G. Bowditch, "Disaster Specialist Attacks 'Monster' of Trauma Counseling," *Times* (London), January 29, 1997.

47. Cited in Edward Linenthal, *The Unfinished Bombing: Oklahoma City in American Memory*, p. 88.

48. Richard Gist and Grant J. Devilly, "Post-Trauma Debriefing: The Road Too Frequently Traveled," *The Lancet* 360 (2002), pp. 741–42.

49. Author Satel was awarded a certificate in basic crisis management for a course given by ICSIF in Columbia Md., May 30–31, 2002.

50. J. T. Mitchell and G. S. Everly, *The Basic Critical Incident Stress Management Course*, p. 25.

51. Ibid., p. 92; see also Ibid., p. 96, "We do not recommend that [not talking in the debriefing group] because that can do more harm than good. We recommend instead that you talk about the incident."

52. Beverley Raphael and John P. Wilson, *Psychological Debriefing: Theory, Practice and Evidence*.

53. S. Rose, J. Bisson and S. Wessely, "Psychological Debriefing for Preventing Post Traumatic Stress Disorder, Cochrane Review," in *The Cochrane Library* 3 (Oxford: Update Software, December 3, 2001); B. Litz, M. Gray, R. Bryant and A. Adler, "Early Interventions for Trauma: Current Status and Future Directions," *Clinical Psychology: Science and Practice* 9 (2002), pp. 112–34; R. McNally, R. Bryant and A. Ehlers, "Does Early Psychological Intervention Promote Recovery From Posttraumatic Stress?" *Psychological Science in the Public Interest* 4, no. 2 (2003), pp. 45–79; Arnold P. van Emmerik, Jan H. Kamphuis, Alexander M. Hulsbosch, and Paul M. G. Emmelkamp, "Single Session Debriefing After Psychological Trauma: A Meta-Analysis," *Lancet* 360 (2002), pp. 766–71; J. Bisson, "Single-Session Early Psychological Interventions Following Traumatic Events," *Clinical Psychology Review* 23, no. 3 (2003), pp. 481–99; S. Rose, J. Bisson and S. Wessely, "A Systematic Review of Single-Session Psychological Interventions ('debriefing') Following Trauma," *Psychotherapy and Psychosomatics* 72 (2003), pp. 176–84; G. Devilly, R. Gist and P. Cotton, "Ready, Fire, Aim: The Evolution of Psychological Debriefing Services and Interven-

tion Outcome Research," submitted to *Psychological Bulletin,* manuscript on file with author; B. Litz, M. Gray, R. Bryant, and A. Adler, "Early Interventions for Trauma: Current Status and Future Directions," *Clinical Psychology: Science and Practice* 9 (2002), pp. 112–34; Van Emmerik et al., "Single Session Debriefing After Psychological Trauma: A Meta-Analysis," pp. 766–71.

54. J. Bisson, P. Jenkins, J. Alexander, and C. Bannister, "A Randomised Controlled Trial of Psychological Debriefing for Victims of Acute Burn Trauma," *British Journal of Psychiatry* 171 (1997), pp. 78–81. Despite randomization, burns were more severe in the debriefed group but when analysis of covariance was applied the debriefed group still fared significantly worse. Also, the sooner debriefing occurred after the burn the worse the outcome.

55. R. Mayou, A. Ehlers and M. Hobbs, "Psychological Debriefing for Road Traffic Accident Victims: A Three-Year Follow-Up of a Randomized Controlled Trial," *British Journal of Psychiatry* 176 (2000), pp. 589–93.

56. G. Parry, "Evidence-Based Clinical Practice Guidelines for Treatment Choice in Psychological Therapies and Counselling," (United Kingdom: Department of Health, National Health Service, 2001), http://www.doh.gov.uk/mentalhealth/treatmentguideline/treatment. pdf (accessed December 31, 2003); NATO, "NATO-Russia advanced research workshop on social and psychological consequences of chemical, biological, and radiological terrorism," NATO Science Programme Workshop, March 25–27, 2002, NATO Headquarters, http:///www. nato.int/science/e/020325-arw2.htm (accessed August 1, 2003); WHO, "Mental Health in Emergencies: Mental and Social Aspects of Populations Exposed to Extreme Stressors" (Geneva: World Health Organization, 2003), recommendation 1.2, p. 4, "Because of possible negative effects, it is not advised to organize forms of single-session psychological debriefing that push persons to share their personal experiences beyond what they would naturally share."

57. National Institute of Mental Health, *Mental Health and Mass Violence: Evidence-Based Early Psychological Intervention for Victims/Survivors of Mass Violence. A Workshop to Reach Consensus on Best Practices: NIH Publication No. 02-5138* (Washington, D.C.: U.S. Government Printing Office, 2002).

58. Ibid., p. 2.

59. A. Ehlers and D. M. Clark, "A Cognitive Model of Post-Traumatic Stress Disorder," *Behaviour Research and Therapy* 38 (2000), pp. 319–45.

60. A. Ehlers and D. Clark, "Early Psychological Interventions for Adult Survivors of Trauma: A Review," *Biological Psychiatry* 53 (2003), pp. 817–26; A. Ehlers, R. Mayou, and B. Bryant, "Psychological Pre-

dictors of Chronic PTSD after Motor Vehicle Accidents," *Journal of Abnormal Psychology* 107 (1998), pp. 508–17; J. Murray, A. Ehlers, and R. Mayou, "Dissociation and Posttraumatic Stress Disorder: Two Prospective Studies of Road Traffic Accident Victims," *British Journal of Psychiatry* 180 (2002), pp. 363–68.

61. A. Coghlan, "Counselling Can Add to Post-Trauma Disaster," *New Scientist*, June 25, 2003.

62. Sarah Baxter and Lois Rogers, "Stiff Upper Lip Beats Stress Counselling," *Times* (London), March 2, 2003, p. 12.

63. D. Spiegel and L. Butler, "Acute Stress in Response to the Terrorist Attacks on September 11, 2001," *CPA Bulletin de l'APC*, August, 2002, p. 17.

64. G. Devilly, R. Gist, and P. Cotton, "Ready, Fire, Aim: The Evolution of Psychological Debriefing Services and Intervention Outcome Research," submitted to *Psychological Bulletin*, manuscript on file with author Satel.

65. J. Lindy, M. Grace, and B. Green, "Survivors: Outreach to a Reluctant Population, *American Journal of Orthopsychiatry* 51, no. 3 (1981), pp. 468–78.

66. G. S. Everly and J. T. Mitchell, "The Debriefing Controversy and Crisis Intervention: A Review of Lexical and Substantive Issues," *International Journal of Emergency Mental Health* 2 (2000), pp. 211–25; R. J. McNally, R. A. Bryant, and A. Ehlers, "Does Early Psychological Intervention Promote Recovery from Posttraumatic Stress?" *Psychological Science in the Public Interest* 4 (2003), pp. 45–79.

67. There is debate among researchers about the extent to which these differences (individual vs. group; direct vs. indirect; victim vs. rescuer) actually matter when it comes to judging the value of debriefing. See B. Litz, M. Gray, R. Bryant, and A. Adler, "Early Interventions for Trauma: Current Status and Future Directions," pp. 112–34; C. Fullerton, R. Ursano, K. Vance, and L. Wang, "Debriefing Following Trauma," American Psychiatric Association Practice of Psychiatry, 2002, http://www.psych.org/pract_of_psych/debriefing_following_trauma3501.cfm (accessed July 15, 2002).

68. R. A. Bryant, M. L. Moulds, R. M. Guthrie, et al., "Imaginal Exposure Alone and Imaginal Exposure with Cognitive Restructuring in Treatment of Posttraumatic Stress Disorder," *Journal of Consulting and Clinical Psychology* 71, no. 4 (2003), pp. 706–12.

69. M. J. Friedman, C. L. Donnelly, and T. A. Mellman, "Pharmacotherapy for PTSD," *Psychiatric Annals* 33 (2003), pp. 57–62.

70. P. Resick and M. Schnicke, "Cognitive Processing Therapy for Sexual Assault Victims," *Journal of Consulting and Clinical Psychology* 60 (1992),

290   *Notes for Pages 191–194*

pp. 748–56; A. Ehlers and D. Clark, "Early Psychological Interventions for Adult Survivors of Trauma: A Review," *Biological Psychiatry* 53 (2003), pp. 817–26; E. Dunmore, D. M. Clark, and A. Ehlers, "A Prospective Study of the Role of Cognitive Factors in Persistent Post-traumatic Stress Disorder after Physical or Sexual Assault," *Behaviour Research and Therapy* 39 (2001), pp. 1063–84.

71. Sharon Kahn, in discussion with author Satel, July 22, 2002.
72. Jerome Groopman, "The Grief Industry," *The New Yorker*, January 26, 2004, p. 35.
73. Rachel Yehuda (paper presented at the annual meeting of the Anxiety Disorders Association of America, Austin Tx., March 21–23, 2002), copy on file with author Satel.
74. Joseph A. Boscarino, Sandro Galea, Jennifer Ahern, et al., "Utilization of Mental Health Services Following the September 11th Terrorist Attacks in Manhattan, New York City," *International Journal of Emergency Mental Health* 4, no. 3 (2002), pp. 143–56.
75. S. Galea, H. Resnick, and D. Vlahov, "Psychological Sequelae of Sept 11," *New England Journal of Medicine* 347, no. 6 (2002), p. 444.
76. J. A. Boscarino, S. Galea, R. E. Adams, et al., "Mental Health Services and Medication Use in New York City After the Sept. 11, 2001, Terrorist Attack," *Psychiatric Services* 55 (2004), pp. 274–83.
77. Erica Goode and Emily Eakin, "Mental Health: The Profession Tests its Limits," *New York Times*, September 11, 2002, sec. A, p. 1.
78. R. Rosenheck and A. Fontana, "Use of Mental Health Services by Veterans with PTSD After the Terrorist Attacks of September 11," *American Journal of Psychiatry* 160 (2003), pp. 1684–90.
79. Ibid., p. 1689; authors cite Dr. Miklos Losonczy, who described to them that mental health administrators of the Veterans Integrated Service Network "3" (which comprises New York metropolitan area VAs) met daily to monitor events and that the uniform experience was of no palpable increase in demand for services; Erica Goode, "Calculating the Toll of Trauma," *New York Times*, September 9, 2003, sec. F, p. 5.
80. R. Rosenheck and A. Fontana, "Use of Mental Health Services by Veterans with PTSD After the Terrorist Attacks of September 11," pp. 1684–90.
81. Ibid., p. 1690.
82. E. M. Weissman, M. Kushner, S. M. Marcus, and D. F. Davis, "Volume of VA Patients With Posttraumatic Stress Disorder in the New York Metropolitan Area After September 11," *Psychiatric Services* 54 (2003), pp. 1641–43.
83. C. Hoge, J. Pavlin, and C. Milliken, "Psychological Sequelae of Sept 11," *New England Journal of Medicine* 347, no. 6 (2002), p. 443.

84. Office of Applied Studies, *Impact of September 11, 2001 Events on Substance Use and Mental Health in the New York Area*, Analytic Series: A-18, DHHS Publication No. SMA 02-3729 (Rockville, Md.: Substance Abuse and Mental Health Services Administration, 2002).

85. J. A. Boscarino, S. Galea, J. Ahern, et al., "Psychiatric Medication Use Among Manhattan Residents Following the World Trade Center Disaster," *Journal of Traumatic Stress* 16 (2003), pp. 301–6.

86. J. Rosack, "Psychotropic Prescribing Patterns Not Impacted by Sept. 11," *Psychiatric News*, September 6, 2002; Data are from IMSHealth and NDCHealth, independent firms that tracks and analyzes prescription drug sales for industry and government. NCDHealth data were specifically requested by *Psychiatric News* (The initial bump in antianxiety medications, most prominent in the NYC area, with smaller bumps in D.C. and across the nation, leveled off around Christmas. Some of these prescriptions were written for people with no previous psychiatric problems, but no one knows how many. Given the fact that individuals with a previous history of depression or anxiety are most at risk for trauma-induced distress it is likely that most of these medications were prescribed for people who had already once taken them.)

87. James Rosack, in discussion with author Satel, July 29, 2003.

88. M. A. Schuster, B. D. Stein, L. H. Jaycox, et al., "A National Survey of Stress Reactions After the September 11th 2001 Terrorist Attacks," *New England Journal of Medicine* 345 (2001), pp. 1507–12.

89. Ibid., p. 1511.

90. S. Reisner, "Trauma: The Seductive Hypothesis," *Journal of the American Psychoanalytic Association* 51 (2003), pp. 381–414; Erica Goode, "Program To Cover Psychiatric Help for 9/11 Families," *New York Times*, August 21, 2002, sec. A, p. 1; J. Groopman "The Grief Industry."

91. S. Galea, J. Ahern, H. Resnick, et al., "Psychological Sequelae of the September 11 Terrorist Attacks in New York City," *New England Journal of Medicine* 346 (2002), pp. 982–87; S. Galea, D. Vlahov, H. Resnick, et al., "Trends of Probable Post-Traumatic Stress Disorder in New York City after the September 11 Terrorist Attacks," *American Journal of Epidemiology* 158, no. 6 (2003), pp. 514–24.

92. Subjects were asked if their symptoms of reexperiencing (nightmares, intrusive thoughts), anxiety and avoidance of reminders or emotional numbing persisted for two weeks; the formal criteria for PTSD require four-week duration. Nor did researchers inquire about severity of symptoms or the impact on functioning which are important determinants of the diagnosis.

93. J. Rosack, "Experts Disagree on the Extent of 9/11 Mental Health Consequences," *Psychiatric News* vol 37, no. 2 (2002), pp. 1, 25.

94. S. Galea, D. Vlahov, H. Resnick, et al., "Trends of Probable Post-Traumatic Stress Disorder in New York City after the September 11 Terrorist Attacks," pp. 514–24.
95. W. Schlenger, J. Caddell, L. Ebert, et al., "Psychological Reactions to Terrorist Attacks: Findings From the National Study of Americans' Reactions to September 11," *Journal of the American Medical Association* 288 (2002), pp. 581–88.
96. C. North and B. Pfefferbaum, "Research on the Mental Health Effects of Terrorism," *Journal of the American Medical Association* 288 (2002), pp. 633–36.
97. R. C. Silver, E. A. Holman, D. N. McIntosh, et al., "Nationwide Longitudinal Study of Psychological Responses to September 11," *Journal of the American Medical Association* 288, no. 10 (2002), pp. 1235–44.
98. Ibid., p. 1243.
99. Greg Gittrich, "9/11 Counseling Shunned: Psychologists Critical of Program," New York *Daily News*, August 22, 2002, p. 23.
100. Chip Felton, Director of Project Liberty, congressional briefing attended by author Satel, Washington, D.C., March 27, 2003.
101. Precentage referrals from Seth Hassett, of Center for Mental Health Services, in discussion with author Satel, June 16, 2004; Trish Marsik of Project Liberty (the FEMA-funded counseling program) projected that forty percent of those counseled would require intensive therapy. Ten percent, in fact, were referred for formal therapy that would be performed by social workers, psychologists, or psychiatrists, according to Hassett.
102. Stephanie Strom, "Finding Cure for Hearts Broken Sept. 11 Is as Difficult as Explaining the Cost," *New York Times*, July 22, 2002, sec. B, p. 1.
103. FEMA, "FEMA-Funded Program Reaches Out to New Yorkers—Largest Crisis Counseling Grant In FEMA's History," May 21, 2002.
104. Project Liberty, full page advertisement, *New York Times Magazine*, October 27, 2002, p. 39.
105. April Naturale, Statewide Director of Project Liberty, in discussion with author Satel, August 21, 2003.
106. Greg Gittrich, "9/11 Trauma Aid in Limbo: Millions Unspent As Relatively Few Seek Counseling," New York *Daily News*, May 27, 2003, p. 8.
107. Robert Fresco, "Therapy Overkill? Some Say Outreach in 9/11 Aftermath Too Wide in Scope," New York *Newsday*, May 3, 2002, sec. A, p. 7.
108. Rachel Yehuda (paper presented at the annual meeting of the Anxiety Disorders Association of America, Austin Tx., March 21–23, 2002), copy on file with author Satel.
109. Lynne Rosen, in discussion with author Satel, May 20, 2002.
110. Bernie Zilbergeld, *The Shrinking of America: Myths of Psychological Change* (Boston: Little, Brown, 1983).

III. R. Wunsch-Hitzig, J. Plapinger, J. Draper, and E. del Campo, "Calls for Help After September 11: A Community Mental Health Hotline," *Journal of Urban Health* 79 (2002), pp. 417–29; in social service circles "satisfaction" with service often counts as proof of necessity, even though evaluations of programs show that perceived helpfulness does not necessarily mesh with improvement in emotional state or functioning. See also K. Hytten and A. Hasle, "Firefighters: A Study of Stress and Coping," *Acta Psychiatrica Scandinavica* 80, Suppl 355 (1989), pp. 50–55; J. A. Kenardy, R. S. Webster, T. J. Lewis, et al., "Stress Debriefing and Patterns of Recovery Following a Natural Disaster," *Journal of Traumatic Stress* 9 (1996), pp. 37–49; M. Deahl, "Psychological Debriefing: Controversy and Challenge," *Australian and New Zealand Journal of Psychiatry*, pp. 929–39; I. V. Carlier, A. E. Voerman, and B. P. Gersons, "The Influence of Occupational Debriefing on Posttraumatic Stress Symptomatology in Traumatized Police Officers," *British Journal of Medical Psychology* 73 (2000), pp. 87–98; V. J. Carr, T. J. Lewin, R. A. Webster, and J. Kenardy, "A Synthesis of the Findings from the Quake Impact Study: A Two-Year Investigation of the Psychosocial Sequelae of the 1989 Newcastle Earthquake," *International Journal of Social Psychiatry and Psychiatric Epidemiology* 32 (1997), pp. 123–36.

112. R. J. McNally, R. A. Bryant, and A. Ehlers, "Does Early Psychological Intervention Promote Recovery from Posttraumatic Stress?" pp. 45–79.

113. D. Gilbert and D. Silvera, "Overhelping," *Journal of Personality and Social Psychology* 70 (1996), pp. 678–90.

114. S. Madon, A. Smith, L. Jussim, et al., "Am I as You See Me or Do You See Me as I Am? Self-fulfilling Prophecies and Self-verification," *Personality and Social Psychology Bulletin* 27 (2001), pp. 1214–24; G. Wiedmann, P. Pauli, and W. Dengler, "Apriori Expectancy Bias in Patients with Panic Disorder," *Journal of Anxiety Disorders* 15 (2001), pp. 401–12.

115. Jacqueline L. Salmon and Lena H. Sun, "Victims at Risk Again; Counselors Scramble To Avert Depression, Suicides After Sept. 11," *Washington Post*, December 19, 2001, sec. A, p. 1.

116. In summer 2002, the September 11th Fund, a charity established by The New York Community Trust and United Way of New York City announced $55 million over the next five years, and the Red Cross announced $40 million over the next three to five years. The FEMA-funded Project Liberty was allocated $150 million, to end by December, 2003. See Stephanie Strom, "Finding Cure for Hearts Broken Sept. 11 Is as Difficult as Explaining the Cost," p. 1; "Red Cross expected to spend $40 million on the program over three to five years.

The September 11th Fund projects spending $45 million to $55 million over five years for treatment and for training professionals how to recognize and treat traumatic stress reactions." See Erica Goode, "Program To Cover Psychiatric Help for 9/11 Families," p. 1.

117. Red Cross, "Three Organizations Coordinate Efforts to Promote 9/11-Related Mental Health and Substance Abuse Services," July 16, 2003, http://www.redcross.org/press/disaster/ds_pr/030717sept11.html (accessed July 19, 2003).

118. G. Langer, "Psychological Sequelae of Sept 11," *New England Journal of Medicine* 347, no. 6 (2002), p. 444 (Pew, Marist, and *ABC/Washington Post* polls cited in Langer); M. A. Schuster, B. D. Stein, M. N. Elliot, et al., "A National Longitudinal Survey of Adult and Child Distress After the September 11, 2001, Terrorist Attacks," in *The Social, Psychological, and Political Impact of the September 11 Attacks on the American Public*, ed. Tom W. Smith, Kenneth A. Rasinski, and Jennifer Berktold (New York: Cambridge University Press, in press).

119. Fran Norris, "50,000 Disaster Victims Speak—An Empirical Review of the Empirical Literature: 1981–2001," September 2001, www.ncdpt.org/docs/Norris.pdf. Norris's report was commissioned by the federal Substance Abuse and Mental Health Services Administration to help officials plan for mental health disaster services. (The report was a compilation of studies of direct victims whose lives were threatened by disaster.)

120. A. Butler, A. Panzer, and L. Goldfrank, eds., *Preparing for the Psychological Consequences of Terrorism: A Public Health Strategy* (Washington, D.C.: Institute of Medicine National Academies Press, 2003).

121. Alan Goodman, administrator of the American Red Cross September 11 Recovery Program, from Red Cross, "Three Organizations Coordinate Efforts to Promote 9/11-Related Mental Health and Substance Abuse Services," July 16, 2003.

122. John Draper, Director of Public Education and the LifeNet Multicultural Hotline Network of the Mental Health Association of New York City, from Red Cross, "Three Organizations Coordinate Efforts to Promote 9/11-Related Mental Health and Substance Abuse Services," July 16, 2003.

123. See http://www.9-11mentalhealth.org (accessed September 7, 2004).

124. Erica Goode and Emily Eakin, "Threats and Responses: The Doctors; Mental Health: The Profession Tests Its Limits," *New York Times*, September 11, 2002, sec. A, p. 1.

125. Erica Goode, "Program to Cover Psychiatric Help for 9-11 Families."

126. Stephanie Strom, "Finding Cure for Hearts Broken Sept. 11 Is as Difficult as Explaining the Cost."

127. Greg Gittrich, "9/11 Counseling Shunned: Psychologists Critical of Program," New York *Daily News*, August 22, 2002, p. 23.

128. Carol North M.D., paper presented at the New York Academy of Medicine, New York, September 9, 2002.

129. See pp. 205–206 in chapter 5 of this book.

130. Erica Goode, "Program To Cover Psychiatric Help for 9/11 Families."

131. Ian Driscoll, "Mental Health Care Providers In Demand Post Attacks," *Reuters*, December 1, 2001.

132. Monica Schoch-Spana, "Educating, Informing, and Mobilizing the Public," in *Terrorism and Public Health: A Balanced Approach to Strengthening Systems and Protecting People*, ed. Barry S. Levy and Victor W. Sidel (London: Oxford University Press, 2002), pp. 118–35.

133. Claudia Dreifus, "A Conversation with Lee Clarke; Living One Disaster After Another, and then Sharing the Experience," *New York Times*, May 20, 2003, sec. D, p. 2.

134. E. H. Quarantelli, "Human and Group Behaviour in the Emergency Period of Disasters: Now and in the Future" (Newark, De.: University of Delaware Disaster Research Center, 1984), p. 8, http://www.udel.edu/drc; note that panic is more likely to occur in enclosed places (e.g., nightclubs). Even then, however, some disasters, such as the 1977 Beverly Hills Supper Club blaze and the deadly 1979 Cincinnati Who concert, there was very little panic. See N. Johnson, "Panic and the Breakdown of Social Order: Popular Myth, Social Theory, Empirical Evidence," *Sociological Focus* 20 (1987), pp. 171–83; W. Feinberg and N. Johnson, "The Ties that Bind: A Macrolevel Approach to Panic," *International Journal of Mass Emergencies and Disasters* 19, no. 3 (2001), pp. 269–95.

135. Public lecture given at Syracuse University, Syracuse, New York, http://www.campbellinstitute.org (accessed March 27, 2003); according to Schoch-Spana, overestimating the likelihood of panic and incompetence in the wake dire events does more than slight the public's fortitude. It can actually compromise safety. If officials feel the need to tailor their remarks to keep from scaring the public, for example, they end up withholding information or they paint an unrealistically rosy picture. Ultimately, their credibility suffers and citizens are less willing to follow directives.

136. E. Quarantelli, "The Sociology of Panic," in *International Encyclopedia of the Social and Behavioral Sciences*, ed. Smelser and Bates (New York: Pergamon, 2001); Ralph H. Turner and Lewis M. Killian, *Collective Behavior*, 3rd edition (Englewood Cliffs, N.J.: Prentice Hall, 1987).

137. In 1932 and 1945 the Japanese attacked Chinese citizens with bubonic plague, anthrax, and cholera. Evidence of panic was minimal. In World

War II, the U.S. Strategic Bombing Survey chronicled attacks on German and Japanese cities; cited in L. Clarke, "2003 Panic: Myth or Reality," *Contexts* Fall 2002, pp. 21–26.

138. Richard Gist, Bernard Lubin, and Bradley G. Redburn, "Psychosocial, Ecological and Community Perspectives on Disaster Response," in *Response to Disaster: Psychosocial, Community and Ecological Perspectives*, pp. 1–16.

139. "In Disasters, Panic Is Rare; Altruism Dominates," American Sociological Association, August 7, 2002, http://www.asanet.org/media/panic.html (accessed April 28, 2004).

140. P. Vernon, "The Psychological Effects of Air Raids," *Journal of Abnormal and Social Psychology* 36 (1941), pp. 457–76.

141. John Rickman, "Panic and Air-Raid Precautions," *The Lancet* 1 (1938), pp. 1291–95.

142. A. B. Stokes, "War Strains and Mental Health," *Journal of Nervous and Mental Disease* 101 (1945), pp. 215–19.

143. Ben Shephard, "Dunkirk, the Blitz, and the Blue," in *A War of Nerves*, Ben Shephard (Cambridge, Mass.: Harvard University Press, 2001), pp. 169–86; see Ibid., pp. 174–75 for reasons why authorities expected widespread panic and mental illness.

144. E. Stengel, "Air-raid Phobia," *British Journal of Medical Psychology* 20 (1946), pp. 135–43; F. Brown, "Civilian Psychiatric Air Raid Casualties," *Lancet* 2 (1942), pp. 175–83.

145. I. L. Janis, *Air War and Emotional Stress* (New York: McGraw Hill, 1951), p. 87.

146. Ibid.

147. Aubrey Lewis, *The Lancet* 2 (1942), p. 179.

148. W. Linford Rees, in conversation with David Healy, "The Place of Clinical Trials in the Development of Psychopharmacology," *History of Psychiatry* 8 (1997), pp. 1–20, 3.

149. R. Hemphill, "The Influence of the War on Mental Disease: A Psychiatric Study," *Journal of Mental Science* 87 (1941), pp. 170–82.

150. S. J. Rachman, *Fear and Courage* (San Francisco: W. H. Freeman and Company, 1978), p. 29.

151. H. Wilson, "Mental Reactions to Air-Raids," *The Lancet* 1 (1942), pp. 284–87; cited in Ben Shephard, *War of Nerves*, p. 181.

152. E. Jones, R. Woolven, B. Durodie, and S. Wessely, "Public Panic and Morale: A Reassessment of Civilian Reactions During the Blitz and World War II," *Journal of Social History*, in press (as of December 20, 2003).

153. A. Freud and D. T. Burlingham, *War and Children* (London: Medical War Books, 1943) pp. 20–21.

154. Ibid., p. 21; See also "Instead of turning away from [destruction] in instinctive horror, as people seem to expect, the child turns to them with primitive excitement," Ibid., p. 23; and also "Children are, of course, afraid of air raids but their fear is neither as universal nor as overwhelming as had been expected," Ibid., p. 25.

155. Norman Garmezy, "Stressors of Childhood," in *Stress, Coping, and Development in Children,* ed. Norman Garmezy and Michael Rutter (New York: McGraw Hill, 1983), pp. 43–84.

156. P. Curran, "Psychiatric Aspects of Terrorist Violence: Northern Ireland 1969–87," *British Journal of Psychiatry* 153 (1988), pp. 470–75.

157. Renee Garfinkle, "Surviving Disaster: What We Can Learn from Elderly Civilians' Surprisingly Successful Coping with Missile Attacks," http://www.fsu.edu~trauma/a5v5i3.htm (accessed December 28, 2003).

158. Ibid.

159. S. Hantman, Z. Solomon, and Y. Horn, "Long-Term Coping of Holocaust Survivors: A Typology," *The Israel Journal of Psychiatry and Related Sciences* 40 (2003), pp. 126–34.

160. L. Eitinger, "Pathology of the Concentration Camp Syndrome," *Archives of General Psychiatry* 5 (1961), pp. 371–79; H. Krystal, *Massive Psychic Trauma* (New York: International Universities Press, 1968); P. Matussek, *Internment in Concentration Camps and its Consequences* (New York: Springer, 1973).

161. Herman M. Van Praag, *"Make-Believes" in Psychiatry: Or The Perils of Progress* (New York: Taylor & Francis, 1993); John J. Sigal and Morton Weinfeld, *Trauma and Rebirth: Intergenerational Effects of the Holocaust* (New York: Greenwood, 1989); Y. Danieli, "The Heterogeneity that is Observed in the Postwar Adaptation of Families of Holocaust Survivors," in *The Psychological Perspectives of the Holocaust and its Aftermath,* ed. Randolph L. Braham (New York: Columbia University Press, 1988); G. R. Leon, J. N. Butcher, and M. Kleinman, "Survivors of the Holocaust and their Children: Current Status and Adjustment," *Journal of Personality and Social Psychology* 41 (1981), pp. 503–6.

162. A. Bleich, M. Gelkopf and Z. Solomon, "Exposure to Terrorism, Stress-related Mental Health Symptoms, and Coping Behaviors Among a Nationally Representative Sample in Israel," *Journal of the American Medical Association* 290 (2003), pp. 612–20.

163. Ibid., p. 618.

164. Ronnie Janoff-Bulman, *Shattered Assumptions—Towards A New Psychology of Trauma* (New York: Free Press, 1992).

165. H. Hendin and A. Hass, "Combat Adaptations of Vietnam Veterans Without Post Traumatic Stress Disorder," *American Journal of Psychia-*

try 14, no. 8 (1984), pp. 956–59; S. Nice, C. Garland, S. Hilton, et al., "Long Term Health Outcomes and Medical Effects of Torture among US Navy Prisoners of War in Vietnam," *Journal of the American Medical Association* 276, no. 5 (1996), pp. 375–81; R. Eberly and B. Engdahl, "Prevalence of Somatic and Psychiatric Disorders among Former Prisoners of War," *Hospital and Community Psychiatry* 42 (1991), pp. 807–13; R. Zeiss and H. Dickman, "PTSD 40 Years Later: Incidence and Person-situation Correlates in Former POWs," *Journal of Clinical Psychology* 45 (1989), pp. 80–87; M. Basoglu, S. Mineka, M. Paker, et al., "Psychological Preparedness for Trauma as a Protective Factor in Survivors of Torture," *Psychological Medicine* 27 (1997), pp. 1421–33; Professor Emilio Mira, chief psychiatrist to the Spanish Republican Army, remarked that the incidence of war neurosis was lowest among, "the 5th and 10th Corps, which were composed of young men of the Communist Party with strong political ideas. The best preventive of neurosis was devotion to the object for which the war was being waged." See E. Mira, in *British Medical Journal*, July 15, 1939, p. 132 at the fifth annual conference of the Ex-Services Welfare Society, on the subject of "The Incidence of War Neurosis"; see also Emilio Mira, "Psychiatric Experience in the Spanish War," *British Medical Journal* 1 (1939), p. 11–61H.

166. Joel Paris, *Nature and Nurture in Psychiatry: A Predisposition-Stress Model for Mental Disorders* (Washington, D.C.: American Psychiatric Press, 1999); Herbert Hendin and Ann Pollinger Haas, *Wounds of War: The Psychological Aftermath of Combat in Vietnam* (New York: Basic Books, 1984); G. J. Elder and E. Clipp, "Combat Experience and Emotional Health: Impairment and Resilience in Later Life," *Journal of Personality* 57, no. 2 (1989), pp. 311–14; N. Yarom, "Facing Death in War—An Existential Crisis," in *Stress In Israel*, ed. Shlomo Breznitz (New York: Van Nostrand Reinhold, 1982), pp. 3–38.

167. A. Butler, A. Panzer and L. Goldfrank, eds., *Preparing for the Psychological Consequences of Terrorism: A Public Health Strategy.*

168. Richard Carmona, M.D., Surgeon General, quoted in S. Barlas, "Responding to Psychological Effects of Terrorism," *Psychiatric Times*, August 2003, p. 39.

169. Lucette Lagnado, "Bracing for Trauma's Second Wave," *Wall Street Journal*, March 5, 2002, sec. B, p. 1.

170. E. S. Susser, D. B. Herman and B. Aaron, "Combating the Terror of Terrorism," *Scientific American*, August 2002, p. 72.

171. Examining case studies of disaster-struck communities that did not fare well illustrate the elements that slow recovery. They include a persistently ravaged environment, derailment of local economy, per-

ceived blame (for the disaster itself or inadequate recovery), or when forces such as prolonged adversarial litigation or political factions tear at the community's social fabric. The 1989 *Exxon Valdez* oil spill off Alaska and the 1972 Buffalo Creek Dam collapse in West Virginia are dramatic examples. See also B. Marshall, J. Picou, and A. Gill, "Terrorism as Disaster: Selected Commonalities and Long-term Recovery for 9/11 Survivors," in "Terrorism and Disaster: New Threats, New Ideas," ed. Lee Clarke, *Research in Social Problems and Public Policy* 11 (2003), pp. 73–96; S. Bland, E. O'Leary, E. Farinaro, et al., "Long-term Psychological Effects of Natural Disasters," *Psychosomatic Medicine 58* (1996), pp. 18–24; B. Green, M. Grace, J. Lindy, et al., "Buffalo Creek Survivors in the Second Decade: Comparison with Unexposed and Nonlitigant Groups," *Journal of Applied Social Psychology* 20, no. 13 (1990), pp. 1033–50; Green et al write: ". . . the low educational levels of most individuals and the limited socioeconomic resources associated with the community may have seriously impaired what would be normal coping and recovery processes in a community with more resources. These factors undoubtedly had some impact on the long-term effects of this event," Ibid., p. 1046.

172. E. Guthrie, A. Wells, H. Pilgrim, et al., "The Manchester Bombing: Providing Rational Response," *Journal of Mental Health* 8 (1999), pp. 149–57; this study describes the psychological response provided by a Manchester hospital to patients admitted after the 1996 Manchester bombing. A decision was made not to offer them debriefing but to screen them eight weeks later and provide treatment for the ones who scored high levels of distress.

173. P. Chodoff, "The Medicalization of the Human Condition," *Psychiatric Services* 53 (2002), pp. 627–28.

174. Richard G. Tedeschi and Lawrence G. Calhoun, "Posttraumatic Growth: A New Focus in Psychotraumatology," *Psych-Talk: Newsletter of the British Psychological Society Student Members Group*, April 2000, http://www.getting-on.co.uk/toolkit/posttrauma.html.

175. R. G. Tedeschi, and L. G. Calhoun, "The Posttraumatic Growth Inventory: Measuring the Positive Legacy of Trauma," *Journal of Traumatic Stress* 9 (1996), pp. 455–71.

176. Jeanne A. Schaefer and Rudolf H. Moos, "The Context for Posttraumatic Growth: Life Crises, Individual and Social Resources and Coping," in *Posttraumatic Growth: Positive Changes in the Aftermath of Crisis,* ed. Crystal L. Park, Lawrence G. Calhoun and Richard Tedeschi (Mahwah, N.J.: Lawrence Erlbaum, 1998), pp. 99–125; See also G. Affleck and H. Tenne, "Construing Benefits from Adversity: Adaptation Significance and Dispositional Underpinnings," *Journal of Personality* 64

(1996), pp. 899–922; C. M. Aldwin, K. J. Sutton, and M. Lachman, "The Development of Coping Resources in Adulthood," *Journal of Personality* 64 (1996), pp. 837–71; Charles S. Carver, and Michael F. Scheier, *On the Self-Regulation of Behavior* (New York: Cambridge University Press, 1998); S. Folkman, "Positive Psychological States and Coping with Severe Stress," *Social Science and Medicine* 45 (1997), pp. 1207–21; J. C. McMillen, E. M. Smith, and R. H. Fisher, "Perceived Benefit and Mental Health After Three Types of Disaster," *Journal of Consulting and Clinical Psychology* 65 (1997), pp. 733–39; P. P. Schnurr, S. D. Rosenberg, and M. J. Friedman, "Change in MMPI Scores from College to Adulthood as a Function of Military Service," *Journal of Abnormal Psychology* 102 (1993), pp. 288–96, the authors found that "combat does not produce uniformly negative outcomes and may well have positive outcomes in some populations."

CONCLUSION: THERAPISM AND THE NATION'S FUTURE.

1. Deirdre Imus, *The Imus Ranch: Cooking for Kids and Cowboys* (Emmaus, Pa.: Rodale, 2004), p. 19.

2. Jack in Ibid., p. 33.

3. Ibid.

4. United Federation of Teachers and New York City Board of Education, "Guidelines For Addressing the Needs of Students in the Aftermath of Trauma," distributed in the weeks following September 11, 2001, http://www.uft.org/?fid=102&tf=631 (accessed July 1, 2004).

5. Alan Wolfe, *Moral Freedom: The Search for Virtue in a World of Chance* (New York: W. W. Norton, 2001), p. 91.

6. Kelly Houston in Ibid., p. 87.

7. Abraham H. Maslow, *Toward A Psychology of Being*, 2nd ed. (New York: D. Van Nostrand, 1968), p. iii.

8. Carl Rogers, *On Encounter Groups* (New York: Harrow, 1973), p. 11.

9. Sigmund Freud, *The Future of An Illusion*, ed., trans. James Strachey (New York: W. W. Norton, 1989), p. 68.

10. Paul Johnson, *A History of the American People* (New York: Harper Collins, 1998).

11. Ibid., p. 976.

Index

Leary, Timothy, 65–67
Lembcke, Jerry, 143–44
Leo, John, 13
Leonard, George, 72–73
Leshner, Alan, 100, 101–2, 107, 108
Levy, Harold O., 215–16
Lewis, Aubrey, 207
Lewis, Michael, 23–25
Life (magazine), 72
Lifton, Robert Jay, 142–43, 145, 146, 151, 153, 175
Lincoln, Abraham, 44, 50, 61
Lindemann, Eric, 133
Lindy, Jacob, 190
Loma Prieta earthquake
    reaction to, 119–21, 126
Los Angeles Times, 13, 178
loss, myths of coping with, 128–30
"Lottery, The," (Jackson), 43
Loveless, Tom, 26
LSD, 65
Lyubomirsky, Sonya, 123

McCleod, Scott, 24–25
McDonald, James, Jr., 172
McEwen, Yvonne, 186
McHugh, Paul, 160, 164
McNally, Richard, 74, 148, 150
Maher, Brendan, 130–31
Man's Search for Meaning (Frankl), 7
Markowitz, John, 192
Marshall, John R., 111–12
Marshall, Randall, 212
Marsik, Trish, 203
Maslow, Abraham, 8–9, 57–59, 59–64, 64–68, 72, 75–76, 216–17
Medical Foundation for Caring
    Victims of Torture, 167
Meet the Press, 100
Menendez brothers, 95
Middleton, Warwick, 134
Milk, Harvey, 95

Mill, John Stuart, 32–33, 91, 113–14, 140
Miller, Kenneth, 169
Miller, Kevin, 17–18
Milton, Joyce, 65–66
Mitchell, Jeffrey T., 181
Mitford, Jessica, 127
Mollica, Richard, 178
Monitoring the Future (survey), 21
Montreal Heart Attack Readjustment Trial, 121
Moore, Michael, 174
Moos, Rudolf, 214
Moral Freedom (Wolfe), 78
moral relativism, 44–46, 46–53
Morrow, Lance, 7–8
Moscone, George, 95
Mourning and Melancholia (Freud), 133
Moyers, Bill, Sr., 100
multiculturalism
    and morality, 41–44
murderers, 85–88
    adolescent killers, 88–90, 90–91
    personal accountability, 95–99
Myth of Self-Esteem (Hewitt), 33–34
"Myths of Coping With Loss, The" (Nussbaum/Silver), 130

Naipaul, V. S., 45
Narcotics Anonymous, 101
National Association of School Psychologists, 126–27
National Education Association (NEA), 5, 39–40, 46–53
National Institute of Mental Health (NIMH), 188
National Institute on Drug Abuse (NIDA), 99–100
National Public Radio, 22
National Vietnam Veterans' Readjustment Study, 152
Neimeyer, Robert, 138
Neuhaus, Father Richard, 82

Neuva Learning Center, 34
New England Journal of Medicine, 195
*New Phrenology: The Limits of
    Localizing Cognitive Processes in the
    Brain, The* (Uttal), 103
New York Academy of Medicine, 192,
    195, 196
New York *Daily News*, 181, 199
New York *Newsday*, 199
New York Post, 181
New York State Office of Mental
    Health, 198
New York Times, 11, 90, 117–18,
    118–19, 143–44, 151, 161, 193,
    204
New York Times Magazine, 23–24, 36,
    78–79, 111
New Yorker (magazine), 81, 125, 192
Newjack: Guarding Sing Sing (Conover),
    173
Newsweek (magazine), 22, 73–74
Nightline (ABC), 22
9/11 (World Trade Center) Project
    Liberty, 197–201
  survivors, 7–8
  trauma industry and, 177–79,
    179–80, 180–84, 184–86,
    186–89, 189–91, 191–95,
    195–97, 197–201, 201–4
"9/11 As History" (curriculum),
    48–52
Nixon, Richard, 74
Nolen-Hoeksema, Susan, 119–21,
    123–24
Non Sequitur (comic strip), 93
North, Carol, 197
Nussbaum, Emily, 129

O'Brien, Charles P., 99
O'Donohue, William, 172
Oathout, Curtis, 80–81
*Odd Girl Out: The Hidden Culture of
    Aggression in Girls* (Simmons), 22

Offer, Daniel, 20
Ofman, Paul, 203
Oklahoma City bombing, 180, 197
On Death and Dying (Kübler-Ross),
    135
One Nation Under Therapy
    (Sommers/Satel), 3, 6–7, 9
"oops phenomenon," 104–5
Oprah Winfrey Show, 22
Overseas Development Institute,
    164

Paltrow, Gwyneth, 174
Pandya, Anand, 186
Pankratz, Loren, 160–61
Parker, James, 88–90
Parkes, Colin Murray, 135–36
"Pathology in the Hundred Acre
    Wood," 1
Pear, Tom, 147
Pellegrini, Anthony, 14–15
personal accountability, 95–99
Petty, Celia, 166
Pfefferbaum, Betty, 197
Pilot (newspaper), 82
Pinker, Steven, 90–91, 94
Pipher, Mary, 2, 19
Plato, 44, 59
*Politics of Readjustment: Vietnam
    Veterans Since the War, The*
    (Scott), 146
Pollack, William, 2, 19
Pope, Denise Clark, 27–29, 29
Portland General Electric, 127
post-traumatic stress disorder
    (PTSD), 8, 141–76
  definition, 171–74
  delayed-onset, 153–56
  economic considerations, 161–64
  and Iraq, 174–75
  and 9/11, 192–95, 195–97,
    199–200, 202–4
  politics and, 145–46

post-traumatic stress disorder (*cont.*)
Post-Vietnam Syndrome, 142–45,
145–46, 151–53, 153–56, 158–59
psychological debriefing, 182–84,
187–89, 189–91
PTSD diagnosis, veterans and,
159–61
traumatic events, response to,
141–43, 148–51, 164–67,
168–70
VA hospitals and, 156–58, 158–59
and warfare, 146–48, 174–76
Post-Traumatic Stress Disorder: How to Apply for 100-Percent-Total Disability Rating, 162
Posttraumatic Growth: Positive Changes in the Aftermath of Crisis (Tedeschi/Calhoun), 214
Post-Vietnam Syndrome, 142–45,
145–46, 151–53, 153–56, 158–59
Powers, Ron, 89–90
Prashant, Lyn, 128
Project Liberty, 197–201
Psychiatric Services, 192
Psychobabble (Rosen), 74
Psychological Science in the Public Interest (APS journal), 31–32
Psychological Society, The (Gross), 74
Psychology Today, 112
Psychosocial Training and Support Program, 165–66
Psychotherapy Finances (newsletter), 181
Public Agenda, 26, 28, 30
publishing
history as affirmation, 38–41, 42
sensitivity and bias committees, 5–6, 15–17, 38–41

Quaraentelli, Henry, 205
Queen Bees and Wannabes (Wiseman), 22
Quindlen, Anna, 48
Quit It!, 13–14

Rachman, Stanley J., 207
Rando, Therese, 138
Ravitch, Diane, 5–6, 15–17, 39, 42
Reach Out to Heal (PBS), 191–92
Reading Rainbow (PBS), 50
Reagan, Ronald, 74
Real Boys: Rescuing Our Sons from the Myths of Boyhood (Pollack), 2, 19
Real Boys' Voices (Pollack), 19
"Real Me," doctrine of, 87–88
Rees, W. Linford, 207
Regier, Daryl, 204
Reich, Wilhelm, 58
Reilly, Rick, 12
Reisner, Steven, 150
Religions, Values, and Peak-Experiences (Maslow), 72
Relman, Arnold, 116
Remembering Trauma (McNally), 150
Report on Bereavement and Grief Research, 139–40
"Repress Yourself" (Slater), 111
responsibility
metaphysics of, 91–95
Reuters, 204
Review of Educational Research, 30
Reviving Ophelia: Saving the Selves of Adolescent Girls (Pipher), 2, 19
Rickman, John, 206
Rieff, Philip, 9
Riverside Publishing, 15–16
Road to Malpsychia: Humanistic Psychology and Our Discontents, The (Milton), 65–66
Robins, Lee, 107
Robles, Richard, 85–88
Rochester, Martin, 39
Rogers, Carl, 8–9, 58–59, 68–71, 71–72, 75–76, 217
Roosevelt, Eleanor, 74
Rosen, Gerald, 178
Rosen, Lynne, 199–200
Rosen, R. D., 74